AMERICA:

PURPOSE AND POWER

AMERICA:
PURPOSE AND POWER

EDITED WITH AN INTRODUCTION BY

GENE M. LYONS

CHICAGO / QUADRANGLE BOOKS / 1965

Published under the auspices of
The Public Affairs Center, Dartmouth College

 For information,
address: Quadrangle Books, Inc., 180 North Wacker Drive,
Chicago 60606. Manufactured in the United States of America.

Library of Congress Catalog Card Number: 65-18243

Preface

THIS book of essays is a publication of the Public Affairs Center at Dartmouth College. In establishing the Center in late 1961, the College sought to meet a threefold task: (1) to strengthen the liberal education which is the indispensable basis for an informed citizenry; (2) to stimulate and begin the preparation of young men for public service; (3) to encourage and provide opportunities for research and writing in the basic issues of public policy by members of the faculty.

One of the first research projects organized by the Center was a study of changing forces in American society, out of which the present publication emerged. The choice of this broad area of investigation was quite deliberate, for it has been helpful in offering a broad conceptual framework for subsequent research projects. It also provided a setting within which to emphasize the multi-disciplinary nature of the Center's research and to carry out a worthwhile exchange on the different approaches of the social sciences.

The research involved in these essays was supported from a grant made to the Center by Mr. Kenneth Montgomery, a graduate of Dartmouth in the class of 1925. We are grateful to Mr. Montgomery and to President John Sloan Dickey and Provost John W. Masland for their continual encouragement in the work of the Center.

G. M. L.

Hanover, New Hampshire

Contents

III

NATIONAL CHANGE

Introduction

IT IS "the irony of American history" that the purposes of American experience seem inadequate to the demands of the contemporary world. This disjunction is particularly cruel to a people that has traditionally seen its commitment to democracy as an historical and universal mission. Yet today we can well ask whether it is the dedication of Americans to freedom that extends the franchise to the Negro—or the power of America's centralized government; and whether it is America's example of moral restraint that helps provide stability in a world in revolutionary turmoil—or the power of the nuclear deterrent. To quote Reinhold Niebuhr, who first explored this "irony": "Our dreams of a pure virtue are dissolved in a situation in which it is possible to exercise the virtue of responsibility toward a community of nations only by courting the prospective guilt of the atomic bomb."

The use of power may not necessarily mean the distortion of high purpose, and what seems irony may be nothing more than the harsh reality of relating means to ends. Americans have always tended to emphasize the goals of their society and to expect that their path would be cleared simply because their purposes were valid and unimpeachable. Even when they have embraced the uses of cold power, they have done so with infinite regret, bemoaning the blindness and irrationality in others that made it necessary.

This emphasis on goals has tended to obscure the limits within which Americans can shape their destiny. Indeed, the tendency toward idealizing and universalizing its own values is contradictory in a nation that characterizes itself as pragmatic. Today these limits are, to some degree, set by the intensity of international involvement and the necessity of accommodating American purposes with those of other nations. But they are also set by forces for change that spring out of the world as it is and do not necessarily respond to the aspirations of American society. Americans may want peace, justice for all, and the preservation and extension of individual dignity. These are fine objectives. But they hardly help define the gap between rich and poor, the frustration of the under-privileged, the inevitable disruptions of technological innovation, the sharpness of national and ideological differences, and the reactions of human character which can lead to violence, hatred, and degradation.

I do not insist that the goals of American society are immaterial to national policy or that Americans should accept a doctrine of historical or material determinism. Yet Americans have too often sought guidance for their actions in the purposes of their society with little or no reference to historical forces for change. At the same time, defeat and disappointment have frequently been attributed to a lack of direction when they might more realistically have been attributed to a misreading of contemporary history. Adherence to traditional aims of freedom and equality is crucial to the integrity of American society, but it does not help identify the practical choices that must be made to reach these goals.

There is little expectation that Americans can meet the challenges posed by modern weapons, technological expansion, economic development at home and abroad, and urbanization without a deliberate relating of power to purpose. It is incongruous and even disastrous, on the one hand, to accept the responsibilities for world peace and individual freedom that the United States has, and, on the other, to reject the requirements of power and action which these responsibilities dictate. The real problem is not to shy away from the use of political power in the name of freedom, but to extend freedom by action that effectively responds to the opportunities and dangers that it faces.

The concept of power is, however, poorly understood by most Americans. For some, power is unlimited; for others, its use becomes a sullied experience. Certainly when power becomes purpose itself, ugly tyranny results. At the same time, ends without means have little chance of fulfillment. When the use of power—in kind, in limit, in method—is determined by both clear purpose and an understanding of historical conditions, then power can serve and need not threaten a society.

No two authors in this book would agree on a definition of power or on a general relationship of purpose and power. And yet each in his own way has dealt with this relationship. Whether describing the development of American society, or dealing with military defense, economic aid, or urbanization, or analyzing world trade, technological innovation, or civil rights, the authors all became involved with the methods and limits of using power, as well as its purposes.

In these essays the authors have also been involved in another area that complicates the relationship of purpose. and power. They have demonstrated how doubtful is the common separation between domestic and foreign affairs and how, contrary to myth, it was always so. American historical development, no less than the present situation, is the product of the dynamic interplay of international and internal forces. Sometimes one set of forces has been more powerful, sometimes the other. Yet never was the United States so detached from the rest of the world that its development could be carried on in isolation from what was happening elsewhere. If isolation was a policy of American governments, it never was a reality of American life.

This melding of the foreign and domestic is more complex than it may first appear; it is more than the integration of two sets of forces which have different roots; it is more like a fusion. Where, for example, do Americans look for the motives for their policies and actions? It is too obvious to say that a strong America means a stable world, and that what is good for Americans is thus good for other peoples. It may be, but there are questions of timing and method that may be crucial. For example, tariff adjustments are likely to affect the interests of domestic entrepreneurs, the development of European integration, and the ability of the emergent nations to earn foreign exchange; the formulation of American trade policy is, in effect, a fusing of all these interests.

In no less meaningful a way, the civil rights issue at home is tied to the rise of colored nations in the southern hemisphere of the world. Americans are right in insisting that the race problem should be solved on the basis of clear American purposes and that there is no need to seek motives or stimuli from abroad. But in the practice of real life, the agonies of Mississippi and the Congo cannot be separated, and nothing can be gained by warning Jomo Kenyatta or Kwame Nkrumah that they have nothing to do with James Meredith, any more than their admonition for us to leave Africa alone means that we could, or should, withdraw our influence from that tortured continent.

The world is highly interdependent, however one may argue about the different degrees of dependent relationships. This fact unfortunately cannot commit us to the ideal of world government as the logical and rational extension of the objective situation. Power resides in national states and in the combinations of national states that respond to political and economic necessities. There is no power base on which to establish a world government. We are thus destined to exist in a divided but nonetheless interacting and increasingly interdependent world. The point of our history is that we have lived in interdependence throughout our development, no matter how much we have tried to glorify our freedom from foreign involvement. The point of our contemporary situation is the qualitative shift in our power relations with the rest of the world.

The highly charged character of contemporary life suggests one final problem that should be emphasized here. How susceptible to rational analysis are the volatile and complex determinants of purpose and power in America today? To respond in the negative is to disdain any possibility of understanding, let alone prognosis, prediction, or control. But to respond in the affirmative does not mean embracing some simple faith in man's ability to manage his own future. There may be unexpurgable original sin, supreme irrationality, divine intervention, or other uncontrollable forces that we shall never be able to fathom, let alone manipulate. Despite these limits upon rationality, there are at least two sources of understanding that allow us a sensible opportunity to be more than puppets in some Olympian tragedy: the key role of science and technology in social change, and the development of intellectual tools of social analysis.

Science and technology have always disrupted social patterns, but technological change today is distinguished by its rapidity and pervasiveness. The accumulation of research and development, the capacity of productive equipment, and the development of facilities for communication and distribution carry new ideas about the nature of the physical world from a point of vague speculation to an outburst of broad utility in a breathlessly short period. For an industrialized society the process of adaptation to change is essential to reasonable order, and for the developing nations even more so since the change, in their case, is such a great leap forward. In both cases a significant lag between technological change and social adjustment can be crippling. There is thus a critical need for planning—for projecting the capabilities of technological changes and preparing social and economic patterns to absorb their impact. There is, moreover, a consciousness of this need that is evident at every level from community planning to national programs for education, economic growth, and military strategy.

The future effects of technology cannot, however, always be precisely estimated. There may, in many instances, be several possible effects (or several possible rates of change) depending upon the mixture of human decisions that are made during the period of development and early application. These decisions, in turn, depend upon the prevailing pressures, the social atmosphere, the nature of the leadership and goals of the society. To gain insight into these phenomena is something quite different from determining the capacity of a new technological system. It requires, among other things, an understanding of historical relevance, social relations, behavioral patterns, and human judgment. These are the realms of history and the social sciences, and there is every evidence that here, too—if the growth of knowledge is not so phenomenal as in the physical sciences—the area of understanding has been widely and deeply increased in recent years.

But the importance of science and technology and the use of systematic social analysis in making public policy are not without their problems. While offering the possiblity of rationalizing the complex and interrelated process of modern decision-making, they present the risks of an expert society. The "expertization" of policy and politics puts a burden on the democratic system. If specialized knowledge is needed in order to relate purpose and power in a meaningful way, then political leaders and expert advisers must be able to communicate with each other, the working atmosphere of government must be receptive to the reflection and inquiry of scientific and scholarly study, and the politicians and the experts have a joint obligation to distill the essence out of the jungle of data and argument and present the core of the issues to the larger public for their ultimate policy decision.

For the expert there is an additional dilemma. Caught up in the operational pressures of public policy, he will be tempted and cajoled to exceed the limits of his role and become involved in the goals-oriented process of making political choice from among technical possibilities. It is a fearsome dilemma, for the line between possibilities and priorities is ambiguous, and what becomes feasible through new study and analysis may decisively influence what is desirable. The expert cannot play it completely safe. But both he and the politician must understand that the role of the scientist or the scholar in public life depends, in the first instance, on his professional competence and integrity; any deviation from the rigorous standards of his discipline makes him something other than what he is supposed to be.

The coming of the expert society puts a burden on the public in a democracy, as well. The people simply must know more about issues of public policy if they are going to play any kind of part in the political process through which decisions are made and leaders are held accountable for their acts. Otherwise we encourage a rule of elitism or put impossible pressures on leaders from an ignorant public. But knowing more about the issues does not (indeed cannot) mean the absorption of as much information as the specialist has and needs. It does, however, mean a decent understanding of the basic issues involved and a realistic perspective on the relationship of purpose and power.

The essays in this book offer a basis for comprehending what is involved in gaining such a perspective. They are both descriptive and analytical. To the extent they are descriptive, they offer an understanding of the development and present state of American society; to the extent they are analytical, they offer a frame of reference for examining its unresolved problems. They will hopefully have meaning for our professional colleagues even though they are ultimately written for our students—past, present, and future—who are part of the public community of the nation.

All but one of the essays are published here for the first time. They profited greatly from a series of meetings held over a period of almost a year, during which most of the authors were able to test their ideas under the criticism of frank colleagues and benefit from the variety of experience and interest in the group. In bringing these essays together, we have sought to retain the individual character of each author's work and the individual responsibility each author assumes. While conscious of each other's motives and commitments, the authors agreed at an early date not to follow any pre-determined model of American society as a base point for their analysis—even if they could have agreed on what that model should be. Nonetheless, out of a good deal of conversation and reading, a kind of unity evolved. It is not the tight unity that can only be the product of one man's mind. But it is a unity that derives from meaningful communication among men who share a common respect for good scholarship and a common interest in understanding the issues that confront their country.

I

The Historical Shaping

1

POLITICS AND IDEOLOGY: THE AMERICAN WORLD MISSION

ROGER H. BROWN

THE theme of a special destiny to improve the lot of man is one that has been apparent in many different phases of American life. From the earliest days of settlement, the belief that this land was uniquely destined for the fulfillment of high and special purposes has been persistent and pervasive in American thought and action. Pursuing a wide variety of aims, Americans have ever felt that their country—broad, rich, spacious, and open—was ordained to be the means of realizing a better order of things—for themselves and all mankind.[1]

The nation's conception of itself as the prototype of a free society is the most important political expression of the American idea of its proper mission in the world. From the very first days of nationhood, Americans have believed that it was their unique purpose to demonstrate just what they as free men could achieve

1. Various aspects of the American mission—religious, ethnic, material, moral—are discussed in Edward McNall Burns, *The American Idea of Mission: Concepts of National Purpose and Destiny* (New Brunswick, 1957).

in the way of a better life for themselves. Ever since that time they have felt a special obligation to prove how much more successfully men could live in freedom than they could under the autocratic and aristocratic systems of society and government that existed in the Old World. The belief in a national mission to demonstrate the vitality and worth of such a society has been a profound and lasting force in shaping the American experience.

The effect of this conviction is especially obvious at periods in American history when the ability of the nation to fulfill its own most vital needs has been challenged. At such times the question was consistently raised whether the nation possessed within itself sufficient purpose, imagination, and will to continue to survive and flourish. Thus, during the first decades of national independence the challenge was the competence of a republican form of government to discharge what were considered to be the essential obligations of government—the protection of citizens in their lives and property, the defense of national honor and national independence, the maintenance of internal order. In the mid-nineteenth century it was the capacity of America to make it possible for the latent abilities of man to develop to their fullest extent. In the twentieth century it was the ability to control the energies and consequences of industrialism and turn them to the service of man's social and economic welfare.

The influence of the idea of mission is also evident in the history of American foreign policy. The belief that America should serve the world by setting an example at home, rather than by actively extending its influence abroad, has long exercised an important restraining effect on the conduct of foreign affairs. Yet it was the original aim of attaining a secure and lasting independence—an essential prerequisite to realizing the American mission—that led the nation into a new period of world commitment and responsibility when new conditions affected its relations with other nations.

Holding to this concept of national mission, Americans have

always conceived of themselves as leading the world to higher and better things. Theirs was an experiment that would benefit all mankind. Yet, in the fulfillment of this purpose, Americans have often looked abroad for aid and guidance. Especially at times when circumstances have cast doubt on the nation's ability to advance and prosper have they turned to other nations for ideas and techniques to solve their most pressing problems. Throughout their history, Americans have been prepared to advance the well-being of all men through their own meaningful application of foreign experience and precedent.

The Establishment of Republicanism

The pervasive concern of the Revolutionary and post-Revolutionary generations for a republican form of government was the earliest expression of the American national mission. Until the 1820's it was the chief preoccupation of most politically conscious Americans to preserve their recently acquired liberty through the secure establishment of their newly organized republican system of government. It was their firm conviction that irresponsible systems of government—monarchy, aristocracy, and dictatorship—reduced men to a state of slavish dependency and stultified them as human beings; self-governing democracies and republics alone furnished the personal freedom and independence that was man's inalienable birthright. It was the nation's special purpose to demonstrate the practicability of a republican form of government for the benefit of all mankind; and the various efforts to establish the republican system on a firm and sound foundation gave politics in the early national period its distinctive character and meaning.

The world watching them was a highly skeptical one. With few exceptions, eighteenth-century political theorists agreed that republican governments were unsuited for large nations with disparate economic, ethnic, class, or religious interests in the population. Politically sophisticated Europeans believed that the average man was too selfish, narrow, and irresponsible to govern himself, much less pay heed to such vital eighteenth-century concerns as the protection of persons in their lives and property, the maintenance of order, the defense of national honor and national independence. Given the inherently irresponsible nature of man, how could a large aggregate of men possibly conduct its own affairs through elected and accountable representatives without doing violence to these vital obligations of government? When even Montesquieu, the great eighteenth-century authority on government, had advised that republics could flourish only in small states with populations of exceptional homogeneity and virtue, it seemed almost presumptuous to expect that America, a broad land of many varied interests, would prove him wrong.[2]

Such was the issue that filled men's minds during the first decades of our national existence. One can detect its influence in the movement that in 1787 gave rise to the Constitution. Scarcely had independence been formally acknowledged than the fitness of Americans for republican government became a matter of high concern. In the first years of peace, state legislatures refused to comply with congressional requests for financial assistance toward common national expenses; passed laws impeding collection of debts by foreign creditors; imposed tariffs on foreign commerce en route to other states; squabbled over rival land claims; and undercut retaliatory commercial legislation aimed at Great Britain. By 1787 over half the legislatures had bowed to the clamor of debtors for stay laws and paper money emissions, and where legislatures had stood firm, court stoppages, riots, and violence had resulted.

2. For recent explorations of republicanism, see Cecelia Kenyon, "Republicanism and Radicalism in the American Revolution: An Old Fashioned Interpretation," *William and Mary Quarterly*, XIX (1962), 153-182; Bernard Bailyn, Introduction, *Pamphlets of the American Revolution, 1750-1776* (Cambridge, 1965); and Roger H. Brown, *The Republic in Peril: 1812* (New York, 1964).

Unable to ignore the evidence of such widespread selfishness and irresponsibility, prominent Americans began to doubt the very premise upon which republican government depended. Were men, after all, incapable of sound and responsible self-government? By 1787 New England leaders had begun to discuss openly the advantages of hereditary monarchy and aristocracy, and more than one agreed with the Massachusetts legislator who avowed that: "Monarchy in our present situation is become absolutely necessary to save the States from sinking into the lowest abbiss [sic] of Misery." In Virginia, George Washington, deploring the trend of affairs, wondered aloud whether the American experiment was not "ideal & fallacious," and James Madison observed that the behavior of the states had "tainted the faith of the most orthodox republicans." [3]

Alarmed for the future of the republican experiment, the Founding Fathers turned for guidance to the constitutions of the states of ancient Greece and Rome and modern Europe, and the political commentaries of ancient and recent writers. The writings of the eighteenth-century Scottish philosopher and theorist David Hume afforded what was perhaps the most significant contribution to their decision to rebuild entirely the republican structure of the nation. No one, not even antifederalists, disputed the fact that the national government was in need of new powers to regulate commerce and raise money. But the complete reconstruction of the national government, with the addition of sweeping new powers over individual citizens, went far beyond this minimum. Inspired by discussion in three of Hume's essays, James Madison advanced the daring proposal that a large re-

3. Brown, *The Republic in Peril,* 5-6; Charles Warren, *The Making of the Constitution* (Boston, 1929); and Neal Riemer, "The Republicanism of James Madison," *Political Science Quarterly,* LXIX (1954), 45-64, stress the importance of concern for republicanism in the thought of the Fathers of the Constitution. A reading of the correspondence conveniently gathered in Department of State, *Documentary History of the Constitution* (Washington, 1905), IV, will further support this point.

public, in which a great multitude of interests competed with and offset each other, would prove a more disinterested agency of authority than would smaller republics, whose legislators were more vulnerable to the pressure of selfish majorities. Improved still more by constitutional devices intended to raise the quality of representation and increase the number of refining stages in the legislative process, Madison's blueprint for a new national government raised fresh hopes for the success of republicanism and became the basis of the final design.[4]

The preoccupation with proving the ability of a republican government to serve the interests of man is also evident in the policies of the Federalists who assumed the initial direction of the newly established government. To provide the federal authority with means for discharging its essential obligations, Alexander Hamilton, the Secretary of the Treasury, proposed his famous economic program. Professing sincere attachment to "the republican theory" and expressing hope for its success, Hamilton considered its competence "as yet a problem," deeming it "yet to be determined by experience whether [republicanism] be consistent with that stability and order in government which are essential to public strength and private security and happiness." The new government must have what the government of the Confederation lacked —the authority and power that comes from an ample purse. Hence the provisions to restore credit, provide an adequate fund of capital, and assure a steady revenue, all contained in the plans for funding and assumption, the national bank, the common protective tariff, government subsidies to manufacturing, and the excise.

The zeal of the Federalists for energetic countermeasures in the Whiskey and Fries Rebellions also showed their concern with proving the new government to be capable of putting down mobs

4. Douglas Adair, " 'That Politics May Be Reduced to a Science': David Hume, James Madison and the Tenth *Federalist*," *The Huntington Library Quarterly*, XX (August 1957), 343-360.

and protecting American lives and property. "The consideration of expense is of no moment compared with the advantages of energy," advised Hamilton in 1799 with reference to the latter uprising. Moreover, the extreme Federalist reaction to the emergence of the Jeffersonian Republican party derived in part from fear that the authority of the new government would be destroyed by legislative fragmentation, obstructionism, and subversive activity widely identified in eighteenth-century minds with party opposition. Thus Washington in the Farewell Address warned his countrymen against "the spirit of party" in governments "of the popular character, in Governments purely elective," and identified Republican party opposition to Federalist policies with a plot to paralyze and destroy the new authority.[5]

Equally, the Jeffersonians, when elected to office in 1800, were preoccupied with proving the competence of republicanism. Less concerned with the threat of popular licentiousness and mob disorder, the Republicans at first narrowly restricted the national government in its functions, trusting more to the common sense and good judgment of the people to preserve order and respect life and property than did their predecessors. Yet when confronted with British and French depredations against American commerce and shipping on the high seas, they were willing to exert the fullest powers of government in order to protect American lives and property and to defend national honor and independence.[6]

Initially Jefferson and his party sought to bring the offending powers to terms through economic pressure—embargo, non-intercourse, non-importation. After these measures had failed, the

5. Hamilton to Edward Carrington, 26 May 1792, *The Works of Alexander Hamilton,* ed. by Henry C. Lodge (New York, 1903), IX, 533-535; Hamilton to James McHenry, 18 March 1799, *The Basic Ideas of Alexander Hamilton,* ed. by Richard B. Morris (New York, 1957), 369; Washington to Lafayette, 25 December 1798, *The Writings of George Washington,* Fitzpatrick edition (Washington, 1931-40), XXXVII, 66.

6. For a full discussion of the coming of the War of 1812, see Brown, *The Republic in Peril.*

Republicans preferred to face the hazards and difficulties of war than risk the loss of prestige that submission would inflict upon republicanism: "Being the only republick," wrote Richard Rush in 1812, "the destinies of that sort of government are in our keeping. Should we stand by and see it longer debased by submission, or sordid avarice, its cause is gone forever." The republic must now prove its competence to stand and fight in defense of vital American interests—the very fate of America and the world depended on the outcome. "God grant us a happy result to this new & untried experiment to which the only free government upon earth is about to be subjected!" wrote Henry Clay in 1812. "That such will be the issue of the contest I entertain no doubt if the people possess the fortitude and firmness which I believe they do."[7]

It was not until after the close of the War of 1812 that Americans began to shift their attention to matters other than the securing of their republican government. Not until war against the world's most formidable naval power had shown the competency of the republic to function as adequately in war as in peace did Americans grow confident that their republican system was well suited to the purposes for which governments were originally intended. Thus Hezekiah Niles, the famous editor, could affirm: "The sublime problem, so long held doubtful by political casuists, is completely solved—man *is* best able to govern himself, and that of a free republic *is* the strongest system yet devised for a social compact amongst men." But succeeding decades would raise new challenges to determine whether this nation of freemen, "the hope of the earth," would continue to inspire the admiration of mankind.[8]

7. Richard Rush to Charles J. Ingersoll, 29 April 1812; and Henry Clay to Thomas Bodley, May 12, 1812, quoted in Brown, *The Republic in Peril*, 84, 86-87.

8. Niles' *Weekly Register*, 29 August 1818, quoted in Leonard D. White, *The Jeffersonians: A Study in Administrative History, 1801-1829* (New York, 1951), 28.

The Cause of Human Betterment

For several decades after independence, Americans centered their efforts for the fulfillment of the national mission on the establishment and preservation of republicanism. By the appeal of their republican example they hoped to encourage men, wherever they might be in bondage, to strike down autocratic and aristocratic domination and be free. In the mid-1820's, however, Americans launched a broad-gauged attack on a variety of social ills in which concern for the republican system was no longer the predominant motive. In a vigorous outburst of reform activity, men began addressing themselves to the cause of human betterment with an intensity and breadth of purpose that their predecessors would not have recognized.

The interests and objectives of these reformers embraced a multitude of causes ranging the full spectrum of social evil. There were prison reformers demanding new approaches to prison discipline and criminal rehabilitation; temperance crusaders exhorting men to abstain from harmful consumption of alcohol; educational reformers organizing state supported, universal, compulsory school systems, teacher training institutes, and worker education programs; feminists insisting on equal access to the professions and equal status before the law for women; humanitarians pressing for better treatment of the blind, deaf, mute, and insane. There were communitarians who founded utopian societies intended to remove men from the brutalizing effects of the competitive struggle; peace crusaders who preached an end to violence among nations; transcendentalists who urged men to reject social convention and trust their own inner convictions; and abolitionists who launched an intense campaign to liberate the Negro from slavery. Everywhere in America men and women were turning critical eyes on institutional deficiencies and injustices and demanding remedy.

A heightened sense of man's moral and physical potential afforded the major psychological drive for the new galaxy of reformist activity. With unprecedented intensity and conviction, the pre-Civil War generation was convinced that man possessed virtually unlimited capacity for moral and intellectual improvement; that the evils and deficiencies of society prevented him from developing these powers; and that men now held within their grasp the ability to reach their full potential. Such heady optimism was the natural outgrowth of profound transformations in the physical world in which men themselves were the agents of change. Steamboats, canals, railroads, the factory system and mass production, the sudden rise in material living standards, the sewing machine, the mechanical reaper—all the great mass of inventions, improvements, new processes, and new products that we associate with the dawn of the industrial age—were awakening men everywhere to a new sense of their own worth and power. If man could attain so much in the physical world, could he not do the same for his own moral and intellectual progress? [9]

High among the ideological sources of the reforming zeal was the feeling that America must fulfill its promise by breaking new roads in the development of man's capacities. Just as America had pioneered in establishing republican freedom for the benefit of man, so now must this nation of freemen lead the way in enabling men to attain their full individual potential. Lyman Beecher, prominent in educational, temperance, and antislavery causes, proclaimed this purpose when he vowed that the success or failure of American reform would determine the fate of all mankind:

9. Among numerous illustrations of the new confidence was the statement of the editor of the *Scioto* (Ohio) *Gazette* which, after reviewing "the astonishing and progressive improvements which have and are now taking place in the world," affirmed that "the intelligence and enterprise of the present age can effect almost any earthly project." Quoted in White, *The Jeffersonians*, 11. For a general discussion of this point, see Daniel J. Boorstin, *The Lost World of Thomas Jefferson* (New York, 1948), 243-248.

> The time has come when the experiment is to be made whether the world is to be emancipated and rendered happy, or whether the whole creation shall groan and travail together in pain. . . . If it had been the design of Heaven to establish a powerful nation in the full enjoyment of civil and religious liberty, where all the energies of man might find full scope and excitement, on purpose to show the world by one great successful experiment of what man is capable . . . where should such an experiment have been made but in this country! [10]

To meet the challenge posed by the new awareness of man's innate resources, reformers did not hestitate to draw on foreign precedents to assist in carrying out the American mission. They copied the organizational techniques of British reform groups—local associations linked to a central head, conventions, paid professional lecturers, pledges, pamphlets, fund-raising, memorials to the government. The success of the British movement for the immediate emancipation of the West Indian slaves not only gave fresh encouragement to American abolitionists but spurred formation of the New England Anti-Slavery and American Anti-Slavery societies patterned on the model of their British counterpart. Americans, concerned with the care of the insane and the cause of peace, drew upon their British equivalents for ideas, resources, and inspiration. In education, the founding of the London mechanics' institute and the English *Mechanics' Magazine* prompted the establishment of similar American institutions; the Boston and American Societies for the Diffusion of Useful Knowledge were modeled after Henry Brougham's London society of the same name; the American Lyceum movement developed out of the background of English pioneering in educating the working classes; the monitorial system of the English educator Joseph Lancaster was incorporated into the schools of the New York Free School Society, the charity schools of Philadelphia, and elsewhere. Reformers also drew from Continental sources. The communitarian theories of the French socialist Charles Fourier

10. Statement of Lyman Beecher, quoted in Alice Felt Tyler, *Freedom's Ferment* (Minneapolis, 1944), 1.

were tried in more than forty American "phalanxes." Horace Mann and Calvin Stowe championed the principle of state-controlled compulsory school attendance after studying the Prussian educational system. The educational ideas of the famous Swiss pedagogue Johann H. Pestalozzi influenced the curricula of several progressive schools established in the period.[11]

In several of their campaigns the reformers made notable and lasting contributions to the cause of human progress. Their efforts led to the construction of hospitals for the care of the physically and mentally handicapped. They obtained improved and enlarged prisons and segregated facilities for minor offenders, youths, and women. Their pressure resulted in the establishment of new and improved public elementary and high school systems, teacher-training colleges, lyceums, and mechanics' institutes. Inexorably, however, a single cause rose to prominence and absorbed the interest and energy of the reform generation. More flagrantly than any other evil, Negro slavery denied a major segment of the population the opportunity for self-development; and more fiercely than any other established group, Southern slave-owners defended the "peculiar institution" against all efforts to grant the Negro his claim to freedom. It was a situation that few men of conscience could allow themselves to disregard.

Never more than a small minority of the entire population, the abolitionists succeeded in turning the existence of slavery in the South into the foremost moral and political issue of the age. Under the spotlight of their exposure and criticism, slavery became a matter that politicians ignored at their peril; and the political history of the 1850's is largely the story of the various ways in which the American parties—Whig, Democratic, and Republican—confronted or failed to confront this great issue.

11. Frank Thistlethwaite, *The Anglo-American Connection in the Early Nineteenth Century* (Philadelphia, 1959), 91-92, 137-142, 144; Gilbert H. Barnes, *The Antislavery Impulse, 1830-1844* (New York, 1933), 29-58; Tyler, *Freedom's Ferment,* 217-220, 245-248.

Though the North as a whole certainly considered the immediate abolition of slavery to be far too radical, as both contrary to the Constitution and dangerous to the Union, Northern antislavery feeling was strong enough by 1860 to play a major role in electing to the presidency a candidate opposed to the territorial expansion of slavery. Southern leaders, meanwhile, alarmed by the rising tide of Northern antislavery sentiment, made ever-increasing demands for the protection of slavery not only where it already existed in the states, but in the federal territories where it did not yet exist. To the extent that the abolitionists aroused Northern opposition to the expansion of slavery, to the extent that they evoked Southern demands for its extra-territorial protection, to this extent were they responsible for creating a conflict that was irreconcilable and irrepressible.[12]

The outbreak of the Civil War signaled renewed and broadened abolitionist efforts in behalf of the Negro. Right up to January, 1863, when Lincoln issued the Emancipation Proclamation, abolitionists continued to pressure the administration, making no secret of their impatience with the apparent reluctance of the government to grant freedom to the slave. Nor did they abandon the freedman after the Proclamation. Abolitionists played a vital role in shaping government policy on the procedures to be followed in bringing the Negro to freedom.

Again, foreign experience was seized upon to assist in carrying out America's mission as a showcase of liberty. An abolitionist-inspired and abolitionist-controlled American Freedman's Inquiry Commission conducted an extensive investigation into the process of Negro emancipation in the British West Indies, and into the contemporary condition of the free Negro in the United States and Canada. On the basis of these studies, the commission rec-

12. Arthur Bestor, "The American Civil War as a Constitutional Crisis," *American Historical Review,* LXIX (January 1964), 327-352, makes the case for the territorial expansion of slavery as the central constitutional issue behind the coming of the Civil War.

ommended a broad program of economic and educational assistance to enable the freedman to establish immediate self-sufficiency. Rather than proceed to freedom by way of apprenticeship or federal guardianship, the commission urged that the Negro receive immediate schooling, an opportunity to earn a living and acquire land, and protection in "those rights, civil and political, without which they are but laboring as a man labors with his hands bound." Accordingly, Congress established a Freedman's Bureau to provide educational facilities and to assist the freedman in obtaining work and land.[13]

Not content with these achievements, abolitionists pressed a campaign to desegregate public facilities and to extend the franchise to the Negro. Here again consciousness of the national mission was apparent. Segregated schools for Negroes, wrote the New York abolitionist Samuel J. May in 1864, were "a perpetual imputation of fault, unworthiness or inferiority, which must tend to discourage and keep them depressed. . . . We are to show the world that *all* men, not white men alone, but all, of every complexion, language and lineage have equal rights to life, liberty and the pursuit of happiness; and that all men, jointly and severally, excepting idiots, the insane and intemperate, are capable of governing themselves and each other, better than they ever have been, or ever can be governed by despots, kings, aristocrats, or any privileged individuals." [14]

Even so, attainment of the major abolitionist objectives came more through coincidental political and military developments than through any genuine commitment of white men to the Negro cause. When Lincoln proclaimed emancipation he did so for

13. James M. McPherson, *The Struggle for Equality: Abolitionists and the Negro in the Civil War and Reconstruction* (Princeton, 1964), 75-133, 178-191, 386-393.

14. Samuel J. May to Andrew D. White, 11 March 1864, quoted in James M. Smith, "The 'Separate but Equal' Doctrine: An Abolitionist Discusses Racial Segregation and Educational Policy during the Civil War," *Journal of Negro History,* XLI (April 1956), 143.

reasons of war strategy, not because of conversion to abolitionist principles. By providing fresh manpower for Northern forces, by undermining the Southern economy, by winning support abroad, by quieting abolitionist criticism of his administration, emancipation would bring new strength to the Union cause—a cause Lincoln identified with the world prestige of popular government. Thus final emancipation owed more to the Lincolnian concept of the war as a test of the validity of government of, by, and for the people than to the abolitionist conception of it as a crusade to free the slave.

Abolitionists pressed hard for the other great constitutional legacies of the Civil War—the Fourteenth and Fifteenth Amendments. Yet here again these guarantees of equal legal protection and the franchise were not the result of a sudden popular enthusiasm for Negro equality, but of fortuitous circumstances that enabled the abolitionists to win their objectives without broadly based support. President Andrew Johnson's stubborn veto of all congressional measures intended to nullify economically discriminatory Southern "black codes" drove Republican moderates into the arms of radicals who wanted iron-clad constitutional guarantees of Negro civil and political rights. Lacking genuine popular support either in the North or the South, the abolitionists could win their most important advances only when political and military exigency happened to coincide with their objectives.[15]

Unable to awaken national support for Negro equality, abolitionists soon realized their most ambitious projects were doomed to failure. Despite limited gains made during peak periods of war idealism, segregation and political disfranchisement remained prevalent in the North outside New England. In the South, by 1900, the Negro had lost much of the ground gained during Reconstruction, as historic assumptions regarding his innate in-

15. Benjamin Thomas, *Abraham Lincoln* (New York, 1952), 257-283, 333-334, 355-364; McPherson, *Struggle for Equality*, 186, 341-366, 417-432; Eric McKitrick, *Andrew Johnson and Reconstruction* (Chicago, 1960).

feriority, together with the racist demagoguery of politicians, reduced him to a position of strict segregation and political and economic limitation. Like other reform causes of the nineteenth century, the cause of Negro equality would require other conditions and challenges to renew its dynamism and regain its momentum.[16]

Control of Industrialism

Nineteenth-century reformers aimed their attacks against ignorance, neglect, self-abuse, and oppression—the worst of the apparent obstacles to human progress. They did not yet deem it necessary to concern themselves with objectives that have become a major preoccupation of their twentieth-century counterparts—social justice and economic welfare. But during the closing decades of the century industrialism completed the transformation of America into an urban, industrialized society. It was a transformation that opened a new chapter in the American quest for ways to demonstrate the capacity of a free society to advance and flourish.

Industrialization involved processes that brought social dislocation and economic hardship to every occupation and class. As a result of the revolution in transportation and production, local manufacturers and merchants lost their ascendancy over regional markets in which slow and costly methods of production and exchange had been a prime condition of their success. Reacting to the intensified pressure of nationwide competition, the most enterprising of them soon organized huge corporate combines, gained control over entire industries, and even threatened the integrity of the legislative process itself. Onlookers wondered whether America was about to become feudalized into an indus-

16. McPherson, *Struggle for Equality,* 430-432; Rayford W. Logan, *The Negro in American Life and Thought: The Nadir, 1877-1901* (New York, 1954), 233-238; C. Vann Woodward, *The Strange Career of Jim Crow* (New York, 1957).

trial plutocracy, the private preserve of an elite of "robber barons."

Farmers also fell victim to the economic pressures of a highly unstable price-cost network. Blaming their troubles on exploitation by railroad capitalists, middlemen, and financiers, they sought relief in Grangerism, the Alliance movement, the Populist crusade, and in the advocacy of such radical programs as silver inflation and government-owned railroads, telegraphs, and credit facilities. In the industrial sphere, strikes, boycotts, violence, and killing reflected hardship and misery in the working classes. Caught in a grim, hopeless world of factories and slums, workers searched for ways out of their predicament through worker-owned co-operatives, industrial unions, socialism, communism, and anarchism. Many observers saw in the misery of the masses, the sullen bitterness of their protest, their class-consciousness, radicalism, and violence, the dark spectre of revolution.[17]

By 1900 the United States led the world in industrial production; yet the nation lagged far behind other industrialized countries in coming to grips with the most prominent ills of industrial development. By the turn of the century, Germany, Great Britain, France, Belgium, Denmark, New Zealand, and Australia had made major advances in such fields as control over public utilities, workmen's compensation, tenement house regulation, and unemployment and old age assistance. Wedded to an historic tradition of personal freedom, Americans were less willing than Europeans to accept government interference in their economic and social lives. A society whose greatest material achievements had resulted from private initiative and private means was naturally more skeptical of public action than it would have been if government had been deeply involved in industrial development. Rationalizing the conditions of late nineteenth-century America, the ideologies

17. Samuel P. Hays, *The Response to Industrialism, 1885-1914* (Chicago, 1957), is the most penetrating recent discussion of industrialism and its group impact.

of laissez-faire and Social Darwinism had attained a position of prestige that seemed almost unassailable.

Nevertheless, during the 1880's and 1890's a small group of middle class reformers, shocked and guilt-ridden by the chaos and misery they saw around them, began attacking the worst evils of the industrial order. Social workers founded settlement houses to provide education, recreation, and welfare to slum dwellers; social commentators portrayed the wastefulness of unrestrained competition and prescribed government regulation and welfare action; ministers called upon employers to provide decent wages and humane working conditions, and upon the state to regulate industry and make provision for the unemployed. These were the first Progressives—middle and upper class reformers who by 1900 had begun a wide-ranging campaign of action against the forces that were bringing misery and want to millions, setting rich and poor against each other, and threatening the very survival of America as a free society.

The Progressives made many vital contributions to the modern American welfare state. Their reforms had a range and depth that went beyond anything theretofore achieved in the field of social and economic welfare. Their aim, in Walter Lippmann's phrase, was "mastery," in contrast to "drift." They sought security for the handicapped and helpless, regulation of business and the public services, better living and working conditions for the laboring classes, an end to the influence of special interests and privilege in government. Progressive legislatures took action that prohibited child labor, determined maximum hours for railroad workers and women in industry, established workmen's compensation, set minimum wage rates for women, and authorized pensions for widows with children. They established public commissions that fixed railroad rates, inspected factories, regulated utility operations, and reformed inequitable tax structures. Cities, too, made significant advances against urban ills. They reorganized government on commission or city-manager plans for more responsible and efficient administration; opened kindergartens, playgrounds and golf courses; enacted tenement house ordinances; instituted special courts for juvenile offenders; and increased the number of municipally owned public utilities—water, gas, electricity, transportation. In the area of national affairs the progressive administrations of Theodore Roosevelt, William Howard Taft, and Woodrow Wilson left an enduring legacy of legislation and government action—the regulation of trusts and railroad rates, control of the meat-packing industry and food and drug manufacture, the conservation and development of forest and water resources, a more flexible and equitable banking system.

Behind these reforms was a strong sense that America would betray her historic obligation by failing to control the processes of industrialism. Once again it was incumbent upon the nation to demonstrate its capacity to resolve its most urgent problems. Thus Theodore Roosevelt, warning against the destructive consequences of unrestrained competition—unjustly divided prosperity, class conflict, government by plutocracy or by mob—called on Americans to "strive for social and industrial justice, achieved through the genuine rule of the people." "We, here in America," he continued in a reference to the American mission, "hold in our hands the hope of the world, the fate of the coming years; and shame and disgrace will be ours if in our eyes the light of high resolve is dimmed, if we trail in the dust the golden hopes of men." In a similar vein, Woodrow Wilson, calling for the renewal of economic opportunity "in this land of ours, the hope of all the earth," could ask: "Are we, in the consciousness that the life of man is pledged to higher levels here than elsewhere, striving still to bear aloft the standards of liberty and hope, or, disillusioned and defeated, are we feeling the disgrace of having had a free field in which to do new things, and of not having done them?" [18]

18. Theodore Roosevelt, Address, 20 March 1912, *The Works of Theodore Roosevelt,* National edition (New York, 1926), XVII, 170-171; Woodrow Wilson, *The New Freedom: A Call for the Emancipation of the Generous Energies of a People* (New York, 1913), 284-285.

Again, Americans, in support of the national mission, turned to outside sources. Many Progressives, finding little in the American experience to guide them in dealing with the ills of city and factory, looked abroad for instruction in the work of reform. Benjamin Flower saw Germany, New Zealand, and other countries as "Foreign Experiment Stations" in welfare legislation; Henry Demarest Lloyd hoped that Americans would adopt "all the good ideas of Europe and Australasia." The concrete results were wide-ranging. After visiting London's Toynbee Hall, Robert A. Woods, Stanton Coit, Vida Scudder, and Jane Addams built settlement houses in Boston, New York, and Chicago. On the basis of their studies of European "municipal socialism," Albert Shaw, Frank Parsons, Robert A. Woods, and Frederic C. Howe forged powerful and persuasive arguments for strong municipal governments that could own and operate public utilities, demolish slums and establish model tenements, build parks, laundries, bath houses, libraries, and gymnasiums. The New York legislature modeled its workmen's compensation law of 1909 on British legislation passed in 1897; the New York Tenement House Commission of 1900 based its recommendations on European housing experience; the first unemployment assistance act ever introduced into a state legislature (Massachusetts, 1916) was patterned after the British act of 1911.[19]

During the 1920's Progressivism continued to gain ground in its effort to improve men's lot under industrialism. The decade witnessed such accomplishments as the extension of state and federal utility regulation, municipal ownership of electric power

19. Arthur Mann, "British Social Thought and American Reformers of the Progressive Era," *The Mississippi Valley Historical Review,* XLII (March 1956), 672-692; Edwin E. Witte, "An Historical Account of Unemployment Insurance in the Social Security Act," *Law and Contemporary Problems,* III (January 1936), 157; Edward C. Kirkland, *Industry Comes of Age: Business, Labor, and Public Policy 1860-1897* (New York, 1961), 249; Robert W. Deforest and Lawrence Veiller, *The Tenement House Problem* (New York, 1903), 11, 33, 45-46.

facilities, the expansion of state and local welfare and educational activities, and the growth of the movement for the multi-purpose development of wasted river valleys. Despite such achievements, however, the nation had not yet learned to combat one of the most destructive features of the industrial order—depression. In facing the great economic crisis that closed the decade, Americans once again were confronted by a challenge that tested the capacity of a free society successfully to manage its own affairs. By 1932 the Great Depression had reduced thirteen million workers to idleness, to tramping the streets, selling apples, waiting in bread lines. The same year over 250,000 families lost their homes through foreclosure; in 1933 evictions were taking place at the rate of more than a thousand a day. Tens of thousands of men, women, and children were already sleeping in tents, in rudely constructed shacks, and even in doorways and on the ground. In the countryside, farmers actively resisted sheriffs attempting eviction, blocked highways, and overturned milk trucks in protest against low prices.

When Franklin D. Roosevelt entered office in March, 1933, the spectre of revolution hung low over the land. Men talked of dictatorship and intelligent people, including leading writers and intellectuals, endorsed a Communist candidate for president. When several thousand unemployed in Ohio marched on the state house at Columbus, Louis Budenz shouted to them: "We must take control of the government and establish a workers' and farmers' republic." A prominent New Deal official recalled several years later that the mood in the country was such that: "We could have got a dictator a lot easier than Germany got Hitler." At the Capitol in 1934, Senator Burton K. Wheeler reminded his listeners that "many in this room" had not long ago wondered whether this government would survive. In the words of Arthur Schlesinger, Jr., "It was now not just a matter of staving off hunger. It was a matter of seeing whether a representative democracy could conquer economic collapse. It was a matter of staving off violence, even (at least some so thought) revolution." Democratic government had to prove, as Roosevelt himself recalled in 1941, that it possessed within itself "the ability to furnish to its citizens the strength, the courage, the assistance, the instruments with which to meet their problems." [20]

In its first phase the New Deal emphasized the rebuilding of prosperity and assistance to bankrupt states and charities in the vast work of relief. It authorized grants to the states and to job-creating public service programs; it enacted huge public works projects, home and farm refinancing, farm crop supports, and industrial codes setting maximum hours and minimum wages. In its second phase it stressed social justice and long-term security: contributory old-age insurance and federal-state unemployment support, minimum wage and maximum hour standards, public housing, low-interest loans to struggling farmers, the right of labor to unionize and bargain collectively with employers on an equitable basis.

In this fight against the worst ravages of industrialism, the New Deal, faithful to the American reform tradition, was quite prepared to reach across national boundaries for ideas. True, as Arthur Link has noted, the New Deal probably drew most of its raw material "from half a century or more of discussion and practical experience and from ideas proposed as well by Republicans as by Democrats." But just as their reformist predecessors had done, so did the reformers of the 1930's discover useful precedents and experience abroad. After investigating European and Australasian unemployment and old-age assistance schemes, administration leaders based the contributory annuity plan for

20. Arthur M. Schlesinger, Jr., *The Coming of the New Deal* (Cambridge, 1959) is replete with references to contemporary fears of revolution. The extensive and detailed study, Bernard Sternsher, *Rexford Tugwell and the New Deal* (New Brunswick, 1964), also shows the fears of a leading New Deal official, 144-146; Franklin D. Roosevelt, Introduction, *The Public Papers and Addresses of Franklin D. Roosevelt* (New York, 1941), 1937 volume, lxxii.

old-age assistance, as well as other features, on the most successful foreign pattern. The three greenbelt communities built by the Resettlement Administration were modeled after the English garden cities of Ebenezer Howard, as well as earlier American adaptations of this prototype. The administration sent one of its housing planners abroad to study European public housing, appointed him chief project planner in the U.S. Housing Authority, and undoubtedly shaped many technical details and specifications in its housing program after European examples. The Bankhead-Jones Farm Tenancy Act of 1937, which extended rehabilitation loans to farmers and granted low-interest long-term loans to selected tenants to enable them to buy family-sized farms, was derived from Mexico's experience in converting peons into peasant proprietors. True also to the reform tradition, Roosevelt conceived of the New Deal as showing the world the ability of a free society to cope with economic disaster. "We of the Republic," the President emphasized, "sensed the truth that democratic government has innate capacity to protect its people against disasters once considered inevitable, to solve problems once considered unsolvable." Thus, in combatting the Depression, "we Americans were discovering no wholly new truth; we were writing a new chapter in our book of self-government." [21]

21. Arthur S. Link, *American Epoch: A History of the United States Since the 1890's* (New York, 1955), 425; J. Douglas Brown, "The Development of the Old-Age Insurance Provisions of the Social Security Act," *Law and Contemporary Problems,* III (April 1936), 186-198; Barbara Armstrong, "Old Age Security Abroad: The Backgrounds of Titles II and VII of the Social Security Act," *Law and Contemporary Problems* (April 1936), 175-185; Roy Lubove, "New Cities for Old: The Urban Reconstruction Program of the 1930's," *Social Studies,* LIII (November 1962), 203-213; William V. Reed and Elizabeth Ogg, *New Homes for Old: Public Housing in Europe and America* (New York, 1940); William E. Leuchtenburg, *Franklin D. Roosevelt and the New Deal 1932-1940* (New York, 1963), 140-141; Roosevelt, "Second Inaugural Address," *Public Papers and Addresses,* 1937 volume, 1.

From Isolationism to World Commitment

No less than in the areas of social justice and economic security, the impact of the national mission is evident in the history of American foreign policy. This mission implied a process in which the American example would encourage the oppressed peoples of the world to overthrow their masters and be free. Instead of seeking to emancipate mankind through political subversion or military conquest, America would achieve the same result through the inspiration of its own successful experiment in freedom. Throughout American history, the concept of America as a model to be emulated, rather than as a pattern to be imposed, has exercised a restraining influence against the kind of aggressive messianism that nations which see themselves as saviors frequently pursue. This concept also helps explain why American policy has been more defensive and self-limiting than aggressively aimed at the liberation of others.

The traditional policy of abstention from European rivalries, alliances, and balance-of-power politics indicates the restraining influence of this approach. If President Washington's policy of neutrality and non-involvement reflected the realities of national weakness and the circumstances of a distant geographical position, it also revealed the logic of affording America the necessary security for the development and display of her own unique destiny. In his first Inaugural Address, Washington reminded his listeners that "the preservation of the sacred fire of liberty, and the destiny of the Republican model of Government, are justly considered as deeply, perhaps as finally staked, on the experiment entrusted to the hands of the American people." Persuaded by the importance of this trust, Washington tried to steer a course that would enable the nation to work exclusively for its own unity and strength apart from European entanglement. Likewise, President Jefferson set a course that would keep the United States beyond the pale of European entanglement, confident that a "just & solid republican government maintained here, will be a standing monument & example for the aim & imitation of the people of other countries." [22]

It seemed only logical that if America should abstain from political interference in the affairs of Europe, European powers should, in their turn, leave the Western Hemisphere alone. Although Jefferson and Madison suggested the principle, it was James Monroe who finally made the doctrine of the two separate hemispheres a matter of public record and policy. Concerned that the autocratic regimes of France, Austria, Prussia, and Russia might seek to restore the newly independent republics of Latin America to Spain, Monroe in 1823 warned Europe against any interference in the affairs of the South American hemisphere. Henceforth, Monroe declared, any intervention on the part of Old World powers "with the purpose of oppressing, or controlling in any other manner, the destiny of the new republics" of Latin America would be "regarded as the manifestation of an unfriendly disposition toward the United States." Nor were "the American continents, by the free and independent conditions which they have assumed and maintain," to be henceforth considered "as subject for future colonization by any European power." While expressing an ideological affinity with the new republics of Latin America, Monroe was also concerned that a restoration of monarchical rule in Latin America would threaten the security of the new experiment in freedom.

Very clearly the American mission was a concept that did not call for the application of American military power in aid of popular or anti-colonial revolutions, however much they might have owed to the American example. There were numerous temptations. Hardly had America achieved her independence than revolution convulsed France, the Low Countries, Switzerland,

22. Jefferson to John Dickinson, 6 Mar 01, *The Works of Thomas Jefferson,* Ford edition (New York, 1904-05), IX, 201-202.

Italy, and Ireland, and similar tides swept through Europe in the 1820's, 1830's, and 1840's. But no American administration ever contributed direct assistance to any of these revolutionary struggles. Neither did the American government participate in the anti-colonial revolutions that brought independence to the countries of Latin America during the second decade of the nineteenth century; and not until the turn of the twentieth century did America actively intervene in the politics of any nation south of the border. Americans might have applauded these independence movements, and occasionally a few Americans enlisted as volunteers in a revolutionary cause. American administrations were not, moreover, entirely averse to granting early recognition to revolutionary regimes. But the majority of Americans did not feel obligated to go further than that—neither by the interests of security nor by their conception of the nation's destiny.[23]

On occasion, however, this concept of mission failed to restrain Americans from attempting to impose their own purposes on others. It gave little concern to those frontiersmen who staged uprisings in West Florida in 1810, East Florida in 1812, Texas in 1819 and 1835, and California in 1846. It gave little pause to President James Polk, whose territorial ambitions led the nation into the most discreditable war in American history, a war that left Mexico despoiled of a third of her territory and nursing an enduring legacy of bitterness toward her northern neighbor. It did not concern men like Theodore Roosevelt, Henry Cabot Lodge, and Alfred T. Mahan, whose campaign for strategic naval bases and trading stations played an important part in transforming the Spanish-American War from a humanitarian crusade for Cuban independence into an unseemly scramble for island possessions.

Still, neither "manifest destiny" nor imperialism reflected the true values of the great majority of the American people. Even in the headiest days of the "roaring forties," expansionism never

23. Dexter Perkins, *The American Approach to Foreign Policy* (Cambridge, 1962), 6, 78-82.

attracted the enthusiastic support of more than a minority. Polk's Mexican policies aroused strong opposition, and even at the peak of the Mexican War the acquisition of additional areas from Mexico failed to arouse extensive approval. Many Americans would have agreed with Albert Gallatin that expansionism betrayed America's true purpose—"to improve the state of the world, to be the 'model republic,' to show that men are capable of governing themselves, and that the simple and natural form of government is that also which confers most happiness on all, is productive of the greatest development of the intellectual faculties, above all, that which is attended with the highest standard of private and political virtue and morality." [24]

Equally, in the 1890's, there was much opposition to the acquisition of overseas possessions. Ex-President Grover Cleveland touched a familiar chord when he denounced the acquisition of Hawaii as a "perversion" of the national mission, insisting that the "mission of our nation is to build up and make a greater country out of what we have instead of annexing islands." The continentalism of the 1840's and the imperialism of the 1890's were never, as Frederick Merk has observed, "true expressions of the national spirit"; they were "traps into which the nation was led in 1846 and 1899, and from which it extricated itself as well as it could afterward." [25]

Nonetheless, the emergence of America to the status of a great power by the end of the nineteenth century created new temptations for the nation to exert its influence in the world by methods not sanctioned by the traditional ideal. National power inevitably made Americans more willing to use this power in behalf of causes analogous to their own. It is significant that the Spanish-American War, undertaken as a crusade to free Cuba from Spanish oppression, occurred at a time when Ameri-

24. Frederick Merk, *Manifest Destiny and Mission in American History: A Reinterpretation* (New York, 1963), 24-41, 144-179, 187-201, 262.
25. *Ibid.*, 261, 263.

cans were awakening to a sense of national strength. Our repeated interventions in the Caribbean during the first three decades of the twentieth century revealed the extent to which the new confidence could carry us, not only to safeguard vital hemispheric interests but to bring American concepts of popular government to the peoples of the area. Significantly, Woodrow Wilson chose war in 1917 when he realized that he could not surrender to unrestricted German submarine warfare without disgracing the nation and its ideals, without betraying the obligation imposed by the growing power of the United States to exert its influence for good in the world. Surely it was a feeling for the nation's new might that gave him confidence to define the struggle as one in which America would make the world "safe for democracy" by achieving a peace in which the whole world would be ordered by "such a concert of free peoples as shall bring peace and safety to all nations and make the world itself at last free." [26]

Still, until World War II the crusades of 1898 and 1917 remained notable exceptions to the historic notion that America's true destiny lay in saving the world through what she did at home rather than what she did abroad. Although a majority of Americans in the immediate aftermath of the war probably preferred American participation in the League of Nations, in time the dominant mood of the country came to favor full withdrawal from the international scene. For two decades American foreign policy vacillated between isolationism and ineffective schemes of collective action, while the nation withheld its power from the world arena and refused to pledge itself to assist in the maintenance of international stability. American aloofness reached its zenith in the 1930's when Congress enacted a series of neutrality laws which, until their repeal after the invasion of Poland in 1939, prohibited all financial loans and sales of arms and ammu-

26. Ernest R. May, *The World War and American Isolation 1914-1917* (Cambridge, 1963), 427, 433.

nition to belligerent powers. So unwilling were Americans to become involved in world politics that even as late as 1941, with the United States already aiding Britain, President Roosevelt felt it necessary repeatedly to deny that his policies sought any other objective but plain national survival. Lend-lease, wrote the President, was "not based primarily on a desire to preserve democracy for the rest of the world," but "primarily on a desire to protect the United States and the Western Hemisphere from the effects of a Nazi victory upon ourselves and upon our children." At the same time it seemed to Roosevelt that America's survival also carried special implications for all mankind. In the words of his Third Inaugural Address in 1941:

> The destiny of America was proclaimed in words of prophecy spoken by our first President in his first Inaugural in 1789—words almost directed, it would seem, to this year of 1941: "The preservation of the sacred fire of liberty and the destiny of the republican model of government are justly considered . . . deeply . . . finally, staked on the experiment intrusted to the hands of the American people."

"In the face of great perils never before encountered," concluded the President, "our strong purpose is to protect and perpetuate the integrity of democracy." [27]

Just as Roosevelt finally exerted American strength when faced with the threat of Nazism, so have the nation's postwar leaders, in defense of the American mission, felt compelled to direct American power and influence overseas. America's new participation in world affairs, total and binding for the first time in its history, is the logical response to the condition of a shrinking world in which it is no longer possible to defend the integrity of the nation by ramparts erected at its own shores. As the shadow

27. Franklin D. Roosevelt, Introduction, *The Public Papers and Addresses of Franklin D. Roosevelt,* ed. by Samuel Rosenman (New York, 1941), 1940 volume, xxx; Roosevelt, Third Inaugural Address, *Public Papers and Addresses,* 1941 volume, 3-6.

of communist domination fell across the world in the chaotic aftermath of World War II, there seemed no other rational alternative than to contain the new threat before it won control of the resources and power of all Europe and Asia. Never before has a nation borne such heavy world burdens and responsibilities to ensure its national survival in time of peace as did the United States in the postwar era: economic, technical, and military aid to countries under direct communist pressure, to war-ravaged Europe, and to the emerging nations; mutual defense and security treaties with nations in the North Atlantic, Middle Eastern, and Southeast Asian areas; the nuclear deterrent; engagement of American military and naval power in the active defense of South Korea, Lebanon, South Vietnam, and West Berlin. To achieve a viable and permanent independence in which to work out its destiny, the United States, in the eighteenth and nineteenth centuries, had withheld itself from active participation in world affairs; aware of a sudden vulnerability in the mid-twentieth century, the nation projected its power and influence to every corner of the globe.[28]

In this new exercise of American strength throughout the world, the nation is entering a new phase in the accomplishment of a mission undertaken nearly two centuries before. Can a free society successfully serve the vital needs of man, providing not only liberty but security, justice, the opportunity for self-fulfillment and happiness? In the earliest decades of our national experience this purpose expressed itself in efforts to prove the competence of a republican government to discharge the obligations of government as then defined. In the mid-nineteenth century it revealed

28. Robert E. Osgood, *Ideals and Self-Interest in America's Foreign Relations* (Chicago, 1953), 429, attributes the "recent national awakening to the dependence of America's welfare upon events abroad" to "the mounting fear since the beginning of World War II that the maintenance of America's democratic institutions and the preservation of America's territorial integrity are seriously threatened by the restless surge of aggressive and antidemocratic powers outside the Western Hemisphere."

itself again in attempts to make it possible for men to develop their full powers and capacities. In the twentieth century it expressed itself once more in efforts to control the forces and consequences of industrialism and turn them to man's welfare. In foreign policy it expressed itself in the search for a firmly independent status and in self-restraint in international relations.

It is this mission that has tied the American experience to the rest of the world, this and the instruction received from abroad in the search for solutions to the nation's recurrent problems. As both example and beneficiary, America has always been deeply involved in world development. It has never been isolated. Yet today, as never before, the nation is compelled to fulfill its mission not only by social and economic achievement at home, but by bearing the heavy burdens of economic assistance and military defense throughout the globe. Forced into this new role by the requirements of its own security, the nation finds itself again required to prove the strength, imagination, and staying power of a free society.

2

AMERICA IN THE WORLD ECONOMY: A RETROSPECT

HARRY N. SCHEIBER

AT a time when modern communications are quickly annihilating once formidable barriers of time and space, it is tempting to dismiss the past record of America's role in the world economy as irrelevant to an understanding of her present economic position in the world. Many of the most urgent questions faced by the United States since 1945, it is true, have sprung directly from the international situation: the need to support postwar European reconstruction, the issues raised by the demands of new nations struggling with the problems of economic development, the perils of a shifting balance of payments, the emergence of regional trade associations, and the impact of a massive defense establishment on the domestic economy in a period of severe world tension. Yet the post-1945 experience does not represent a complete departure from an earlier era. Despite the presence of rich resources in an unsettled continent, despite the vaunted impact of the frontier on American development and the distances that separated this country from the Old World, the American economy was never isolated nor was American economic growth ever shaped exclusively by internal forces.

In its colonial era, America was on the western perimeter of Europe's imperial trade area, an appendage of the Old World's economy. Even after the American Revolution, the United States continued to hold an essentially colonial position in relation to the European economy; and so close were trade ties (and mutual interdependence) with England and the British Empire that the North Atlantic area was practically a "common market." Following the Civil War, internal forces—expansion of the resource base, the growth of cities, and extensive railroad construction—were more important than before as basic determinants of American growth. But American industry remained dependent upon European supplies of labor, capital, and technology; the West Coast region was reliant upon Asian labor; American agriculture sold much of its surplus in foreign markets, and indeed, exports of farm produce played a major role in determining short-run fluctuations in the domestic economy.

Beginning with World War I, the American role in the world economy began to assume its more familiar "modern" form, as developments within the United States became a key determinant of change in global economic affairs. But the relationship was never merely one-way: even then, the capability of the American economy for sustained development was closely tied to the healthy growth of international trade and the world economy. This became tragically clear in 1929 with the onset of the Great Depression. During the depression years the United States adopted essentially nationalistic measures to combat stagnation. But even in the New Deal years, the potential of expanded foreign trade as a means for promoting recovery was not lost upon those who planned the Reciprocal Trade Program; and, tragically, exports to the European belligerents played a central role in finally pulling the U.S. out of the depression.

The American national economy has thus developed historically within the context of world-wide scientific and technological change, social dislocation, and political and military conflict. No matter how impressive the depth and complexity of America's involvement in the present-day world economy, it would be a distortion to think of it as drama without prologue.

The Colonial Economy and the Mercantilist Heritage

The formative role of "foreign" influences on American economic life before the Revolution is self-evident. Prior to 1776 farmers, artisans, and merchants of thirteen related but separate colonies operated within the British Empire, and American development went forward in the context of British commercial policy. The English encouraged migration to America from the home islands and permitted private colonizing ventures. They did not circumscribe unduly the privileges of American self-government, nor did they seek (as the French did) to build an American empire upon the slim base of the fur trade. Had the British imperial design been like that of Spain or France, the destiny of the mainland colonies assuredly would have been entirely different. As it was, a principal aim of British mercantilism was to encourage large-scale permanent settlement and to foster economic development of the colonies. Mercantilism was not entirely restrictive; it was, in fact, clearly advantageous to certain economic interests in America, offering protected markets, bounties, special privileges, and the protective arm of the British army and navy. But always its avowed purpose was to mold American development in a way that would subordinate the colonies to the needs and growth of England.

The dual forces of geography and American enterprise combined to frustrate British mercantilist aims. The natural resources of New England and the Middle Atlantic area drew colonial producers into competition with the fishing, shipbuilding, and shipping industries of the home islands, and forced American merchants into legal or illicit trade in competition with their counterparts in England. Although the agrarian economies of the Southern colonies were better suited to the mercantilist scheme, their leadership constantly sought a greater measure of economic self-sufficiency, a drive which produced increasing tension between them and the imperial government. Prior to 1763, moreover, the British trade acts went virtually unenforced in essential respects; and pursuing a policy of "salutary neglect," the British permitted illegal trade with the West Indies to emerge as a vital element of the North American economy.

So long as the trade acts were administered with a light hand, the imperial tie remained on the whole advantageous. After 1763, however, a series of new statutes, Council orders, and administrative reforms thoroughly disrupted the established economic and political relationships between the colonies and the mother country. The British conquest of Quebec and consolidation of the region north of the Ohio River with that province, prohibition of American settlement west of the Appalachian "fall line," enforcement of customs duties in a way which imperiled the lifeblood of American commerce, and the imposition of new monopolies and restrictions on colonial currency—all went far toward establishing the conditions for revolution.

These new restrictions were a threat to America not solely because of the related assault on political liberties, but also because they were imposed on a maturing society. By the late eighteenth century the coastal ports had spawned a merchant class with deeply vested economic interests in illicit trade and with capital to invest in new enterprises. The American West, now apparently closed permanently to exploitation, had been an object of concern and a region which promised new opportunity to simple farmers and great land speculators alike. Boston fought the new restrictions because it had a thriving commerce to defend. New York was shaken by the incorporation of the Ohio country into Quebec because she had already proved her ability to compete successfully with Montreal for the rich fur trade of the interior. And Southern planters were willing to risk a breach with England because they were confident that they could market their tobacco more profitably in Continental Europe; and they despaired of their ability to escape the web of indebtedness that bound them to English and Scots merchants unless they had liberty to establish their own currency and debtor laws. In sum, this was a society in which perceived (and indeed very real) economic opportunities and vested interests alike were being threatened. An imperial tie which had fostered American growth in the past now was proving hostile to present and future needs.

Frustrated in their efforts to achieve a peaceful resolution of the conflict with English authorities, many colonial leaders accepted the necessity for revolution. Ironically, one basic premise on which American revolutionary leadership acted was peculiarly eighteenth-century European in origin: the mercantilist assumption that the state should be deeply involved in the national economy and should guide the growth of the economy in the national interest. As Curtis P. Nettels has observed, the colonists, "having lived so long under the rule of mercantilism, had become imbued with mercantilist ideas. If the British imperium would not allow them to grow and expand, . . . the colonists would have to take to themselves the right and power to guide their economic development." [1] When British mercantilist policy ran counter to their

1. Curtis P. Nettels, "British Mercantilism and the Economic Development of the Thirteen Colonies," *Journal of Economic History,* XII (1952), 113-114.

common interests, Americans saw political independence as essential.[2]

Attainment of American independence permitted the new nation to establish its own mercantilist policies. There was no wide consensus as to what these policies should be. On the contrary, from 1783 until well into the 1830's, American politics was marked by a sustained conflict between contending interest groups. This conflict pitted certain agrarian elements and urban artisans who stood for decentralized government against industrial and commercial groups which pressed on the whole for a powerful federal government, a national developmental program, and encouragement of industry and trade. Despite such conflicts, however, in the half-century after American independence a mature society formulated its own economic programs. Thus, in the decade after the 1787 Constitution went into effect, Congress erected a common external tariff, enacted a series of laws favoring American shippers and shipbuilders, and established a nationally chartered bank (financed with private and federal funds) to perform financial services for the government and to aid American commerce. The Constitution itself provided for a single national coinage, eliminated legal barriers to internal commerce, and stabilized business conditions by preventing the states from adopting laws which would impair legal contracts. Congress also enacted laws for the disposal of the public domain in the West that served the dual function of providing a source of revenue and encouraging settlement; and a colonial policy was adopted, unique in that it provided for absorption of territories into the Union on an equal basis with older states.

The state governments also retained a wide area of autonomy

2. In the last analysis, the political issues were foremost. Yet the political questions of the Revolution concerned primarily the suspension of traditional American liberties and prerogatives in the post-1763 British effort to raise revenue in the colonies and to enforce new (as well as old, but long-neglected) economic restrictions.

in economic affairs within the federal system. The states established major public enterprises, including canals, roads, and banks; and they regulated corporate practices and conditions of labor, including slave labor. Withal, the vigorous economic programs of the states and the federal government alike perpetuated eighteenth-century mercantilist conceptions of government's proper place in the economy, and they revealed a strong bent toward public action that departs markedly from the popular conception of the early nineteenth century as the heyday of American laissez-faire policy.[3]

But even this wide range of mercantilist policies fell short of making the United States fully master of its own economic destiny. Autonomous as the new nation was in formulating policy, certain economic forces were largely beyond the control of government. One of the most important was the continuing interdependence of this nation with others, especially England, within the international economy. In fact, American international economic relations placed important constraints upon growth in some respects, while in others they stimulated the development of the United States economy from the Revolution to the Civil War.

America in the Atlantic Economy, 1790-1860

Far from destroying the vital international context of American economic development, the Revolution permitted still deeper involvement of the American nation in world trade.[4] Thus a

3. Henry W. Broude, "The Role of the State in American Economic Development, 1820-1890," *The State and Economic Growth,* ed. by H. G. J. Aitken (New York, 1959); Carter Goodrich, *Government Promotion of American Canals and Railroads, 1800-1890* (New York, 1960).

4. The ensuing analysis of foreign trade in its relation to domestic growth owes much to Douglass C. North, *The Economic Growth of the United States, 1790-1890* (Englewood Cliffs, 1961); and Frank Thistlethwaite, *The Anglo-American Connection in the Early Nineteenth Century* (Philadelphia, 1959), Chap. 1.

Massachusetts editor heralded the attainment of independence, declaring: "Our commerce is freed from those shackles it used to be cramped with, and bids fair to extend to every part of the globe, without passing through the medium of England, that rotten island." [5] His optimism was, to be sure, premature, for the uncertainties of the post-Revolutionary world in part offset the advantages of trade free from British control. Undaunted by the risks of trading under the flag of a small new nation in a world of empires, American merchants sent out their ships to regions previously forbidden to them by the British navigation laws. India, China, and the East Indies were quickly sought out by American vessels. The Baltic states, Russia, the French West Indies, southern Africa and the Philippines were also drawn into the expanding, though still flimsy, web of United States commerce.

But the mainstay of American commerce from 1783 to 1807 continued to be trade with Europe. Out of American ports to England and the Continent went lumber, rice, tobacco, and foodstuffs, which together amounted to three-fourths of total American exports. From Europe entered manufactures, wine, and processed foods; from both European middlemen and the tropical areas came tea, spices, sugar, and Negro slaves.

It is ironic that a period dominated by a dramatic clash of political-economic programs, posing the neo-mercantilist doctrines of Hamilton against the agrarianism of Jefferson, was also a period when neither the factory producer nor the self-sufficient yeoman dominated the American economy. Instead, the central role was played by the merchant prince of the Atlantic Coast, with his fleet of compact schooners and stout square-rigged freighters. The merchant's primary place in the economy was assured by the outbreak of war in Europe in 1793, with England and France locked in a prolonged death struggle. Immediately, European demand for neutral ships and shipping, foodstuffs and products

5. Quoted in Merrill Jensen, *The New Nation* (New York, 1950), 154.

of sea and forest, carried foreign trade into new prominence in the American economy.

Never since the years of the Anglo-French wars has foreign commerce so absorbed the energies of the American nation and governed short-run fluctuations in the American economy as it did from 1793 to 1807. The decks of United States ships and the walks of the Atlantic shipyards were as much a frontier for enterprise as the new lands to the West; and even Western lands were a promising field for settlement largely because of active overseas demand for American staples. The statistics of foreign commerce reflected this pattern of change. Exports climbed from $20 million in 1790 to $67 million (current prices) in 1796. At the peak of trade in the pre-War of 1812 period, in 1807, exports reached $108 million. Imports increased as well, reflecting the growth of American trade in and production of staples and the rising purchasing power of the new nation. Some $23 million in 1790, imports were $139 million in 1807. In the tradition of the great maritime nations, American vessels showed their neutral flag and became merchantmen to a world at war. Despite havoc wrought on United States shipping by belligerent navies, American shipping earnings rose from some $6 million in 1790 to $42 million in 1807. During the same period, earnings of the U.S. merchant fleet increased almost sevenfold, and the value of re-exports rose from $300,000 to over $60 million.[6]

The post-1807 embargo legislation and the War of 1812 with England closed this distinct epoch in American development. Military and civilian demand stimulated manufacturing after 1807, as sources of foreign supply were cut off, while rising wholesale prices during the wartime inflation attracted idle merchant capital into industry. During the war with England, 1812-1815, U.S.

6. Douglass C. North, "The U.S. Balance of Payments" in National Bureau of Economic Research, *Trends in the American Economy in the 19th Century* (Princeton, 1960), 590-592, 595, 600; John G. B. Hutchins, *The American Maritime Industries and Public Policy* (Cambridge, 1941), 227.

foreign commerce dropped sharply. But the prominent role of foreign trade was revealed once again immediately after the war, when, despite the emergency tariff of 1816, imported manufactures flooded the American market. While domestic manufacturers suffered, the economy was buoyed until 1819, this time by continued European demand for farm products. When the European nations adjusted to peacetime economic needs, aided by bumper crops in 1818-19, the foreign market for American staples suddenly declined; the expansive influence of a land boom in the West, which had been a response to the boom in demand, now collapsed; and monetary derangement and a prolonged depression set in. Once again, the state of foreign demand had proven critical to the prosperity of the United States and governed the timing of business cycles in the domestic economy.

A persuasive argument has been made that restoration of prosperity in the mid-1820's, and indeed the entire growth of the American economy from 1820 to 1840, was mainly dependent upon the course of the United States cotton trade with Great Britain. The cotton textile industry was the leading edge of the industrial revolution in England, and rising British demand for this staple crop carried cotton into new prominence in the American export trade following the introduction of Eli Whitney's cotton gin in the 1790's. In 1807 cotton comprised less than 10 per cent of exports. By 1835, however, cotton amounted to more than half the value of exports, a position it held until the Civil War. The profits to be made in cotton-growing fastened a single-crop agricultural pattern on much of the South. This embedded the slave plantation system in the region and made the South dependent upon the Northeast for capital, shipping services, and manufactures, both domestic and imported. At the same time, a rapid shift westward of cotton production occurred in response to soil exhaustion in the old regions, and the slave plantation system was allowed to shape the economic and social structure of the Southwest. This dominance of the plantation left the

South reliant upon outside sources for foodstuffs; and because the Mississippi River was the chief export route for surplus Western staples, this meant a growing market for the agricultural products of the West.

In this manner, the westward movement of settlement into the Ohio country was tied to the fortunes of the cotton trade. So, too, were the shipping and shipbuilding industries of the Atlantic seaboard, for cotton was the mainstay of the trade in which middlemen and coastal merchants engaged. For the economy as a whole, moreover, the profits of cotton exports underwrote the continuing flow of merchandise imports into the United States. Taking into account the strategic place of cotton, both in the United States and in the British economies, it is understandable that this crop should have been termed "king, not only of the southern states, but of the Atlantic world itself." [7]

Although the cotton trade had a key role in American development before 1860, it was not the only important bridge between the economies of America and the Old World. The contribution of immigration to population growth in the United States was another reflection of interdependence within the Atlantic economy. Immigration from Europe ranged from 6,300 to 23,000 persons annually in the 1820's. But from 1831 to 1840 the annual average rose to more than 60,000, mainly from the British Isles and northern Europe.

The development of improved transportation facilities in the United States similarly was reliant upon economic contact with Europe. Transport improvements speeded the emergence of an integrated national economy and permitted regional specialization, and were therefore a major force in American economic development. A large part of the new system of canals, roads, and railways was built with the aid of British and European capital. The canal network, constructed mainly by the state governments, was

7. Frank Thistlethwaite, *The Great Experiment* (Cambridge [England], 1955), 73.

financed in large part by sale of public bonds to British investors: for example, in the years 1834-44, at the height of the American canal movement, more than 90 per cent of the $72 million expended in construction was obtained abroad.[8] Similarly, foreign investors poured capital into western lands; they extended, through the commercial banking houses of London and Paris, short-term loans that were vital to both the import and export trades; and in the 1850's purchased a large part of the railroad bonds issued to support new construction.

Finally, the development of the American economy involved exploitation of foreign technological innovations and scientists. In canal planning and construction, for example, the influence of the British and French was considerable; in fact, many of the early American-born engineers were foreign-trained, and even the Army Engineers and the West Point faculty relied in part upon French personnel until the mid-1820's. In agriculture, such foreign innovations as tile draining techniques were rapidly adapted to American needs; and in manufacturing, especially in textiles and mining, some of the most successful of the earliest firms relied heavily on foreign craftsmen and machines modeled on foreign designs.

The cotton trade continued to play a central role in American development after 1840, influencing as before the pace of Southern and Western settlement and providing the chief source of exports. But in both internal commerce and manufacturing, the early 1840's witnessed major changes with important long-range effects. [9] In domestic commerce, the forties brought a massive increase in the volume of trade between the Atlantic Coast and the new agricultural regions of the West. This was the result of the completion of the major canals begun during the previous decade, and

8. Harvey H. Segal, "Cycles of Canal Construction," *Canals and American Economic Development,* ed. by Carter Goodrich (New York, 1962), 180 ff.

9. Cf. George Rogers Taylor, *The Transportation Revolution* (New York, 1950).

it permitted introduction of cheap food supplies into the East from the high-yield new lands of the West. Eastern agriculture suffered a relative decline as a result, and the new sources of foodstuffs, together with the expanding market the West offered for eastern manufactures, impelled the movement toward industrialization and urbanization in the East. In manufacturing, the depression of 1839-43 marked what Victor S. Clark has termed "a dividing line between two industrial periods." [10] In many of the industries founded earlier (e.g., textiles, metal-working, and clothing manufacture), the economic crisis forced small firms into bankruptcy or produced mergers with larger, more efficient units. Household manufacture gave way increasingly to the factory system, a shift in basic business organization that portended the shape of industrialization in the future. The depression also destroyed much of the flimsy banking system which had blossomed in the 1830's; and in many states the crisis forced banking onto a more stable basis, thereby strengthening the sources of capital for industrial investment. After 1840 short-term interest rates declined and the increasing availability of long-term capital permitted manufacturers to expand plant operations by means of bond issues, instead of relying upon sales of equity stock. In the realm of industrial technology, moreover, the late 1830's brought significant changes in the manufacture of cotton textiles, woolens, and iron. The new inventions were costly, and they served to stimulate the movement toward more highly capitalized firms.[11]

The resultant growth of industrial output made the 1840's a period of fundamental change in the structure of the economy. At the time of the 1840 census, agriculture comprised 72 per cent of total commodity output, while manufacturing accounted

10. Victor S. Clark, *History of Manufactures in the United States* (New York, 1929), I, 381.

11. Alfred H. Conrad, "Income Growth and Structural Change," *American Economic History*, ed. by Seymour E. Harris (New York, 1961), 29 ff; H. J. Habakkuk, *American and British Technology in the 19th Century* (Cambridge [England], 1962), 102 ff.

for only 17 per cent. Ten years later, however, the manufacturing share was 30 per cent and the agricultural 60 per cent; in 1860, manufacturing was up to 32 per cent and agriculture's share had declined to 56 per cent, despite a vast increase, during intervening years, in area of land under cultivation.[12]

Most of the expanded industrial ouput was consumed in the domestic market. Industrialization itself involved an increase in the growth of urban centers. On the farms, commercial specialization (made possible by improved transport and heavier reliance upon mechanized equipment) increased consumption of manufactures; and, especially in the 1850's, the quickening pace of railroad construction stimulated demand for heavy machinery and iron and forest products. Moreover, the impact of the railroads was not restricted to the consumption of manufactured goods: they reduced transport costs (often suffering bankruptcy as a result), made possible winter shipment of foodstuffs to expanding urban markets, and quickly brought farmers even in the remote Western regions into the market economy.

During this surge of industrial growth, foreign trade continued to act as a major expansive force. Raw cotton continued to dominate exports. But grain products became a more important factor in the export trade in the mid-1840's, when crop failures abroad created a sudden demand overseas for American wheat and flour; a decade later, during the Crimean War, American producers again moved their crops into European grain markets. The rise in agricultural exports was great: in 1841-45, the value of wheat, cotton, and tobacco sold abroad averaged $60 million annually, whereas in the period 1856-60 the same staples accounted for an average of $186 million yearly in export receipts. Thus the products of the land helped to finance import of such vital industrial materials as iron rails, and supported interest payment on renewed foreign investment in America.

12. NBER, *Trends*, 26.

The continued movement of goods and capital across international boundaries was matched in importance by movements of people. An estimated 4.4 million aliens passed through Atlantic ports to make permanent homes in America in the 1840's and 1850's. This country welcomed, and to an extent induced, the migration: there were no legal barriers to entry, and American shipping companies and railroads actively sought the business of European immigrants. On this side of the Atlantic, the new railroads made cheaper Western lands accessible, while rising industrial employment offered a still more accessible opportunity to the alien newcomer. After 1842, moreover, the expulsive forces of the Old World took on new significance: there was pressure on agricultural prices, land reform, displacement of peasants and yeomen, political upheaval, and famine, especially the Great Starvation in Ireland. Immigration reached its highest levels when employment opportunities were greatest in the United States. Foreign labor provided a more elastic labor force and offered special labor skills, and the influx of new workers meant an enlarged market for the products of American farm and factory.[13]

Technology too moved relatively freely across national boundaries, despite efforts by some nations to prevent the export of machinery and engineering data. In the iron and steel industry, the blast furnace was introduced into the United States by a German-born New Yorker. Similarly, anthracite smelting was adapted to commercial production in 1839 by Benjamin Perry, a British-born ironmonger living in Pennsylvania. The power loom was introduced at Taunton in 1837 by William Crompton, a year after he had migrated from England. Even in the development of interchangeable parts, which is usually characterized as a uniquely American innovation, many of the pioneer concepts

13. Brinley Thomas, *Migration and Economic Growth* (Cambridge [England], 1954).

and processes were foreign in origin, though applied most quickly in the United States.[14]

The federal government demonstrated its awareness of the importance of America's foreign trade by its commercial policy, just as its recognition of the value of foreign labor found expression in the free-immigration policy. This country became the world's most eloquent and consistent advocate of free navigation in international trade, and a succession of commercial treaties concluded with foreign maritime powers opened their own and their colonial ports to American vessels. As England and the other European nations began to surrender portions of their older mercantilistic shipping regulations, the United States also liberalized its port restrictions, and after 1826 the President was empowered to negotiate bilateral treaties providing for mutual concessions in the quest for freer navigation. The magnificent timber resources of New England and the skills of American shipwrights and naval designers combined to give this country substantial advantages in the era of wooden ships. As a result of new opportunities and continued success in shipbuilding, American registered tonnage increased from 600,000 in 1820 to nearly 2.4 million in 1860. On the eve of the Civil War, American vessels carried more than 70 per cent of goods in U.S. foreign trade.

In tariff policy as well, the United States recognized its need for expanded trade. Tariffs were maintained on a protective basis until the mid-1840's, when the Walker Act reduced the levies on foreign imports almost to a free-trade level. England meanwhile lowered its traditional protective barriers, and its repeal of the Corn Laws in 1846 opened the door to massive imports of American grain. In 1849, moreover, the British repealed their navigation acts, and the United States responded by opening her

14. W. Paul Strassmann, *Risk and Technological Innovation* (Ithaca, 1959), 25; R. S. Woodbury, "The Legend of Eli Whitney and Interchangeable Parts," *Technology and Culture,* I (1960).

ports to all British vessels, regardless of cargo or port of origin. Then, in 1854, the Canadian-American reciprocity treaty brought virtually free trade in primary products and opened the coastal fisheries on an equal basis to Canadian and U.S. fishing vessels. This series of dramatic concessions on all sides promised for a time to unify still further the already interdependent Atlantic world.

On the eve of the Civil War, American foreign trade was dominated by cotton exports to England, and the United States was the principal customer for British exports of manufactured goods.[15] Thus the revision of trade and navigation restrictions, welding a commercial alliance of the Anglo-American nations, produced in the 1850's a community of economic interests which was then as important a force in the world economy as are the European Common Market and the British Commonwealth in our own day. Far from marking a golden age of self-sufficiency when the American continent was isolated from the mainstream of world economic development, the pre-Civil War years were a period when America was heavily dependent upon the Old World for labor, capital, technology, and markets. It was an era when fluctuations in European money markets had immediate repercussions on trade, public finance, and banking in the United States. Conversely, panics, depressions, and periods of boom in this country affected the cycles of business in England and on the Continent. Not only had industrialization already begun to transform the United States economy by 1860, but a pattern of international interdependence which is often considered uniquely modern had played an essential part in shaping American development.

15. See J. Potter, "Atlantic Economy, 1815-60," *Studies in the Industrial Revolution,* ed. by L. S. Presnell (London, 1960).

Internal Growth and Economic Interdependence, 1860-1914

An export-dominated economy, based in large measure on overseas markets for primary products—chiefly cotton—had begun to shift by the 1850's toward a more heavily industrial base. On the eve of the Civil War, America had only some of what have been termed the basic pre-conditions of rapid, self-sustaining industrial growth: "creation of national markets, the mechanization and extension of transportation and industry, the development of power, mineral fuel and metal technology, as well as the evolution of better business and managerial technique."[16] In the half-century after the Civil War, these requisites all were amply fulfilled. By 1870 the United States produced almost one-fourth the world's manufacturing output, second to Great Britain which produced over 30 per cent. By 1881-85, however, the United States had passed Great Britain as the leading manufacturing nation; and in 1900 this country was producing about 30 per cent of world manufactures, compared with 20 per cent for Great Britain, 17 per cent for Germany, and 7 per cent for France.[17]

The dynamics of economic change in the late nineteenth century were dominated by factors that may be termed internal to the American economy. That is, by comparison with development before 1860, the pattern of growth was more autonomous and shaped less by ties with the international economy. Clearly, the course of development would have been altered substantially if the United States had not enjoyed access to labor, capital, and technology from overseas, as well as to expanding foreign markets. Yet it may be argued that domestic sources of capital, the growing

16. Samuel Rezneck, in NBER, *Trends,* 215.

17. Brinley Thomas, *Migration,* 120; S. R. Patel, "Rates of Industrial Growth in the Last Century, 1860-1958," *Economic Development and Cultural Change,* IX (1961).

domestic consumer market, the advent of the modern integrated corporation, and the enlargement of the American resource base by development of railroads were the principal formative influences in the process of industrialization.

One of the most striking features of the period was the ability of the United States to expand agricultural production simultaneously with industrialization. This was a matter partly of land and partly of technology. Settlement was extended into the trans-Mississippi West at the very time when a basic revolution in agricultural technology was improving labor productivity, and farms were increasingly highly capitalized. Gross farm product more than tripled during the last half of the century, permitting American agriculture to sustain an expanding industrial labor force without the import of basic food supplies from abroad—and even permitting the export of large agricultural surpluses that served as an important source of income for the economy as a whole. Together with expansion of agriculture went rapid exploitation of mineral resources. To cite only a few examples, bituminous coal production increased from 9.1 million tons in 1860 to 212.3 million tons in 1900; output of petroleum, which was first refined in 1859, went from 5.3 million barrels in 1870 to 63.6 million in 1900; and iron ore production increased from 2.9 million tons in 1860 to 27.3 million in 1900. The windfall combination of two strategic resources, iron and coal, permitted the American steel industry to apply a new technology (especially the Bessemer and open-hearth processes) and gave the United States a rapidly expanding supply of this metal, so vital in an age of machine production. By 1913 U.S. steel production exceeded all of Europe's. While steel and other heavy industries made immense gains, light manufacturing—and especially food-processing, which was the leading American industry in value of output in 1900—underwent equally rapid changes in technology of production and achieved output levels that dwarfed pre-Civil War levels.

The pattern of industrial growth and resource exploitation was closely related to changes in transportation. During the late nineteenth century the railroad network was extended from its formerly concentrated position in the northeast quarter of the nation, reaching out into the South and Southwest as well as across the Great Plains to the ports of the Pacific Coast. Railway construction and equipment provided the chief American market for coal and metals, and the building of new lines involved major infusions of capital into many thinly settled regions. The railroads also tapped such formerly inaccessible sources of minerals as the Rocky Mountain copper district, opened up the South to industrial development, and carried the agricultural surplus of the Midwest to Eastern cities. The building of new lines was accompanied by a decline in railroad rates.

As mileage of American railroads increased from 30,000 in 1860 to 200,000 in 1900, competition between rival companies became more keen and resulted in a marked drop in average rates, despite the instances of local discrimination so hotly denounced by the Grangers and the Populists. The reduced cost of transferring goods and people by rail permitted a more effective integration of the expanding national market; indeed, the Founders' dream of a great internal free market, unhampered by legal restrictions on trade, was given concrete meaning by the railroad. This took on added importance in the 1880's, when a great surge in urban development took place. As the result of rapid industrial growth, urban population, which was 28 per cent of total population in 1880, had reached some 40 per cent of the total by 1900. Urbanization involved rising consumer demand for food, fuel, clothing, and construction materials, and all these products were carried to the cities at relatively low cost by the railroads.[18]

18. Urban population, as used in the text, refers to residents of cities with populations 2,500 or larger. On the impact of urban demand, see Alfred D. Chandler, Jr., "Entrepreneurial Opportunity in 19th Century America," *Explorations in Entrepreneurial History, Second Series,* I (1963).

No discussion of internal factors affecting industrialization can ignore government policy. The federal laws, adminstrative policies, and judicial record of this period are familiar enough: protective tariffs, generous land grants to railroads, aid to public education, repeal of the Civil War income tax, adherence to the gold standard after 1879 (a policy of questionable benefit, but one widely advocated within the business community), land laws favorable to the lumber, mining, and cattle industries, and hostility to organized labor. In these policies, government was reflecting accurately the values and aspirations of a society which gave high priority to material development and was willing to defer calculation of social costs. Conflicts over government policy (including regulatory legislation affecting transportation and industrial combinations) ranged around narrow issues of economic advantage. Indeed, even the much-vaunted "agrarianism" of the West was less an expression of genuine radicalism than the defense of the agricultural business interest. It was symbolic of the age that its leading social philosopher, William Graham Sumner, should have labeled reformers as "sentimentalists," and that the indifference of businessmen to both outright poverty and the more subtle social costs of industrialization (an indifference that courted violence and invited utter disruption of society) should have been regarded as "realistic." [19]

As much as these internal factors governed the course of industrialization, the United States did not achieve unparalleled economic progress independently of changes in the world economy. The history of the great European migration to America revealed continued economic interdependence, and the rapidity of industrialization here served as a magnet to the immigrant. But the economic growth of the United States also caused profound dislocations in European society, and it contributed to the undermining of roots that had held potential migrants to their native lands. The rich

19. On business mores and their perils, cf. Edward C. Kirkland, "Divide and Ruin," *Mississippi Valley Historical Review,* XLIII (1956).

grain crops of the American West, for example, were carried at low cost by lake vessels and railroads to the East Coast and then shipped overseas, handled by a marketing organization whose efficiency was uniquely high. In order to meet the competition of low-priced American crops, European producers had to reorganize agriculture, and they tore apart the ancient fabric of peasant holdings. The rural poor of Europe were driven to the cities of their own countries, and then overseas to America. Because there were no significant legal barriers restricting European immigration to the United States, a rising tide of European labor followed in the wake of shifting economic opportunity, across the Atlantic.

Of the total international migration of about forty-five million persons in the broad period 1861-1920, the United States received 28.6 million; the second largest receiving country, Canada, absorbed only five million.[20] For the United States, immigration provided an elastic labor force, and, no less important, it contributed toward enlargement of the domestic market for industrial and agricultural products. As Brinley Thomas has argued, moreover, the presence of a large laboring group that spoke no English and had no special craft skills may well have been an incentive to manufacturers to adopt highly mechanized processes which simplified the worker's tasks. This, in turn, enhanced efficiency in manufacturing.[21] The immigrant influx affected the pattern of urban growth, for most of the newcomers settled in the cities. By the 1890's, urban demand for new housing was beginning to rival railroad construction as a leading expansive force in the economy—a phenomenon closely related to the mass migration from Europe.

While the United States continued to provide foodstuffs and raw materials to foreign markets, it remained a borrowing nation.[22] The proportion of foreign to domestic capital invested in American

20. William Ashworth, *A Short History of the International Economy, 1850-1950* (London, 1952), 177.

21. Brinley Thomas, *Migration,* 165.

22. Net indebtedness of the U.S., estimated at about $500 million in 1863, grew to about $3 billion by 1899. (NBER, *Trends,* 706-707.)

transportation and industry was smaller after 1865 than it had been earlier. This inflow of foreign investment played a strategic role in development, however, because the bulk of it went into railroad securities. By thus aiding in construction of the railway network which carried American agricultural surpluses from the interior of the continent to the Atlantic ports, foreign investors were in effect assisting in the expansion of American export trade.[23]

Scientific knowledge, like labor and capital, continued to move freely across international boundaries. Even as early as the 1830's, American manufacturers had provoked frequent comment on their uncanny ability to apply foreign inventions to their own purposes. This exploitative strain became even more pronounced in the late nineteenth century. Among the numerous innovations which revolutionized mining were the diamond drill, first developed in France, and the Nobel Patent dynamite. In steel manufacture, the Bessemer process was developed in England and improved by a Scots metallurgist, while the open-hearth process was perfected by a German in England and a team of French inventors. Later in the century, American advances in the application of electricity for illumination and power were derived from the pioneering work of Hungarian, English, Scots, German, and Italian inventors. Moreover, the international technology on which American manufacturing was built reached into the sphere of industrial organization: introduction of expensive machinery and new processes raised the capital requirements for efficient production and impelled the movement toward combination and integration in key industries.[24]

23. Cf. Ragnur Nurske, "International Investment Today in the Light of 19th Century Experience," *The Economic Journal,* LXIV (1954); D. C. North, "International Capital Movements in Historical Perspective," *U.S. Private and Government Investment Abroad,* ed. by R. F. Mikesell (Eugene, Oregon, 1962).

24. Edward C. Kirkland, *Industry Comes of Age: Business, Labor, and Public Policy, 1860-1897* (New York, 1961), treats technology and industrial growth.

The composition of American foreign trade reflected the shifts in production within the domestic economy. By the turn of the century, American exports of industrial products exceeded imports; and in 1913 industrial products were double the value of foodstuffs in the American export sector. The volume of imports increased from $824 million in 1880 to $1.49 billion in 1905, while exports rose from $668 million to $1.12 billion in the same period. The American *share* of world trade remained constant, at about 10 per cent of total commerce, but within the United States export sector the proportion of manufactures rose quickly in the 1890's, indicative of the increasing ability of American industry to compete in world markets.

In summary, American economic growth in the late nineteenth century was influenced by immigration, international capital movements, and foreign advances in technology—yet all of these conditioning factors were operating in a pattern of growth shaped primarily by expansive forces internal to the national economy. So far as American foreign trade was concerned, Europe continued to be the major supplier and customer and England continued to be America's leading trade partner in Europe. Yet the formative influence which the Anglo-American connection had exerted before the Civil War had given way to a much more autonomous course of development.

The spectacular course of long-run growth was ostensibly threatened by the depression of the mid-1890's. The sense of crisis that grew out of falling prices, overcapacity, and reduced consumer demand was compounded by labor unrest and violence in the 1894 railroad strikes. The alleged "closing of the frontier," prematurely announced by the Census Bureau after the 1890 population survey, contributed to the growing sense of despair among those who assessed the future of the American economy.

Crisis psychology might well have been expected to paralyze business leadership. But powerful instruments with which to combat the challenge of stagnation seemed ready at hand in the form of the investment bankers' giant capital holdings. The "captains of industry" now turned to Wall Street for their salvation, and the tirelessly repeated expressions of belief in competitive individualism were now seldom heard. Instead, businessmen spoke of a new order, more rational and more stable; and they heralded the reorganization of industry for the express purpose of eliminating competition. Even the word "competition" acquired a new sense and was characteristically presented in business rhetoric as "ruinous competition." Integration of firms and large new corporate organizations were championed as means of insulating industry from the impact of depressions, of permitting long-run price stability, and of planning "flexible" (i.e., sub-capacity) production by which crises could be weathered without liquidation.

The merger (or "trust") movement reached a climax during 1897-1903, when there were some 280 mergers involving more than $1 million capitalization each, as compared with eighty-six during 1887-97. The move toward giant, integrated enterprise was given additional impetus by discoveries of gold in the mid-1890's, recovery of export trade for agricultural products, and the revival of wholesale prices during the Spanish-American War. No less important was the development of a broadly based market for industrial common stocks, carefully nurtured by Wall Street investment bankers, notably J. P. Morgan & Co. and Kuhn, Loeb & Co. Together with the movement toward larger firms came a broadening of the functions of large corporations, which now undertook production and transportation of their raw materials, wholesaling, and even retailing of their finished products. Multilevel organization and other management reforms were themselves innovations of prime importance. Indeed, by 1910 the largest corporations had already assumed their modern form in terms of internal organization.

Americans viewed these rapid changes in the structure of industry with mixed reactions. Reformers sought to combat the merger trend, fearing that monopoly would close opportunities for small entrepreneurs and reduce consumers and laborers to mere vassals of industrial overlords. During the Progressive era of the early twentieth century, some moved to revitalize a statute, the Sherman Act, which had been on the books since 1890. Popular support was readily evoked for what Woodrow Wilson termed "laws which will look after the men who are on the make rather than the men who are already made." And yet the effort to achieve basic structural reforms through anti-trust legislation clearly failed. In 1919, after anti-trust prosecutions had tapered off, fewer than 4 per cent of American corporations accounted for 68 per cent of industrial output and employed 57 per cent of all manufacturing workers.[25]

The prophets of the new industrial order did not lose sight of the older view that competition was in the natural order of things. They had long justified acute social distress and ruthless corporate treatment of consumers and small enterprisers as inevitable social costs accompanying progress through competition. Once competition proved ruinous to themselves, however, they shifted their emphasis, now advocating the strategy of combination and monopoly in the context of a different competitive order: the international economy. Thus Charles Van Hise, as quoted approvingly by Theodore Roosevelt in his Progressive party acceptance speech of 1912, asserted in his book *Concentration and Control:*

> Concentration and co-operation in industry in order to secure efficiency are a world-wide movement. The United States cannot resist it. If we isolate ourselves and insist upon the subdivision of industry below the highest economic efficiency, and do not allow co-operation, we shall be defeated in the world's markets. We cannot adopt an economic system less efficient than our great competitors, Germany, England, France and Austria. Either we must modify our present obsolete laws regarding concentration and co-operation so as to conform with the world

25. Harold U. Faulkner, *The Decline of Laissez-Faire* (New York, 1951), 155, 161; Alfred D. Chandler, Jr., "The Beginnings of 'Big Business' in American Industry," *Business History Review,* XXXIII (1959).

> movement, or else fall behind in the race for the world's markets.

Van Hise justified combination as a means of assuring American ability to compete in world markets. Fearful that stagnation had become a permanent feature of the domestic economy, American businessmen staked their hopes upon the expansion of overseas markets. In its November, 1894, number, *The Banker's Magazine* thus declared that industrial exports would thenceforth be the key to American growth, as cotton and other agricultural surpluses formerly had been. The achievement of "manufacturing supremacy over Europe," the magazine asserted, would eliminate the old pattern of cyclical business crises. As a result, there would be

> slow and steady improvement . . . and [with] our surplus manufacturing capacity turned to the production of goods we may be able to export hereafter at reduced cost [and] thus keep all our industries permanently employed, as England does, having the world's markets in which to unload any accumulation.[26]

Rising business pressure for aggressive exploitation of foreign markets contributed toward the new economic diplomacy pursued in Latin America and Asia. Republican Presidents from McKinley to Taft appointed men to consular and embassy posts who were sympathetic with the expansionist aims of domestic business leaders. This development was hailed by Willard Straight, the American diplomat and banker, who thought Taft's appointments in Latin America promised that "the Monroe Doctrine for the first time . . . [might become] a practical question out of which the honest bankers ought to be able to make a small but satisfactory percentage." [27] He was not to be disappointed.

With the quest for new markets came a rising interest in op-

26. Quoted by Walter LaFeber, "The Background of Cleveland's Venezuelan Policy," *American Historical Review,* LXVI (1961).

27. Letter of Willard Straight to E. S. Morgan, October 12, 1907, Willard Straight Papers, Regional History Collection, Cornell University Library.

portunities for foreign investment of American capital. Although the United States remained, on balance, a debtor nation, an outflow of investment had begun in the 1880's, at first mainly into Cuba, Mexico, and Canada, and later into Asia and Latin America. By 1897 American foreign investment had reached a level close to $700 million. Only a decade later, it was $2.5 billion, and by 1914 it was some $3.5 billion.[28] This capital outflow was closely related to the combination movement. Not only was it an allied business response to threatened stagnation at home: it was also an outgrowth of the merger movement itself, which had swelled the coffers of investment banking houses and given them means with which to compete with European powers in overseas capital markets.

Despite the desperate fears of the 1890's, stagnation proved to be illusory. In the first fifteen years of the twentieth century, American industrialization underwent another surge of growth, given impetus by a set of new forces in the economy. Manufacturing output more than doubled from 1900 to 1915. Of critical importance was the introduction of hydroelectric power which freed industrial firms from the necessity of capitalizing their own steampower plants or building factories close to sources of coal. The internal combustion engine was adapted to industrial purposes, and its use for wheeled vehicles led to a spectacular growth of the automobile industry, which in turn created a vast new market for petroleum products, stimulated road construction, and contributed to urban and suburban growth. The rise in industrial output was closely related also to changes in technique associated with mass-production processes, pioneered by Henry Ford, and with the institution of "scientific management" principles typified in the work of Frederick W. Taylor.[29] Meanwhile,

28. Faulkner, *Decline of Laissez-Faire,* 87.

29. Estimated output per unit of labor input—the best measure of productivity—rose in manufacturing from 46.2 in 1900 to 67.6 in 1915 (1929 = 100). (John W. Kendrick, *Productivity Trends in the United States* [Princeton, 1961], 465.)

agriculture entered an era of prosperity, attributable to a slowdown in the rate of settlement of new lands, rising farmland values, and growth of urban demand for food and fiber products. And so farm prices reached the levels of the era of "parity," 1910-14; and immigration, once again attracted by a rapidly expanding economy, reached its historic climax in the 1909-13 period.

Under the impact of industrialization, per capita wealth increased nearly 100 per cent, in real terms, during the period 1880-1915. The basic transformation of the economy was vividly reflected in the growth of the labor force from 10.5 million in 1860 to 36.7 million in 1910. Whereas manufacturing, mining, and construction had employed only 20 per cent of the 1860 total, their share rose to 30 per cent in 1910; meanwhile the proportion engaged in agriculture fell from 60 per cent in 1860 to about 30 per cent in 1910, and employment in service and trade industries rose threefold to 10 per cent in 1910. The heart of the American continent had been settled and a massive trans-Atlantic migration absorbed into the national economy; the basic transportation network was complete; corporate organization had assumed its modern form; and, despite periodic depressions of a major magnitude, the gross national product was increasing at an average rate of nearly 50 per cent each decade.[30] Already the world's leading industrial nation, the United States had begun to exhibit the central characteristic of its subsequent growth: rapid expansion of mass consumer markets at a rate sufficient to sustain the growth of mass-production industries. This pattern of development had occurred within the context of relatively open international order, in which America had imported labor, capital, and technology and exported its agricultural surplus and, by the mid-1890's, a rising quantity of manufactured goods. However, the full significance of America's emergence as the world's largest industrial power did not become clear until 1914-18, when Europe

30. Simon Kuznets, *Capital in the American Economy* (Princeton, 1961), 74.

plunged into war. Immune from the war's devastation, this nation underwent an economic boom while Europe was bled white. Its comparative advantages in world trade thereby enhanced, the United States achieved undisputed hegemony in the international economy in the postwar years.

The Crucible of War, 1914-45

The guns of August, 1914, sounded not only the beginning of a world war but the end of the international economy as men of that era had known it. The period from the mid-nineteenth century to World War I had been unique in commercial history. Only minor international wars had disrupted a century of relative political stability and peace. International trade had grown rapidly, and it had been marked by a high degree of freedom for the movement of men, capital, and goods across national boundaries. On the whole, tariffs had been maintained at less than restrictive levels, and the growing volume of trade had given impetus to economic specialization. Many underdeveloped areas had been drawn (either as colonies or as independent states) into the network of world commerce and had become dependent for growth upon their foreign exports. Industrialized countries had met their needs for primary materials by extending trade lines to remote corners of the globe; international migration had permitted labor to shift into areas of most rapid development; and international capital flows and the gold standard had provided the essential balance mechanism for the far-flung international commercial system.[31]

World War I ended this epoch. Aside from the enormous physical costs of the war itself, the peace treaty created new states in eastern Europe, all of which pursued their own commercial policy in the 1920's, setting up currency and tariff pro-

31. Cf. Ashworth, *Short History,* Chap. 6; J. B. Condliffe, *The Commerce of Nations* (New York, 1950), Part 2.

grams that fragmented a once-integrated European economy. Soviet Russia was virtually isolated from the world economy for a long period after the war. Germany was burdened with enormous war reparations, and the problems of postwar adjustment were complicated by the debts the Allied powers had incurred to the United States. In an effort to restore their own industry and to renew profitable trade ties with Asia, Latin America, and Africa, the European nations concluded new treaties and threw up quota and licensing systems that stifled the atmosphere of commercial freedom.

After 1930 the Great Depression deepened still further the inroads already made on the open international economic order. Desperately seeking to revive their economies, Great Britain established a system of tariff preferences for Commonwealth nations, Germany exacted special trade concessions from east European and South American nations, and Scandinavia and the Low Countries moved toward regional trading-bloc arrangements. Both in the 1920's and during the Great Depression, American commercial policy contributed to this fragmentation of the international economy. Low tariffs established in 1914 were overturned by protectionist forces in Congress, and average tariff rates rose markedly during the period 1921-30. Even the United States Reciprocal Trade Program, which began in 1934, was a hard-headed move to improve American terms of trade in essential imports and exports. Although it resulted in a considerable reduction of U.S. tariffs, it also tended to foster American trade at the expense of countries outside the bloc with which treaties were negotiated.[32]

The First World War also weakened international adherence to the gold standard as the mechanism for maintaining liquidity

32. W. Arthur Lewis, *Economic Survey, 1919-1939* (London, 1949), 149 ff; Grace Beckett, "Effect of the Reciprocal Trade Agreements upon the Foreign Trade of the United States," *Quarterly Journal of Economics,* LIV (1940).

and balancing international accounts. Restored briefly in the 1920's, the gold standard fell victim first to ruinous inflation in the European countries and then, after 1930, to the currency manipulation that marked the programs adopted by various national governments to cure depression problems.

A crisis affecting the poorer, primary-producing nations introduced still another element of instability into world trade following the war. After 1920 the volume of trade failed to recover prewar levels as quickly as manufacturing output or other economic indicators. But this slowdown in trade growth operated most detrimentally against the poorer nations by reducing both their volume of exports and the prices they received for their primary products. This occurred, first, because of a reduced rate of population growth in the industrial countries of Europe, the result of casualties during the war. This retarded the growth of demand for basic foodstuffs and fiber products. Secondly, in the 1920's manufactured synthetics were substituted widely for some of the older primary products used by industry. Third, a technological revolution occurred in the agriculture of the advanced nations through mechanization and the application of chemical fertilizers to the soil. The new capital-intensive farming techniques were not viable for underdeveloped countries with large peasant populations on the land.[33] Increased farm productivity accrued most to the advantage of the industrial nations with large agricultural sectors; for example, the United States enjoyed almost a 50 per cent increase in agricultural productivity during the interwar

33. Thus the Yugoslav foreign minister declared in 1933 that his country could not weather the economic disaster that would be produced if modern landownership and farming techniques were forced on the peasant population. To accomplish an agricultural revolution, he asserted, Yugoslavia would have needed the vast frontiers of Canada or the Argentine. "We could not sacrifice our people by shooting them, but they would nevertheless be killed off by famine—which would come to the same thing." (Quoted in E. H. Carr, *The Twenty Years' Crisis* [New York, 1964], 58.)

years. This development added to the burden of lower farm prices and world surpluses of agricultural products, which bore hardest on the poorer nations. Worse, the poorer countries were often dependent on one or two export products for their economic growth. As a result, the underdeveloped nations raised high tariff barriers, both to reduce imports (and therefore improve their trade balances) and to promote infant industry. This development cut still further inroads into the older, open order and adversely affected the growth of total trade.[34]

There remains to be explained the relationship of American economic growth to these changes in the interwar world economy. During World War I the United States had become the arsenal, the granary, the banker, and the shipper for the Allied nations. Exports had been $1.7 billion in 1910 and $2.8 billion in 1915, but rose to $7.9 billion by 1919—representing 10 per cent of current national income, an historic twentieth-century high that compared with 5 per cent in 1910. During the war itself, American industry reached a new productive plateau from which it would enter a period of equally impressive, continued growth in the 1920's. War demand force-fed new industries such as chemicals and automobiles, and it brought rapid increases in the output of steel and other basic products. It impelled the movement toward integration and combination, stimulated the application of new manufacturing processes, encouraged product standardization, and produced an increase in the area of land under cultivation. Although real wages gained only about 4 per cent during 1914-18, the work force was swelled by the addition of women and formerly unemployed persons, and a marked expansion of total consumer buying power occurred.[35]

During the "new economic era" of the United States in the

34. See *ibid.*, 59, for the remarks of Colombia's president on protectionist policy as a "return to a kind of primitive struggle for existence."
35. George Soule, *Prosperity Decade* (New York, 1947), 74 ff.

1920's, a fabled business boom was stimulated by pent-up consumer and investment demand, low tax rates, and limited government restraints. Gross national product increased more than 40 per cent (in constant dollars) over the course of the decade. Economies of mass production and enlarged markets for new consumer goods, especially electrical and automotive products, gave further thrust to the industrial advance. However, there were important elements of instability: the share of national income that went into wages rose more slowly than the share going into dividends and interest; the increase in consumer buying power was to a large extent provided by expanded installment credit; the farm sector suffered from declining prices and income in the latter part of the decade; stagnation was evident in certain industries and regions; a real estate boom assumed all the features of a speculative bubble, which it proved to be exactly; and an overextended corporate structure was built upon the quicksand of pyramided holding companies and inflated stock prices. Not least important of the forces which carried the potential of disaster, however, was the relation of the American economy to the rest of the world.

The American share of total world trade stabilized, in the twenties, at about 15 per cent of exports and 12 per cent of imports. Thus any fluctuations in the domestic economy would naturally have vital ramifications for all other trading nations. The First World War had also brought a reversal of the traditional U.S. debtor position. In 1914 the United States had owed some $3.6 billion to foreign investors, but it emerged from the war in 1919 a creditor by some $12.6 billion, including both private investment and government loans. Nor was this entirely unplanned. Thus a new investment banking firm, the American International Corporation, was formed in 1916 to make loans to the Allies and then to direct American foreign investment to the underdeveloped countries once the war was over. "The Corporation," one of its founders wrote, "does not wish our friends on this side [i.e., in England and France] to think that we are attempting to pick things off the bargain counter. We believe it will be very much sounder policy if we can work out some scheme under which by furnishing capital now required we may be able to buy ourselves, so to speak, into a partnership with British and French interests in various parts of the world." [36]

During the 1920's American exports consistently exceeded imports, preventing foreigners from meeting their debts through sale of goods to the United States. As a result, maintenance of foreign demand for American exports became vitally dependent upon continued outflows of American capital to overseas borrowers. Because the pattern of American industrial development in the 1920's siphoned off most of the returns of increased productivity to stockholders rather than to labor, there was a growing surplus of investment capital available for such foreign investments. From 1919 to 1929, therefore, some $12 billion in private long-term foreign investments were made by the United States.[37] Yet the continuation of this capital outflow was entirely at the mercy of market conditions. Much foreign investment went into the bonds of foreign governments which were financially unstable, and by 1928-29 there was rising wariness of further loans to such governments. Then, when the panic struck Wall Street in October, 1929, the foundations of American investment banking were undermined, and a massive withdrawal of capital from abroad followed, affecting adversely the ability of foreign countries to continue purchasing American export goods.

36. Letter of Willard Straight to Col. House, March 17, 1916, in Straight Papers, Cornell.

37. Brinley Thomas makes the argument that the new American immigration restrictions after World War I contributed to this capital outflow. In the presence of a vast supply of cheap immigrant labor, surplus American capital might have gone into new manufacturing facilities and housing for this country. Instead, such funds flowed to Canada, which still permitted free immigration, and to Europe. (Thomas, *Migration*, 200.)

America's favorable trade balances during the 1920's also complicated the settlement of international accounts throughout the world. The bulk of the world's gold supply was concentrated increasingly in this country, and international trade settlements became dependent upon the continued outward flow of dollar loans from the United States. Therefore, the 1929 crash also forced foreign governments to protect their dollar and specie reserves and to reduce imports. The withdrawal of American investment capital from Europe during 1930-31 put severe pressure upon European banks, and in 1931 the Creditanstalt of Austria proved insolvent, setting off a financial panic on the Continent and in England. By the end of the year the gold standard had been almost universally abandoned, and depreciation of domestic currencies became endemic. Meanwhile, the collapse of American demand for imports had caused a drop in primary prices, putting the national treasuries of many non-industrial countries in jeopardy; and by 1935 some 38 per cent of American foreign loans were in default. And so the dollar crisis, the financial panic of 1931, and the retrenchment measures and currency manipulation adopted to combat the panic were all directly related to the recklessly myopic economic policies of the United States during the previous decade.[38]

Under both Herbert Hoover and Franklin Roosevelt, economic nationalism was the hallmark of the American government's antidepression policies. But economic nationalism was not unique to the United States. All other major trading nations pursued nationalistic programs during the depression years. Even in 1933, when the London Economic Conference was held amidst optimistic expressions of hope for a change, there was little evidence that the great powers would undertake effective economic cooperation.

38. Hal B. Lary and associates, *The United States in the World Economy* (U.S. Department of Commerce, Economic Series, No. 23, Washington, 1943); Gunnar Myrdal, *An International Economy* (New York, 1956), Chap. 8; Cleona Lewis, *America's Stake in International Investment* (Washington, 1938), 351 ff.

Recognizing the world trend toward insulation of domestic economies and recovery through internal reform, Henry Wallace, Roosevelt's Secretary of Agriculture, declared in *America Must Choose* (1934):

> We have come perforce to think in terms not of free production and trade, but of planned production and trade, within and between nations. . . . Accordingly, the present administration is conducting an orderly retreat from surplus acreage.

Such realistic pessimism about the efficacy of international measures to solve price deflation (let alone the problems of declining employment and wages and structural weaknesses in the American banking system) had led President Roosevent to assert candidly in his 1933 inaugural message:

> Our international trade relations, though vastly important, are, in point of time and necessity, secondary to the establishment of a sound national economy. I favor as a practical policy the putting of first things first. I shall spare no effort to restore world trade by international economic adjustment, but the emergency at home cannot wait on that accomplishment.

The New Deal pursued agricultural recovery in 1933 through a national program of regulation and price control. Mining and manufacturing were subjected to production controls, price agreements, and fixed wages. The currency was manipulated, and to "prime the pump" and promote employment a massive public works program was undertaken. Large-scale government refinancing of private debt was accomplished through farm mortgage and home loan programs. Government loans to banks and industry (begun under Hoover) and institution of basic banking and corporate reforms checked the spiral of bankruptcy and liquidation. Long-term goals such as conservation and regional planning were linked with employment opportunity in the Tennessee Valley Authority and the Civilian Conservation Corps.

Beginning in 1935, New Deal measures were marked increasingly by permanent reform objectives. The agricultural program was continued with modifications, despite invalidation of the 1933 farm act by the Supreme Court. The National Recovery Act for industrial codes and price-fixing was abandoned when the Court struck it down; the administration instead pursued the goal of higher wages by supporting the Wagner Act, which established labor's legal right to collective bargaining in all industries—thus redressing a balance of power, under which the weight of federal law had long been used mainly against organized labor. A social security program was instituted, valuable both because it reduced uncertainty in the lives of many and also because it helped provide a "built-in stabilizer" to sustain income payments during depressions. A broad-ranging employment program was instituted in the Works Progress Administration. Like the public works agencies, the WPA built housing, roads, libraries, and schools, in addition to sponsoring professional and arts projects. Perhaps most important, the Roosevelt administration accepted as permanent, after 1937, the policy of compensatory public spending to reduce unemployment and offset the effects of reduced private expenditure during business downturns.

Many of these reforms were far-reaching, and a large number were in conception and even in form to become permanent. Yet as Calvin B. Hoover has argued, many of the fundamental shifts in the economic order itself had occurred much earlier; not only had industrialization already come to characterize the economy, but so too had large-scale corporate organization, mass employment in the manufacturing industries, emergence of a farm problem in terms of overcapacity for production, and so forth. "Old-style, individual-enterprise capitalism" had disappeared, in good measure, long before 1933, and laissez-faire policy was absent even in the 1920's, when the weapons of government policy were vigorously employed to aid American business. Indeed, "this transformation was largely responsible for the New Deal's coming into existence and . . . it determined the character of the economic program enacted under the Roosevelt regime." [39]

It was ironic that the New Deal's essentially nationalistic program was often defended in terms of foreign precedents. For example, in *Half-Way with Roosevelt* (1936), an influential pro-New Deal book, the distinguished journalist Ernest K. Lindley declared that Roosevelt's farm program, currency-manipulation policies, and industrial regimentation merely reflected what had been done in every other democratic industrial country. Key sections of Lindley's book catalogued with detailed precision the extensive programs for lifting agricultural prices, suspending farm debt, refinancing mortgages, and the like, adopted everywhere in Europe, Latin America, and Asia.[40] President Roosevelt himself adduced similar evidence in defending his program at his famous March 31, 1935, press conference, following the Supreme Court's adverse decision on the 1933 farm bill and the National Recovery Act. The administration, Roosevelt declared, was asking only that it be given "the powers which exist in the national governments of every other nation in the world to enact and administer laws that have a bearing on, and general control over, national economic problems and national social problems."

While Roosevelt and his supporters used foreign experience as a touchstone for domestic action, they did not neglect the possibility of closer cooperation with the governments whose programs they cited as examples for America. The most important international gesture of the period was the 1934 Reciprocal Trade Agreements Act. The law was framed specifically in terms of depression needs, asserting its object to be "expanding the foreign

39. Calvin B. Hoover, *The Economy, Liberty and the State* (New York, 1959), 88.

40. Ernest K. Lindley, *Half-Way with Roosevelt* (New York, 1936), Chap. 1. See also Hoover, *op. cit.,* 239.

markets for the United States" in order to aid "in restoring the American standard of living, in overcoming domestic unemployment and the present depression, in increasing the purchasing power of the American public. . . ." The act empowered the President to negotiate, within certain limits, treaties for reciprocal tariff reductions on a selective basis. In practice, the program worked to the advantage of the United States by obtaining lower tariffs on American manufactures exported in return for reductions on raw materials needed by American industry. Yet its total impact was to establish pressures for lower tariffs generally in world trade.[41]

By 1937 the American recovery program had restored domestic consumer demand and industrial output to 1929 levels. The quantity of American imports—composed largely of crude materials and semi-manufactures used by industry—rose with the general level of economic activity. And yet these raw materials were the products hardest hit by the depression. Since their prices did not rise commensurately with average price levels, the value (as opposed to quantity) of American imports did not keep up with the quantity increase. This proved "an important factor limiting the supply of dollars made available to foreign countries in the 1930's." [42] Faced with a continuing, acute dollar shortage—compounded by the rapid decline of American foreign investment and the withdrawal of loan capital—foreign countries were forced to curtail imports from the United States. Thus, even after the volume of world trade revived in the mid-1930's to pre-depression levels, there were built-in restrictions hampering a proportional rise in U.S. exports.[43]

41. See Walter Adams Brown, Jr., *The United States and the Restoration of World Trade* (Washington, 1950); and Beckett, "Effect of Reciprocal Trade Agreements," *loc. cit.*

42. Lary, *op. cit.,* 43.

43. *Ibid.,* 54 ff.

With the outbreak of war in Europe, however, American manufacturers immediately experienced a massive increase in export demand. There resulted a sharp general increase in the U.S. price level; then, in 1941, lend-lease aid to the Allies stimulated domestic industry, and the rapid growth of defense expenditures meant that America entered the war, after Pearl Harbor, with the economy functioning at better than pre-1929 levels. Between 1940 and 1945 physical output of industrial goods increased by more than half. Production of durable goods, used mainly for military purposes, had increased to an estimated 360 per cent of the 1935-39 average.

> While destruction stalked the earth and the economies of many rival nations were ruined, the U.S.A., simply by exerting full effort and without detriment to current standards of material consumption, was able vastly to increase its productive ability. During the war the size of the productive plant within the country grew by nearly 50 per cent. . . . At the end of the war, more than half the total manufacturing production of the world took place within the U.S.A., which, in fact, turned out a third of the world production of goods of all types. . . . Even two years after the war it supplied one-third of the world total of exports while taking only one-tenth of the imports.[44]

In sum, the Second World War had magnified still further the dominance attained by this country in the international economy during the first world conflict.

44. Ashworth, *Short History,* 227-228. See also G. A. Lincoln and others, "Mobilization and War," *American Economic History,* ed. by Seymour Harris (New York, 1961), 220 ff.

Since 1945—The United States and Three Worlds

The record of the American economy since 1945 is a mixed one.[45] Gross national product rose, in 1954 prices, from $280 billion in 1948 (a good benchmark, since the postwar readjustment had ended) to over $470 billion in 1962. Yet there were serious recessions in 1948-49 (just prior to the Korean War), in 1953-54, 1957-58, and in 1960-61. The growth of GNP was much more impressive in the years 1948-56 (when it increased at an average rate of 4.7 per cent annually) than it was after 1956: for the rate of increase dropped, on the average, to only 3 per cent during 1957-62. The index of industrial production makes even more vivid the nature of the post-1956 decline. In the 1948-56 phase, the index rose 5.7 per cent annually, as compared with only 1 per cent during 1957-62.

Equally important in an assessment of recent U.S. growth is the role of what may be termed Cold War forces. During the 1948-56 phase, economic growth was given a major push by the effects of defense expenditures for the standing military establishment and for the Korean War. Defense spending increased at a rate of 22.4 per cent annually during that time, as compared with 2.9 per cent annually during 1956-63. The rate of increase of private spending also slowed after 1956, and the slack was taken up by a rise in aggregate government expenditures for civilian purposes. The latter increased 4.1 per cent annually during

45. I have relied heavily in this analysis of postwar cyclical patterns upon the valuable study by Alvin H. Hansen, *The Postwar American Economy* (New York, 1964). Also Bert G. Hickman, *Growth and Stability of the Postwar Economy* (Washington, 1960), and Harold G. Vatter, *The U.S. Economy in the 1950's* (New York, 1963). Douglas F. Dowd, "America and the World Economy," *Yale Review*, Winter, 1964, is a most useful interpretive study.

1948-56 and augmented at a 7.4 per cent rate during 1956-62. Yet even this increase was insufficient to maintain the GNP growth pattern, and, what is worse, the average level of unemployment has increased markedly in the post-1956 phase.

Aggregate figures for government spending obscure another aspect of the public expenditure pattern: its effect upon industrial productivity. It is now well recognized that technological developments, including automation and the creation of synthetics, have come to play an important role in setting the pace of economic growth. The strategic importance of government in this field is reflected in the statistics of research and development financing: of all R & D funds expended in the economy, well more than half have represented federal moneys. Second, certain key industries—including aircraft and missile production (which is today the largest manufacturing employer), electronics, and chemicals—have been heavily dependent upon defense contracts. Defense appropriations, which have represented by far the largest items in the federal budget throughout the Cold War years, represent the key impact of external forces upon the American economy.

With rising productivity in manufacturing and the development of new industries, population growth generally and urban growth in particular have been critical in shaping the course of American growth. During the 1950's urban population increased by one-fourth, compared with an 18 per cent increase in total population; and within suburban areas population rose 47 per cent. With the "sprawl" produced by suburban development has come a crisis in the cities, many of which have suffered from the flight of middle class residents to surrounding metropolitan communities. The tax resources of urban governments are already strained to meet the immense current social welfare needs of their population, let alone to solve accelerating problems of traffic congestion, deterioration of downtown core districts, public transportation and auto access, or law enforcement crises. Because of the regressive tax structures typical of state and local government in the United States, moreover, the ability of even the suburbs to provide adequate schools, recreational facilities, and other social needs is already in question.

The dizzying pace of change in urban centers is matched in its poignant human costs by the slow deterioration of entire regions. The Appalachian area, the cutover districts of the northern Great Lakes country, and other well-known "depressed areas" reflect vividly the enormous dislocations that can accompany rapid economic change. Finally, one may point to the costs exacted by inflation in the periods of most vigorous economic development since 1948. Since easing of the inflation that occurred immediately after the war, the long-term price increase has been moderate. And yet inflation's impact upon savings, salaried income groups, industrial-labor relations, and, not least, American export industries cannot be discounted altogether.[46]

An even more disturbing element in the recent economic record is the persistence of poverty in American society. One-fifth of American families still live on incomes of less than $4,000 per year, and in 1957 more than seven million families earned incomes of less than $2,000. The weight of poverty is borne most heavily by racial minorities: in 1960 median income of non-white families was only $3,233 as compared to a median for white families of $5,835. There continues to be a significant difference in opportunities for employment, in health, mortality rates, and housing, and in educational levels between the white

46. See Arthur F. Burns, "Some Reflections on the Employment Act," *Political Science Quarterly*, LXXVII (1962). Even more disturbing is the ability of firms in the basic industries to maintain a trend of slow price increases even during periods of recession and reduced demand, as well as in the face of sharp competition from foreign producers. In this connection, a recent (1964) indictment of the major steel firms for conspiratorial price-fixing may provide a clear answer to the mystery.

and non-white populations.[47] The civil rights issue itself, the economic manifestations of racial prejudice, and the more embracing question of poverty have critical implications for public policy affecting relations with other countries. A massive assault on domestic poverty and on welfare and educational gaps, which perpetuate the difference in living standards among races, will require public spending in magnitudes that might possibly affect the international standing of the dollar; area redevelopment programs often evoke political demands for maintaining obsolescent plant or tariff protection for such products as shoes and textiles, whose manufacture often centers in poverty-stricken areas; and efforts to raise the living standards of the poor may conflict with such established domestic programs as farm price supports or such trade policies as international price-fixing agreements.

More promising aspects of the recent economic record are not altogether obscured by such dark features. There is increased leisure time in the society as a whole; health standards are high (albeit at costs often crippling to family budgets, and with new risks from such phenomena as water, air, and food pollution); mass purchasing power exists sufficient to support mass production of revolutionary consumer items such as air conditioning; and, not least, in an index of well-being that defies quantification, a large measure of personal freedom is maintained within the society. The cardinal issue today has nothing to do with whether economic affluence prevails in the United States, but rather whether prosperity can be extended to all segments within the society.

As in the New Deal period, the recent policies adopted to achieve basic economic goals have been both nationalistic and

47. President's Council of Economic Advisers, 1962 Report, in *Economic Growth: An American Problem,* ed. by P. M. Gutmann (Englewood Cliffs, 1964), 165. See also the provocative attack upon common assumptions about race, poverty, and economic growth rates in William A. Williams, *The Great Evasion* (Chicago, 1964).

internationalist in conception. The nationalistic element was most strikingly embodied in the 1946 Employment Act. This law, which became a symbol of the "permanent New Deal," established the Council of Economic Advisers and required the President to report annually on the state of the economy, with a view toward promoting "maximum employment, production and purchasing power." Although merely a declaration of principle, the Employment Act bespoke the determination of the postwar generation to employ public resources to promote growth through anti-cyclical spending, tax policy, monetary policy, a domestic farm support program, and the like. Evaluating the Employment Act in 1962, Professor Arthur Burns remarked:

> You will look in vain in the Employment Act for any mention of the outside world, or of the need to conduct economic policies, both domestic and foreign, so as to enable us to discharge the political, economic, and military responsibilities that history has thrust upon us.

The law was a product of the depression, Burns claimed, and most Americans were still thinking in terms of possible renewed unemployment such as was known in the thirties. It revealed a naive sense, he asserts, that America was self-sufficient.[48]

Professor Burns' analysis of the Employment Act is valuable for its emphasis on the essentially nationalistic character of many economic programs and policies pursued since 1945. Yet it is rather a distortion to represent Americans' awareness of the need for healthy world economic growth as an entirely recent phenomenon. Throughout the Second World War the United States pressed its allies to commit themselves to postwar cooperation for the revival of world trade and to a new international order. One important part of this policy was the creation of new agencies that would foster the smooth functioning of the inter-

48. Burns, "Some Reflections on the Employment Act," 485-486.

national economy. Obstacles to trade, such as tariff and quotas, and impediments to settlement of international accounts which had plagued the world economy since the collapse of the gold standard, were key targets of the American policy.

It was under pressure from the United States that the representatives of forty-four governments met at Bretton Woods, New Hampshire, in 1944 to consider the problems of postwar trade. Out of this conference emerged two new agencies, the World Bank and the International Monetary Fund (IMF). The World Bank (or International Bank for Reconstruction and Development) was designed to pool the capital resources of the member nations to finance major economic development projects. The IMF was designed to promote monetary strength by stabilizing international exchange rates and expediting multilateral settlement of trade balances. Both new agencies were financed, in the first instance, largely through American capital subscriptions.

Fearful that economic autarky would revive after the Second World War, the United States also pushed consistently for the reduction of trade barriers. With continuous prodding from the American government, more than thirty countries in 1947-48 signed the protocol agreement termed the General Agreement on Trade and Tariffs (GATT). The signatories committed themselves in principle "to promote on a reciprocal and mutually advantageous basis the reduction of tariffs and other barriers to trade and the elimination of discriminatory treatment in international commerce."

Radical as these new departures were, they proved inadequate to meet the economic and political emergency that struck Europe immediately after the war. From 1945 to 1947 the spectre of widespread fuel, food, and clothing shortages in Europe threatened to produce social chaos. Aggravated by the threat of communist expansion, these problems were far beyond solution by trade treaties or new agencies. The United States contributed more than $12 billion in loans, grants, and emergency goods through direct relief, government lending, and the United Nations Relief and Rehabilitation Administration (UNRRA). By modifying the restrictionist immigration policy which dated from 1921, the United States absorbed about 1.5 million European refugees in the eight-year period 1945-53, and extensive American support was extended both to UN resettlement programs and to private charitable efforts.

After a long debate in 1947, Congress accepted a radical shift in approach and approved a program of large outright grants to European nations under the Marshall Plan. This was done, as Senator Arthur Vandenberg asserted, in recognition of "the grim truth—whether we like it or not—that American *self-interest, national economy, and national security*" were linked inseparably with European reconstruction.[49] The $11 billion in Marshall Plan aid poured into Western Europe served the explicit political purpose of the program: containment of the advance of communism. It also generated demand in the domestic economy by providing these foreign nations with purchasing power for importation of American goods. With astonishing rapidity, the European nations recovered to prewar production levels, and by the mid-1950's the economies of America's chief trading partners had been restored.

A major political by-product of the Marshall Plan was the movement toward regional economic cooperation in Continental Europe. As *quid pro quo* for American aid, this country required the recipient nations to coordinate their economic planning and to administer the program multilaterally through the Organization for European Economic Cooperation (OEEC). The OEEC provided for exchanges of economic and planning data, and it coordinated the effort to re-integrate West Germany into European

49. Quoted in Harry B. Price, *The Marshall Plan and Its Meaning* (Ithaca, 1955), 63-64. Italics added.

trade. Most significantly, it subjected tariff and quota schedules to joint scrutiny and worked toward reciprocity in trade. In 1950 the European Payments Union was formed to expedite settlement of international balances within Europe, and two years later the European Coal and Steel Community was founded. The ECSC in turn spawned the Common Market, or European Economic Community. The EEC, founded under the 1957 Rome Treaty, represents the apogee of the postwar movement toward trade liberalization within Europe itself. And yet regional economic agreements are not the same as liberalization of trade, as the French veto of Great Britain's application for membership made clear. Meanwhile, the "outer seven" countries of Europe founded the European Free Trade Association (EFTA), and Great Britain continued to foster its commercial ties with the Commonwealth countries. Finally, the integration movement began to take hold elsewhere: in Latin America, where two loose regional trade agreements have been concluded, and in Africa, where a Pan-African movement for economic cooperation is gaining strength despite deep political divisions.

The type of autarky that prevailed in the world economy before 1940 is no longer dominant. By continued liberalization of its tariff policy and by aid to Europe through grants rather than loans, the United States has contributed toward the restored vigor of world trade. The World Bank and GATT have expanded their roles, and new agencies for international loans have been established. And yet there has been a shift toward a new autarky in the form of regional trade blocs. The industrial nations of the West have realigned themselves in bloc organizations, and the communist countries too are moving toward closer coordination of national planning and centralization of trade policy in the Russian-dominated Council for Mutual Economic Assistance. There also survives an overlay of special economic arrangements between the old imperial powers and their former colonies. It is a moot question today whether new world trade barriers will be any less rigid than those they have replaced.

As bloc arrangements harden, the position of the underdeveloped countries continues to deteriorate. Hence one of the most dangerous trends of the 1920-40 period is still running its course. The industrial nations have expanded their productive capacity and raised living standards rapidly. The poorer countries, however, still labor under the dual strain of severe price fluctuations and declining terms of trade. The statistics of world trade during the decade 1950-60 reflect this dilemma. The industrial countries (excluding the Soviet bloc) increased the value of their total foreign trade at a 6.9 per cent annual rate. But the underdeveloped countries increased their exports at only a 3.6 per cent rate; meanwhile, they increased their imports at a 4.6 per cent rate; and many of them were forced to obtain loans merely to maintain levels of consumption.[50]

The widening gap between rich lands and poor has forced Americans to think in new terms about their role in the world economy. In addition to stimulating financial aid from all industrialized countries, the United States, in cooperation with European nations, has taken hesitant first steps toward "one-way free trade," by which the industrial nations reduce tariffs on selected products imported from the underdeveloped countries but without expectation of immediate reciprocity. In still another effort to combat deteriorating terms of trade for primary producers, the United States has participated in controversial international "price-fixing": price stabilization agreements affecting coffee, tin, sugar,

50. Taking the longer period 1937-38 to 1957, the underdeveloped countries increased their exports by only 50 per cent, as compared to a 104 per cent increase in imports. Of the export increase, moreover, in excess of half represented petroleum sales, affecting only a few countries, among them several with no effective social welfare programs. (Joint Economic Committee, *Employment, Growth, and Price Levels,* Part 5, 86th Cong., 1st Sess., 1063.)

and wheat. These measures have been taken only partially out of altruistic motives; there is a "harder" side to American policy. As noted earlier, measures to bolster the poorer nations reflect a fear of social chaos that might accrue to the benefit of the Soviet bloc.

The United States continues to be the largest trading nation in the world, and it looks to growing overseas markets, especially in the underdeveloped countries, for sale of exports—particularly now, in view of the competitive climate generated by the Common Market. The value of U.S. foreign trade has ranged from about 7 to 9 per cent of GNP since 1947. But the share of U.S. products in total world trade presents a different view. American exports are about 17 per cent of the total, and U.S. imports about 13 per cent. The impact of stagnation in the poor countries upon American trade was readily illustrated by events from 1950 to 1962, when the U.S. share of all manufactures exported fell from 27 per cent to 21 per cent. This relative decrease was the result, to some extent, of the economic revival in Europe. But the demand side of the equation also played a key role. During this period, markets such as Latin America, where the United States dominated as a supplier of manufactures, suffered under depressed conditions, affecting adversely the rate of expansion for American exports.[51] The continuing economic crisis in such areas as Latin America cannot help but damage the U.S. export potential in a very direct way.

The recovery of Europe's industrial nations and the deteriorating position of the underdeveloped areas both contributed to the U.S. balance-of-payments problem after 1958. In trade alone, this country continues to produce a surplus, averaging more

51. 88th Cong., 1st Sess., Joint Economic Committee, *The U.S. Balance of Payments* (committee print, 1963), 30. See also C. P. Kindleberger, "International Trade and United States Experience," *Postwar Economic Trends in the United States,* ed. by Ralph Freeman (New York, 1960).

than $4 billion annually since World War II. And yet U.S. gold reserves have come under increasing pressure in recent years because exports and other earnings have not increased enough to offset imports, expenditures abroad for military purposes, the outflow of investment capital, and the costs of government aid programs. Despite the efforts of the International Monetary Fund, the settlement of international accounts has been strained by the weakening American payments position. Since the dollar holdings of foreign nations are used to supplement gold payments in international settlements, a threat to the stability of the dollar is a danger for the entire world economy. And so other governments, sometimes grudgingly, have cooperated to bolster the American position. The IMF has been used to strengthen U.S. reserves; bilateral "swap" arrangements (advances of informal international credit) have been concluded; and the Treasury Department has obtained gold from governments (including the Soviet Union) which for their own reasons wish to expand their dollar holdings. Moreover, the payments crisis in the United States has fostered new efforts to strengthen the international monetary system. The American government has also attempted to shift part of the financial burden of European defense to other NATO countries; the possibilities of increased trade with the Soviet bloc are being explored; and a large variety of proposals is under study for reform of the international payments mechanism.[52]

The balance-of-payments difficulties have illuminated the international effects of what were once regarded as exclusively domestic economic policies. For example, any Federal Reserve Board action affecting interest rates obviously now entails a balancing of domestic economic needs against the possible flight of investment capital to high-interest money markets abroad. Similarly, there

52. See *The U.S. Balance of Payments: The International Monetary System,* Hearings before the Joint Economic Committee, 88th Cong., 1st Sess., Nov. 12-15, 1963; and *New York Times,* September 30, 1963.

is increasing pressure for balanced federal budgets as a means of strengthening confidence in the dollar, though resisted by those who regard domestic expansion as the best antidote to the payments deficit. Despite such differences over policy, there is general acceptance of the impatient view that "the United States has been severely impeded in pursuing the objectives of the Employment Act of 1946, by the need to bring its balance of payments into equilibrium." [53] On the other hand, the payments crisis has contributed to a sense of frustration and resentment, expressed in a recent statement of Congress' Joint Economic Committee, that "foreigners . . . [thereby] exercise a powerful influence on United States policy which, on the basis of realities, should not be theirs." [54]

The balance-of-payments question is one of several major issues in contemporary political discussion which have deepened Americans' awareness of interdependence in the contemporary world economy. Closely linked to the debate over the 1962 Trade Expansion Act, which President Kennedy made an issue of highest priority in his program, the payments crisis has placed in sharp focus the relationship of domestic economic growth to the health of the world economy. The ability of this country to support economic aid to the underdeveloped nations, to expand markets for primary products, to maintain the flow of military aid entailed in the cold war, to meet the competitive challenge of the Common Market, and to defend the stability of the dollar—all of these, it is now popularly understood, depend in large part upon the rate of economic growth at home.

There is also increasing awareness, within both business and consumer groups, of the potential of foreign markets and sources of supply. The American business corporation has become more international in its outlook and, in many cases, in its organization

53. *The U.S. Balance of Payments,* Joint Economic Committee, 88th Cong., 2nd Sess., Report No. 965 (1964), 5.
54. *Ibid.,* 7.

as well. American investment in foreign countries, for example, averaged less than $700 million annually from 1946 to 1955. Since that time new investment has increased rapidly, and in 1960-62 annual private investment outflow was more than $2.6 billion per year. Domestic firms continue to rely heavily upon foreign sources of raw materials, ranging from Canadian wood pulp to Bolivian tin and South American coffee. Some American oil firms own nearly all their reserves abroad, and the major international corporations often maintain overseas managerial bureaucracies whose size dwarfs that of the resident State Department staff in many foreign countries. The horizons of the American consumer have expanded, as reflected in the share of the U.S. market now held by foreign producers of autos, typewriters, business machines, and other manufactures.[55]

Finally, popular thinking has been jolted severely by the emergent threat of world population pressure. Until now, technological advances have managed to keep pace with, and even ahead of, resource shortages. And yet the consumption of natural resources by industrial societies (particularly when maintaining $50 billion annual defense expenditures) has raised basic questions about the future of man on earth. The rising pace of world population growth threatens to become a dominant variable, wiping out the gains of the new technology and placing an intolerable strain on resources. If the industrial nations ever approach success in the imperative effort to raise living standards for the two-thirds of human population who now exist without basic necessities, the pressure on resources will be magnified proportionally. Even the new technology itself has produced hazards which transcend national limits: "the dangers to life from widely disseminated radiation, the burden of man-made chemicals, fumes and smogs of unknown biological effect which we now absorb, . . . and the

55. *Employment, Growth and Price Levels,* cited n. 50, *supra,* 951, 956; Adolph A. Berle, Jr., *The 20th Century Capitalist Revolution,* Harvest edition (New York, 1954), Chap. 4.

potential of totally destructive war."[56] Who would term any of these merely an "American problem"?

In fact, neither the problems nor the basic determinants of economic development in this country have ever been "exclusively American." In the nineteenth century, the course of American growth was influenced vitally by foreign markets, an influx of labor and capital from abroad, and the contributions of foreign technology. In the twentieth century, the United States has emerged as the world's wealthiest nation, its leading supplier and purchaser of goods in international trade, and its center for the advancement of industrial technology. This long-term reversal of position has occurred within a world economy twice disrupted by total war, strained for many years by economic autarky and prolonged depression, and now facing stagnation in the underdeveloped areas and radical shifts in the institutional structure and composition of world trade. However much the United States may be dominant where it once was secondary, the vital stake of this country in the expansion of the world economy and the economic strength of its trading partners has remained a constant factor. Such critical contemporary issues as the need to stimulate domestic economic growth cannot be treated, as they were in the 1920's, without regard to effects upon the outside world and ultimately upon this nation. Rather, we must recognize that the record of our history reveals no golden age of entire self-sufficiency in any time past. Interdependence within the world economy is deeply rooted, and it has conditioned the basic course of economic growth in America since the settlement of Jamestown and Plymouth Bay.

56. Arthur A. Ekirch, Jr., *Man and Nature in America* (New York, 1963), 134.

3

THE AMERICAN SOCIAL ORDER

ROWLAND BERTHOFF

WHAT is the proper subject matter of social history? The history of society need not be, as it usually has been, a merely residual field, "left after every other group has defined the boundaries of its interests." [1] It pertains instead to a quite specific area of human affairs which, as it happens, has already been conveniently marked out for study by the sociologists: the social order—the structure of society—and the functional interplay of the various institutions and population groups that compose it. In American society such groupings as local or regional communities, social and economic classes, ethnic groups, business corporations, trade unions, political machines, voluntary associations of many kinds, and of course the family have all been conspicuous. The evolution of a society composed of such groups and, in America, of a large proportion of more or less unattached

---

This essay first appeared in the *American Historical Review*, LXV, No. 3 (April 1960), and is reprinted here, with revisions, by permission.

1. John A. Krout, "Reflections of a Social Historian," *Approaches to American Social History*, ed. by William E. Lingelbach (New York, 1937), 61.

individuals, presents the appropriate subject for the social historian.

It would be difficult to say precisely where the boundary lies between social history so defined and cultural history, since the content of the life of the groups within the social order is their culture; a description of the organization of a group that did not advert to its mind or culture would be threadbare indeed. Yet social history and cultural history can differ in emphasis much as sociology differs from literary criticism. By the same token, social history and intellectual history are related to each other, most elementarily in the fact that social institutions are no more substantial than their members and others think they are. Furthermore, the intellectual pattern of a nation—certainly of America—derives in large part from its past and present social pattern. And yet ideas, whatever their social subsoil may have been, do come to have their own flowering which the intellectual historian can clip and dissect. On an earthier level, the economic base, past or present, from which any social order is largely derived has an objective physical existence partly independent of human ideas and purposes, so that no argument is needed to justify economic history as a subject distinct from social or intellectual history.

This is by no means to assert a simple economic or social determinism in history. Ideas, whatever their origins, do react upon the social order, and both ideas and social institutions together help to determine the uses to which we put the objective phenomena of the natural environment. But in examining the oft-praised seamless web of history, we can distinguish, in terms of a carpet, economic history and social history as the basic warp and weft of the coarse backing, cultural history as the finer substance of the carpet, and intellectual history as the figure that both rests upon and gives form to the other materials. If the ultimate goal of historians—no less than carpet weavers—is to construct a whole fabric, still they must first perfect the elements of their carpets or of the grand historical synthesis.

As social historians we have included in our courses and books material relevant to the structure and functioning of the American social order, though it has been rather aimlessly tangled with all manner of more or less extraneous things. What is evidently still needed today, no less than twenty or thirty years ago, is an adequate central theme around which to arrange this material, a synthetic rather than a merely eclectic principle. What I have to suggest may seem only to reflect the odd preoccupation of our time with problems of social status. I am encouraged, however, by the number of perceptive recent studies by historians and social scientists which are essentially consistent with the assumption that the central and continuous factor throughout the history of American society is its characteristic mobility.

The concept of mobility clearly furnishes us with a principle adeqate at least to comprehend a number of conventional concerns of American historiography. The westward movement, which since Frederick Jackson Turner's time has figured as a special field claiming fundamental importance, had better be considered as only one of a number of kinds of physical and social movement. For that matter, along with the even more extensive movement of people to the cities, it proves to have been only one kind of internal migration. Immigration history has grown in recent years into another such primary field. A third, as yet only beginning to be developed by historians, is the occupational and social mobility—the constant vertical movement up and down the ladder of wealth and status—that characterizes any modern industrial country, England or Japan not less than the United States.[2]

Furthermore, each of these three well-known kinds of movement in our history has given rise to certain of our most characteristic social institutions and population groups. The process of settlement, whether westward or cityward, produced our regions and sections and our urban communities. The process of immigra-

2. Seymour Martin Lipset and Reinhard Bendix, *Social Mobility in Industrial Society* (Berkeley, 1959), 11-75.

tion successively introduced a great variety of ethnic and religious groups into the population. Social or vertical mobility, fostered both by the free land of the frontier and by opportunities in expanding commerce and industry, has been with us virtually since our beginnings and has created our characteristic structure of social classes. These three kinds of mobility, and likewise the three kinds of resultant social groupings, of course have always been closely interrelated. We expect to find a certain coincidence in the South, for example, of British ancestry, Protestant religion, and well-defined class distinctions; or in a northern coal-mining town of people of Slavic descent, Catholic or Orthodox religion, and the working class. While there have no doubt been individuals who incorporated in themselves every conceivable regional, ethnic, and social mixture, still our history has made some combinations of ancestry and religion, locale, and class more likely than others.

This interrelationship between the different kinds of mobility makes mobility a useful concept for social history. And likewise the lack of such a concept has misled many historians of the frontier or of immigration to claim too exclusive an importance for these special subjects—to suppose that egalitarian democracy came only out of the frontier forests, or that the end of both the frontier and unrestricted immigration presaged the demise of economic opportunity in America. It will still be convenient to separate these fields of history for monographic research, but otherwise to isolate them is unlikely to produce work of general importance.

If the social order is agreed to be the proper concern of social history, and mobility the central theme in American social history, a general hypothesis can be proposed for the peculiar evolution of the American social order. This evolution has followed a long cycle. The first phase, comprising the seventeenth and eighteenth centuries to about 1815, was characterized by relatively low mobility (though high by European standards) and the establishment of a fairly stable social order in the various colonies and new states.[3] The second phase, the nineteenth century, was an epoch of enormous migration, immigration, and social mobility, during which the recently established social order became badly disorganized and in fact disorderly. Finally, after a transitional period from about 1900 to 1930, during which free land and free immigration came to an end and a profound effort to reorganize the economy began, we have in the past thirty years established a society which, although still highly mobile, is better integrated than that of the nineteenth century and is in this respect more comparable to that of the eighteenth.

How well does this hypothesis fit the familiar annals of frontier history? Well enough, I think, to confirm one of the main points of the Turner thesis of the frontier as the leveler and safety valve of American society. In so far as Turner's critics have denied the *exclusive* significance of the frontier, they have the better case; but free land, considered as one of several sources of mobility, by and large was the egalitarian social force that the frontier school has always maintained it was. By establishing this point statistically for an ordinary district in Wisconsin, Merle Curti's study of Trempealeau County has broken through the timeworn pattern of debate on the matter.[4] Some qualification is necessary; as Paul W. Gates has shown, the land laws permitted various speculators to monopolize vast tracts here and there throughout the West.[5] But as in Trempealeau County, so we may suppose elsewhere, if "the rich became somewhat richer, the poor became a good deal less poor." [6]

3. The best description of this society, in its last days, is still Henry Adams, *History of the United States of America during the First Administration of Thomas Jefferson,* 2 vols. (New York, 1889), I, 1-184.

4. Merle Curti, *The Making of an American Community: A Case Study of Democracy in a Frontier County* (Stanford, 1959), 140-221.

5. Paul W. Gates, "Frontier Estate Builders and Farm Laborers," *The Frontier in Perspective,* ed. by Walker D. Wyman and Clifton B. Kroeber (Madison, 1957), 143-163.

6. Curti, *Making of an American Community,* 445.

The leveling force of free land was, of course, already at work in the seventeenth and eighteenth centuries, so that almost everywhere there was established the self-reliant and comfortable yeomanry whom foreign observers thought so remarkable. And yet mobility and stability were still in balance. The process of settlement was relatively gradual before the Revolution, especially in New England, where until late in the colonial period it proceeded in organized groups of like-minded people strictly controlled by authority. In the South it took more than a century for the east-west migration of tobacco planters and farmers to cross the Blue Ridge, and then only to find back-country migrants already moving down from Pennsylvania. Even with these reinforcements, Southern settlement did not pass west of the mountains in any great numbers until near the end of the eighteenth century. This low rate of migration presumably contributed to the stability and homogeneity of the society in which the class of self-made country squires figured so prominently among the generality of yeomen in both North and South. Another notable result was the strength of local or regional attachments which these relatively stationary Americans evidently felt at that time. The more than a dozen distinct dialect areas which exactly mirror the pattern of colonial settlement between the seaboard and the mountains are telling evidence of this parochialism.[7]

In the nineteenth century, the westward migration which had been measured in hundreds of miles rapidly preempted the remaining thousands. However admirable we have been accustomed to think the restless individualism of the westward migrants, the movement was a disorderly process. Although in general these individuals succeeded, as the Trempealeau study indicates, in their effort to maintain or improve their economic and social status, their migration tended to break down the social order which had been painfully attained in the East in the previous two hundred

7. Hans Kurath, *A Word Geography of the Eastern United States* (Ann Arbor, 1949).

years. The rush for free land inhibited the development of any stable hierarchy of social and economic classes, except, of course, in those parts of the Old Southwest where the introduction of Negro slavery, which had been the most extreme class distinction in the eighteenth-century Tidewater, perpetuated an anachronism. The social and economic leveling of the frontier is still commonly applauded and indeed has become an essential part of our liberal tradition.

Besides social classes, however, other and less dubious forms of social organization, such as local communities, were likewise stunted. Although a score of new regions, from fertile prairie and rugged upland to arid plains and barren desert, were settled, the social differences that these physiographic conditions produced were hardly more remarkable than the social resemblances between the new regions.[8] Even the cattle kingdom of the Great Plains, which rightly lives on in national legend as the last high-water mark of the westward movement, was much like the earlier livestock ranges of the savannas and canebrakes of the Old Southwest, although there it had often been hard to see the cowboys for the trees.[9] What almost all parts of the nineteenth-century West had in common was a disorderly or at best a yet unordered society, whose population was too transient, and consequently too mixed in its origins, to permit the growth of integrated local communities. The townships, counties, and cities may have been "settled," but their inhabitants were not.

This tenuousness of local attachments had a result besides the

8. Obviously, American history is full of sectional conflicts, but these have for the most part, and with the notable exception of the Civil War, arisen from economic rather than social differences. Even the incompatible societies of North and South, for that matter, went to war only after their social differences had been transmuted into antipathetic moral and ideological convictions.

9. Compare Walter Prescott Webb, *The Great Plains* (New York, 1931), 205-269, with Frank Lawrence Owsley, *Plain Folk of the Old South* (Baton Rouge, 1949), 23-50.

undifferentiated nationalism for which Turner praised the West. Although Western settlements did share a fairly homogeneous culture, to the extent that the folk customs of the Old Northwest and Southwest, the Plains and the Far West were in many particulars identical, this common culture was necessarily rudimentary. It was as conservative as possible of the institutions and values of Eastern society, but distance and the half-settled state of the New West were uncongenial. The rawness of the West is one of our great traditions, and rightly so; even the most careful listing of churches, newspapers, libraries, theatres, literary societies, and other infant amenities of the cultural frontier can hardly convince us that the West sprang into being as a highly developed or creative social order. It was not a seedbed of innovation and reform; it was merely unformed. The theology of the frontier camp meeting, for instance, was an old doctrine rudely preached. More thoroughgoing novelties in religion were the work of long-settled Eastern communities which could afford to be liberal.[10]

How the twentieth century removed the influence of the frontier from American society is an old story. As settlement approached its natural limits between 1890 and 1920, so did the egalitarian effect of free land. Class distinctions hardened, not only in Western cities and towns but on the land itself. Farm laborers and tenants no longer could confidently expect to rise into the class of landowning farmers. (The same thing in effect had happened long before in the Old Southwest, where the suitable cotton land had virtually all been entered before 1860.) Alarm over this situation, so novel in the West, was heightened around the turn of the century by the misconception, endorsed by Turner, that

10. Compare, e.g., Owsley, *Plain Folk of the Old South,* 90-149; R. Carlyle Buley, *The Old Northwest: Pioneer Period, 1815-1840,* 2 vols. (Bloomington, 1951), I, 138-394; Everett Dick, *The Sod-House Frontier, 1854-1890: A Social History of the Northern Plains from the Creation of Kansas and Nebraska to the Admission of the Dakotas* (New York, 1937), *passim;* Louis B. Wright, *Culture on the Moving Frontier* (Bloomington, 1955), *passim.*

mobility had been due solely to the influence of the frontier. That a less restless Western population—including an accepted upper class which in time could set a higher tone to Western culture—might have a certain social value was a possibility that nobody seemed to consider worth expressing.

In any case, it is clear that the end of the frontier movement was by no means the end of internal migration. This had long since started to turn toward the cities, in large part because of the other two factors mentioned above, immigration and social mobility.

Like the westward movement, of which it was literally a part, immigration from the Old World in the seventeenth and eighteenth centuries was a relatively gradual process. Although it was the source of the entire white and Negro population of some four million in 1790, in the course of nearly two hundred years it had involved probably not as many as a million persons. Even that degree of movement was cut down during most of the forty years between 1775 and 1815. More important (since numbers are only relative), the colonial immigration established, with only a few local exceptions, a homogeneous population of English origin and culture. Other European and African peoples came, but mostly in the eighteenth century, after the English had already set the pattern of colonial society. Even though some of the others managed to maintain their separate ethnic identities, in general the persistence of immigrant culture meant the persistence of a variant of English culture. Americans were Englishmen established in a new environment. The New World modified the social order that they established, but in the circumstances it was a remarkably orderly society which in many particulars approximated, often quite consciously, that of the mother country.

After 1815, however, and throughout the hundred-odd years before the immigration restriction acts of the 1920's, the enormous influx of some thirty-five million persons—numbering more than four times the entire American population of 1815 and coming from all the countries and cultures of Europe—contributed as much as any factor to the general disorder of nineteenth-century American society. Recent scholarship has made the essential facts of this migration as familiar as those of the westward movement.[11] It has already become a commonplace to remark on the uprooting of the immigrants, especially the peasants among them, out of their accustomed Old World communities, and their equally abrupt transplanting as so many isolated individuals into the unfamiliar and often inhospitable American social climate. Like the westward movement, immigration was not effectively managed by society; in most cases it was undertaken voluntarily by individual families as their particular response to economic and social circumstances that endangered their accustomed status at home or promised a better one in America. But their quest for security, ironically enough, often had unwelcome results when peasants found themselves piled on top of each other in urban slum tenements, where they were too crowded for their taste, or scattered across remote Midwestern prairies on farms which were too isolated.

To be sure, the social confusion suffered by these people was somewhat relieved by the ethnic associations which they organized for themselves. But the immigrants' clubs, newspapers, singing societies, even their churches, were at best fragile substitutes for the social order they had once known and feeble custodians of the old culture they had never intended to abandon. Most of these associations eventually dwindled and dissolved, unable to withstand the atomization to which American social mobility subjected the American-born second generation. (There was at least as great a cultural loss in this uprooting as in the restless

11. William I. Thomas and Florian Znaniecki, *The Polish Peasant in Europe and America: Monograph of an Immigrant Group,* 5 vols. (Boston, 1918-1920); Oscar Handlin, *Boston's Immigrants, 1790-1865; A Study in Acculturation* (Cambridge, 1941), and *The Uprooted: The Epic Story of the Great Migrations that Made the American People* (Boston, 1951).

mobility of the frontiersmen.[12]) Moreover, even in so far as the ethnic group succeeded for a time in providing the warmth of community for first-generation immigrants (most of whom as workingmen were already isolated from Americans of other classes), it compounded the general lack of integration in American society. Our retrospective compassion for these "strangers in the land" may extend also to the Yankees who objected to them as disruptive intruders.

Within the span of the same early twentieth-century generation which saw the end of the frontier migration, free immigration likewise was brought to its end by the national-origins quota acts. The racial theory running through this legislation has since been exposed as pseudoscientific quackery, but the situation of social disorder which made so ill-considered a theory credible to Americans (especially to those anxious for their own status) was real enough.[13] Immigration was no more exclusively the cause of the disorder than were the westward movement and the Industrial Revolution, both of which most Americans considered salutary, but it was one cause. In the 1920's, as Nathan Glazer has put it, "America had decided to stop the kaleidoscope and find out what it had become." [14]

By that time the homogeneity of 1815 had been transformed into a wild complexity of peoples and cultures in various stages of assimilation. Although the immigration acts, by cutting off further additions to this mosaic from abroad, have tended to consolidate the myriad of ethnic groups into a single new American culture, somewhat as was intended, the new homogeneity is still incomplete. In place of an unstable cultural pluralism we now have simpler divisions between Protestants, Catholics, and Jews which

12. Nathan Glazer, "The Immigrant Groups and American Culture," *Yale Review,* XLVIII (Spring 1959), 382-397.

13. John Higham, *Strangers in the Land: Patterns of American Nativism, 1860-1925* (New Brunswick, 1955).

14. Nathan Glazer, "The Integration of American Immigrants," *Law and Contemporary Problems,* XXI (Spring 1956), 269.

seem likely to persist as a permanent social heritage from the nineteenth century.[15] For that matter, partly because of the crudity of the racial notions embedded in the immigration acts, they have in one notable way failed to accomplish even their sponsors' goal of ethnic homogeneity. Since the First World War fresh waves of migrants have been set in motion within the United States, among them Puerto Ricans and poor Southern Negroes and whites, who have come north to take the places now denied to Italian and Polish immigrants. But however imperfect from any point of view, the immigration acts of 1921 and 1924, and of 1952, are at least symptomatic of the twentieth-century impulse to reintegrate a shaken social order.

This impulse has been more consciously expressed, curiously enough, in this century's anxiety to maintain social mobility—the vertical movement of individuals from one class to another. Social mobility in America has been the product of an expanding economy, of which Western settlement and immigration were parts no less than commercial expansion and the Industrial Revolution. In the seventeenth and eighteenth centuries the economy expanded at a slower rate than it was to do thereafter, industrialization having hardly begun here. It was commonly agreed at that time, furthermore, that in economic affairs there were certain narrow standards of fair dealing which limited private enterprise and which should be enforced by government.

The opportunity was at hand, however, in commerce and in land speculation or large-scale cultivation, for many a humble immigrant and his descendants—even for indentured servants after their time was up—to prosper and become gentlemen after the model of the merchants and gentry of England. Even in Pennsylvania and the New England colonies, which were settled for a less earthly purpose, society had its higher ranks, and it was not long before the foremost among these were the merchants

15. Will Herberg, *Protestant—Catholic—Jew: An Essay in American Religious Sociology* (New York, 1955), 18-58.

of the ports and such landed magnates as the Connecticut Valley "river gods." [16] There and elsewhere—especially in South Carolina and the Chesapeake colonies after the mass importation of Negro slave labor—the social order consisted of this aristocracy and of various inferior social classes, distinct from each other and accepting the distinctions.[17] These distinctions were kept from becoming as extreme as in England by the availability of land; nearly everywhere the broad class of roughly equal yeoman freeholders established itself as the bulk of the population. As we may again surmise, however, this leveling was itself limited by the slow pace of settlement. Even after the political Revolution won independence from the mother country, in most of the new states society continued on the whole to acquiesce in domination by a class of "gentlemen freeholders." [18]

It was not immediately apparent that after 1815 this social order was to be swept away nearly everywhere. It became plain in the early 1830's, the time of the great rush of settlers to the West, when in both East and West the rough equality of the class of yeoman farmers was transmuted into an egalitarian ideology. As recent studies of Jacksonianism have demonstrated, the new industrial entrepreneurs as well as the small farmers and handicraft artisans adopted this ideology. These new and old groups alike hated privileged monopoly, though for opposite reasons. The yeoman farmers and artisans were looking backward, seeking to preserve the society of the eighteenth century in which, even

16. Bernard Bailyn, *The New England Merchants in the Seventeenth Century* (Cambridge, 1955); Frederick B. Tolles, *Meeting House and Counting House: The Quaker Merchants of Colonial Philadelphia, 1682-1763* (Chapel Hill, 1948); Robert J. Taylor, *Western Massachusetts in the Revolution* (Providence, 1954), 11-26.

17. Thomas Jefferson Wertenbaker, *The Planters of Colonial Virginia* (Princeton, 1922), 134-161.

18. Charles S. Sydnor, *Gentlemen Freeholders: Political Practices in Washington's Virginia* (Chapel Hill, 1952); Robert E. Brown, *Middle-Class Democracy and the Revolution in Massachusetts, 1691-1780* (Ithaca, 1955).

though there were class divisions, the lower classes had a kind of security that kept them from sinking too low. The new group of rising capitalists, on the contrary, looked forward to a liberal society in which none of their competitors would enjoy a monopoly established by government to block their own individual progress to success and fortune.[19]

From that time on, this ambiguous egalitarianism gave direction (or rather, lack of direction) to both the industrial and the frontier expansion of the nineteenth century. Thus, just when industrialization opened a myriad of opportunities for individuals to rise in position, wealth, and status, the checkrein of governmental regulation was thrown off. The irony of the inadvertent result is another familiar fact: unregulated industrial expansion quickly produced both a glittering plutocracy and a depressed proletariat, far more widely divided in sentiment and interest than colonial social classes had ever been. The fact that the proletariat consisted largely of immigrants of foreign culture widened still further the social divisions. On the other hand, the egalitarian yeoman tradition was by no means dead, and indeed in so far as industrial expansion kept alive a semblance of equal opportunity for the individual, Americans tolerated the actual inequality of wealth and status at any given time within their society.

Well before the end of the century it became abundantly clear that the industrial revolutionaries had produced an American social disorder almost without parallel in the modern world. A self-made plutocracy recognized little responsibility for the working classes; the latter repudiated whatever common interest they had once felt with their employers; ethnic groups regarded each other with little sympathy; the farming regions resented their exploitation by businessmen and bankers; and individuals in general acknowledged few social duties except to themselves, their families,

19. Marvin Meyers, *The Jacksonian Persuasion: Politics and Belief* (Stanford, 1957); Bray Hammond, *Banks and Politics in America: From the Revolution to the Civil War* (Princeton, 1957).

and their narrow interest groups. Even so elemental an institution as the family, for that matter, was feared to be in a state of disintegration, as divorce became a common practice, women left the home to work, and each new generation of children—even those who did not have to work for a living—seemed to have less respect for parental authority.

The forces of social reintegration were feeble. Symptomatic of the need for a new sense of community was the fraternal order. It is customary for historians to dismiss the lodges of Masons or Odd Fellows which sprang up everywhere as an unimportant eccentricity of a "nation of joiners," and yet they were highly significant of the lack of other forms of community in American society in their day.[20] Despite the extravagant flummery of these lodges and the evident lack of cultural taste among their millions of members, perhaps the invention and maintenance of any kind of social community was in itself a sufficient cultural achievement for the time. (Much the same might be said of the still ineffectual trade union movement.) The American's habit, when taxed by a European visitor with the poverty of American culture, of pointing with pride to "our institutions"—meaning, of course, primarily political institutions—was not altogether irrelevant. Europeans might not value either political or social institutions among the higher forms of "culture," but in America the ever-present task of shoring up the social framework inevitably exhausted energies that might otherwise have been devoted to filling the structure with finer things. Like the contemporary English working class culture in the view of Raymond Williams, American popular culture in the nineteenth century created social institutions rather than art, literature, or science—in its context, a remarkable achievement indeed.[21]

Apart from such palliatives, however, the chief resistance to

20. Charles W. Ferguson, *Fifty Million Brothers: A Panorama of American Lodges and Clubs* (New York, 1937), 3-15.

21. Raymond Williams, *Culture and Society, 1780-1950* (London, 1958), 327.

social disorder came from various old-fashioned groups, some of them numbered, to their eventual discomfiture, among Jackson's original supporters, who resented being superseded by the Industrial Revolution. It has recently been suggested that even the humanitarian reformers of the 1830's and 1840's, who have hitherto been ranked as the vanguard of liberalism, in fact included many whose concern for the downtrodden reflected their conservative anxiety over their own loss of prestige or influence in the society. Thus a large proportion of the abolitionist leaders were genteel folk of the old order, and it might be added that at least a few, like Garrison himself, came from the class of artisans whose handicraft skills were already obsolescent.[22] If it is true that the impulse of these reformers was essentially conservative or even reactionary, this may account for their remarkable proneness, when attempting to liberate the individual from bondage to alcohol and other evils, ultimately to resort, with no consciousness of incongruity, to legal prohibition and other restrictions not at all welcome to the individual drinker.

The history of the second quarter of the nineteenth century abounds in similar examples of the reformer who resists change. The clearest is the labor movement, which until the 1850's was composed largely of pre-industrial workingmen with a reactionary program.[23] Again, the most perceptive account of the "burned-over district" of upper New York State suggests that the susceptibility of the small farmers there to novel religious cults in this same period was in some degree the reaction of a settled rural backwater that had already been left behind by the march of progress.[24] Among these groups only the Mormons achieved their

22. David Donald, *Lincoln Reconsidered: Essays on the Civil War Era* (New York, 1956), 19-36.

23. Norman J. Ware, *The Industrial Worker, 1840-1860: The Reaction of American Industrial Society to the Advance of the Industrial Revolution* (Boston, 1924), 198-240.

24. Whitney R. Cross, *The Burned-Over District: The Social and Intellectual History of Enthusiastic Religion in Western New York, 1800-1850* (Ithaca, 1950), 55-109.

own kind of success, and it is significant that they did so by utterly repudiating liberal individualism when they built their own hierarchic social order in the Western deserts.

In recent years the agrarian crusaders of the late nineteenth century have likewise been denied their reputation as radicals and demoted to the ranks of reactionaries. Populism, it now appears, was the unrealistic attempt of unsuccessful rural capitalists to take refuge in an outworn myth. It is true that, in Richard Hofstadter's words, "when times were persistently bad, the farmer tended to reject his business role and its failures [and] to withdraw into the role of the injured little yeoman." [25] But it should be noted that this yeoman tradition evoked nostalgia for a social order in which the small farmer had enjoyed a more secure status. It harked back to the pre-Jacksonian society of the eighteenth century more than to the individualistic disorder of the nineteenth in which these farmer-speculators had injudiciously indulged. In this sense the Populists were double-dyed reactionaries, longing not merely for the past epoch but for the epoch before that.

Nostalgia, however, is sometimes more than a perverse rejection of reality. All these so-called radicals of the nineteenth century, reminiscent as they are of various modern yet archaic European groups of "primitive rebels," may have been only reactionaries out of step with their progressive industrial age, but in the end they were not wholly ineffectual.[26] Their spirit has infused a good deal of the twentieth-century movement to reorder society, and in the process something that was obsolete in 1890 has in effect been restored.

This fundamental task of reintegrating the social order had hardly been begun by 1900, when Americans for the first time came seriously to grips with it. This is the meaning of the Pro-

25. Richard Hofstadter, *The Age of Reform: From Bryan to F. D. R.* (New York, 1955), 47.

26. E. J. Hobsbawm, *Primitive Rebels: Studies in Archaic Forms of Social Movement in the 19th and 20th Centuries* (Manchester [England], 1959).

gressive movement for our social history. Politics from that point on no longer merely followed the lines of the underlying economic and social foundations of the country, but dug down and reshaped them by an act of will.

At the outset, a nineteenth-century habit of speech dictated that honest anxiety be expressed for the survival of equality of opportunity, that is, of social mobility, mortally wounded as it was supposed to be by the closing of the frontier and the spread of industrial monopoly. The trust movement no doubt had thrived on the egalitarianism of liberal American democracy; still, the cure for the ills of democracy was said to be more democracy. But while it is true that the Progressive movement was literally "the complaint of the unorganized against the consequences of organization," in particular such organizations as trusts and political machines, nevertheless by force of circumstances Progressives themselves had to organize in order to control these institutions.[27] Thus the Progressive movement, though undertaken to liberate opportunity for the individual, tended rather to encase it in new regulatory institutions alongside the objectionable institutions. This proliferation of interlocked institutions was a conservative counter-revolution. In its course, the big business corporation eventually would shed its early reputation as a monopolistic monster and in effect become esteemed as the pioneer of modern institutional society, and the urban political machine would be affectionately recalled as the prototype of the welfare state.[28]

Americans of all classes after 1900 preached the Progressive gospel of mutual responsibility, even though we may suspect some of them, like earlier reformers, of more anxiety over their own insecure economic and social status than over the general welfare.[29] Others who still denied their social duties had responsi-

27. Hofstadter, *Age of Reform,* 213-269.

28. Samuel P. Hays, *The Response to Industrialism, 1885-1914* (Chicago, 1957), 48-70.

29. Hofstadter, *Age of Reform,* 131-163; Robert Bremner, *From the Depths: The Discovery of Poverty in the United States* (New York, 1956).

bility forced, at least gingerly, upon them by the Progressive regulation of railroads, labor conditions, banks, food handling, natural resources, and so forth. The Progressive legislative record hardly amounted to a root-and-branch social revolution, but for a time in the 1920's it appeared sufficient. The big business corporation, though still growing, seemed a beneficent monster to middle class investors, and to many other Americans as well it appeared that social reform had been consummated by the legislation that ruthlessly cut back immigration and thought to restore morality through the prohibition of drink.

After 1929 the Great Depression provoked the more thorough reforms of the New Deal, differing in detail from Progressivism but directed more consciously than before at the same essential purpose of social reconstruction. For a time in the 1930's it seemed that the industrial depression would, like the closing of the frontier, be permanent, and that at best the old social mobility of the individual might be succeeded by the stability of a mature economy kept in balance by the government. Social security for all was to be the surrogate for the vanished equality of opportunity. The fear was mistaken; the renewal of industrial expansion since 1940 has also renewed social mobility, even in the absence of the frontier and of free immigration.

And yet the reorganization of the economy by the Progressives and New Dealers, which was part of the broad reaction against the general disorder (often miscalled the status quo) of the nineteenth century, has helped to impose a new social order. As suggested above, this twentieth-century revolution has in the long view been essentially a counterrevolution to reintegrate society somewhat as it was before 1815. True, the bulk of the population no longer consists of yeoman farmers, but the welfare state does secure a minimum subsistence as the family farm once did. (The Farm Security Administration for a time even tried to restore the yeoman farmer himself.) Likewise, since the depression the erstwhile proletariat, with a few still conspicuous exceptions, has climbed back to a comfortable standard of living, while the relative income of the erstwhile plutocracy has declined by about one-third.[30] In a sense, the broad middle class homogeneity of the eighteenth century has been restored. To complete the parallel, now that Roosevelts, Tafts, and Rockefellers not only accept the responsibility of their class to lead the common voter but are in turn accepted by him, it is evident that we once again have an established upper class with privileges and duties roughly equivalent to those of the eighteenth-century gentry.

There is more to our complex social order, of course, than classes, and it would take more confidence than present evidence warrants to assert that such institutions as the family and the local or regional community have regained the stability of their eighteenth-century counterparts. On the other hand, just as vested economic interests were subject to public regulation in the eighteenth century, so are they now.[31] It is no longer doubted, for instance, that capital and labor bear a responsibility, however tentatively defined, to each other and to society at large; indeed, the responsibility is enjoined by law. There is no need to rehearse the familiar list of special economic interests, minority groups, and other segments of the American population whose social rights and duties now are or can be supervised in the common interest by government.

To the extent that, partly as the result of the New Deal, our economy is made up of a balance between such groups as big business, organized labor, the farmers' associations, and government itself, these "countervailing powers" are likewise components

30. Simon Kuznets, *Shares of Upper Income Groups in Income and Savings* (New York, 1953), xxxvii.

31. That public regulation of economic affairs is no foreign "ism" but a return to an American precedent of great age and respectability is the discovery of the considerable body of recent research into such activity in the early nineteenth century. For a review of this literature, see Robert A. Lively, "The American System," *Business History Review,* XXIX (March 1955), 81-96.

of the mid-twentieth-century social order.[32] Recently a spate of sociology has lamented the enmeshing of the individual in a network of institutions, from the mammoth business corporation with its uniformly clad executives and its ambitionless workingmen—both groups tied to the job by pension plans and seniority rights—all the way to the suburban family enslaved to its peer group. But the institutions and even the new elite of our social order, though they shock traditional liberals not only by their imperfections but by their very existence, would seem to be only the latest manifestations of the reordering of American society. The liberal critics of institutional society can take heart from the fact, exemplified by their own criticism, that the individualistic tradition of the nineteenth century does endure at least as a counterweight to the main trend of the twentieth, certainly to no less a degree than eighteenth-century conservatism lingered on in the liberal nineteenth. The individualist crying out against conformity played a role in the 1950's like that of the status-conscious "reformers" of the 1830's or 1890's who resisted excessive individualism.

One can also speculate that the gradual decline since about 1920 of those makeshift communities, the fraternal lodges, is no less significant in our society than their rise was amid the social confusion of the nineteenth century. The psychic energy that Americans formerly expended on maintaining the jerry-built framework of such "institutions" as these has in our more assured institutional structure of recent years been freed, at least potentially, for the creation of more valuable kinds of "culture." The same end may likewise be served if the new social order can allay the kind of personal anxiety over one's social status which, as we have seen, preoccupied the individual members of such varied groups as middle class Progressives and agrarian Populists, Yankee nativists and peasant immigrants, yeomen and artisan Jacksonians and genteel humanitarian reformers, and presumably others whom

32. John Kenneth Galbraith, *American Capitalism: The Concept of Countervailing Power* (Boston, 1952), 115-193.

historians have not yet reinvestigated. The evidence is already becoming plain that status-striving is no latter-day degeneracy of Americans; rather, since such insecurity was a by-product of excessive mobility, it preoccupies the individual today not more but somewhat less than two or three generations ago. If so, the recent popular success of books deploring the unworthiness of status-striving indicates that Americans are throwing off this obsession and making it, as in other societies, including pre-industrial America, merely one concern among many.

No doubt, in so far as Americans have gained a certain freedom to turn from these purely social problems to the task of evolving a cultural tradition for their new society, they have tended to be "other-directed"—unduly subservient to a still inchoate public opinion—as indeed they already were coming to be when Tocqueville observed their lack of "independence of mind and freedom of discussion" shortly after the start of the disorderly nineteenth century.[33] How else could an individualistic people be expected to evolve an indigenous cultural tradition out of social confusion but by consulting, observing, and censuring each other? The result may turn out to be good or bad, but that the process has taken so long to approach a result is due to the ultraliberal nineteenth century, some of the cultural and intellectual effects of which still linger with us in the socially conservative twentieth.[34]

33. David Riesman, *The Lonely Crowd: A Study of the Changing American Character* (New Haven, 1950), 19-25; Alexis de Tocqueville, *Democracy in America,* tr. by Henry Reeve, 2 vols. (New York, 1838), I, 244.

34. The way in which the recent preoccupation of historians with intellectual history has tended to obscure this essential social difference between the nineteenth and twentieth centuries should be evident. To the historian of ideas and culture, the nineteenth century appears, and rightly so, as a period of "formalism" characterized by abstract, deductive thought and derivative cultural standards, while the twentieth has been a time of pragmatic rebellion in the name of relativism in ideas and cultural norms. But in social history the term "formalism" can hardly be applied to the disorder of the nineteenth century. In fact, the "formal" ideas themselves—

Today there are European traditionalists who lament the recent "Americanization" of the Old World, by which they mean the erosion of genteel manners, parental discipline, working class subservience, and aristocratic patronage of art and literature of a certain standard. In the sense that the old European social order has about vanished, they are right. The American example, however, has been less important a cause of this than the continuing industrialization of Europe itself. In the nineteenth century, America, with far less "feudal" tradition to restrain it, did succumb far more rapidly than Europe to the social mobility that accompanies industrialization—succumbed indeed almost at one blow, since the impact of modern industry here was multiplied by the coincidence of massive immigration and the westward movement.[35] But America in the present century has itself undergone a sort of Europeanization, though this did not proceed from Europe, as its opponents have suspected, any more than Americanization really went full-grown across the ocean to Europe. In either case the causes were essentially indigenous.

In effect, Western Europe has recently adopted a social pattern

---

the Protestant ethic, classical economics, even the Malthusian inspiration for Social Darwinism, with which apologists defended social disorder—were drawn largely from the previous, pre-industrial age and were already out of date as descriptions of contemporary reality. Likewise, when after 1880 certain intellectuals revolted against this formalism, their own ideas reflected the liberalism of a nineteenth-century society that was already about to pass away. This is in some degree an illustration of the usual lag with which social ideas follow behind social changes. On the other hand, since at the same time the foremost intellectual rebels, as preachers of what has been called "historicism" and "cultural organicism," were among the prophets of the new, more formally integrated social order, evidently the usual characterization of twentieth-century America as an age of pragmatic disintegration needs to be re-examined. See Morton G. White, *Social Thought in America: The Revolt against Formalism* (New York, 1949), 11-31, 94-103.

35. Louis Hartz, *The Liberal Tradition in America: An Interpretation of American Political Thought Since the Revolution* (New York, 1955), 3-32.

which, as early as the eighteenth century, already was distinctively American: orderly and adequately regulated, yet strongly infused with a robust egalitarianism. In the past, Europe has lacked the practical egalitarianism, and in the nineteenth century America temporarily lost its orderliness and regularity. Recently the Old and New Worlds have become more alike. Like Europe, America no longer has vast immigration or a frontier of free land, but both America and Europe are being continually transformed by the social mobility inherent in their industrial economies, a force that works, however, within the solid and coherent structure of a new institutional order. Whether an equally impressive Western popular culture will also arise on these social foundations is not yet so certain.

International Change

4

THE PRESSURES OF MILITARY NECESSITY

GENE M. LYONS

THE Cold War has created powerful pressures on American society, pressures which by their persistence and ubiquity could have a fundamental influence on the direction the American people move in the future. For the Cold War has strained the bonds of the democratic process, challenged the effectiveness of the American governmental system, and tested the mettle of American leadership and the American people.

The impact of the Cold War on American society can be measured in a number of ways: in terms of the size of the annual defense budget, the existence of a large standing military force, the dependence of important sectors of the national economy on military contracts, an increasing centralization of power in the executive branch of the federal government, and the psychological threat of obliteration through thermonuclear war. It can also be measured in terms of the energies it has released: advances in science and technology that have been carried ahead by defense requirements; and national programs in training, education, and anti-discrimination that have served as a catalyst for moving toward the American dream of equal opportunity for all.

Involved in the Cold War is a concept of the relationship of military force to foreign policy which is new to the American experience. This is not to suggest that the United States has never used force in seeking political objectives, or that Americans have been uncommonly pacifistic. The consolidation of the United States during the nineteenth century and subsequent American expansionism in the Pacific and the Caribbean were accompanied by a deliberate exploitation of military power. At the same time, the American Civil War was the greatest armed conflict between the Napoleonic Wars and World War I, and the first total war under modern technological conditions. Moreover, in both world wars the United States not only mobilized its full resources in support of the military efforts of the allied powers but used its considerable influence in turning allied war aims toward the military objective of unconditional surrender.

The requirements of military policy are thus not unknown in the American experience despite the tradition of anti-militarism and the relative freedom from international conflict that the United States enjoyed until the early part of the twentieth century. The Cold War is nonetheless different from earlier situations. The difference lies principally in America's new role of world leadership and in the incredibly destructive capacity of modern weapons.

The United States has come to a role of world leadership at a time of revolutionary change. The emergence of new nations from the disruption of former colonial empires, the opportunities for rapid technological development and resultant social dislocations, the development of world-wide systems of communication, and the ideological challenge of communism have combined to create an international environment of continual turmoil and tension. Within such a setting, the element of force has become a major instrument of change and military power a central factor in dealing with the problems of foreign policy. All important issues of diplomacy must be dealt with in an atmosphere highly influenced by considerations of military power.

The centrality of military policy is nevertheless complicated by the special nature of modern weapons. Nuclear weapons and long-range delivery systems offer the major powers the means of destroying their opponents in all-out war. While nations may survive a thermonuclear war to the extent that men will try to rebuild a society out of utter chaos, the destruction will be so great that it can truly be said that "total" victory is, for the first time in history, a possibility. For it would certainly be two or more generations before a nation devastated by thermonuclear war became viable once again. The use of modern weapons thus poses a moral issue of deep consequence. At the same time the issue is also one of great practical risk. Modern weapons are essentially offensive, and until a completely effective defensive system is developed, the condition in which the victor finds himself at the end of such a war may be only relatively better than the vanquished. The United States and the Soviet Union, in effect, hazard the perils of self-destruction in becoming engaged in a thermonuclear war.

The situation is also one of extreme paradox. Military power is an indispensable element of international involvement, yet the utility of military power is limited by the risks of its very use. The American response to this paradox has been a "mixed" doctrine combining the policy of deterrence and the concept of control over conflict situations. The policy of deterrence is directed against the threat of aggression and requires the maintenance of sufficient military power to threaten other major nations with unacceptable destruction if they undertake aggressive action. The concept of control involves the moderation of critical areas of tension or conflict before they reach a point where the major powers confront each other without a margin of safety and risk the danger of all-out war. The methods of achieving moderation may vary from bilateral negotiation between the two major nuclear powers to the establishment of international peace-keeping machinery under the United Nations.

One of the most important implications of the current situation, in terms of its impact on American society, is the limits which this policy places on American military power. Military power becomes a requirement but not an active instrument of policy. The usefulness of military might is measured by the extent to which it can be translated into political power. It is an umbrella under which diplomacy, economic activity, and propaganda can be employed to further American interests. Military power might have to be used, especially in response to aggression or equally serious provocation. But even when force is brought to bear, the measure of success is not the crude calculation of military victory but the more difficult dimension of political achievement.

The use of military power as a deterrent is not new in history. Deterrence was an essential function of the British navy in the era of *Pax Britannia,* and in the American experience it was a function of military outposts in protecting Western settlers from Indian attack, and of the fleet in maintaining American footholds in Central America and in the Philippines. But if the function is not new, the scope and requirements of deterrence today are broader and more complex than before, both because of the nature of modern weapons and because of the dynamics of contemporary world politics. The material requirements of developing, maintaining, and perfecting a deterrent capability, the intellectual requirements of planning and anticipating the situations in which the deterrent will have to be brought to bear, and the psychological requirements involved in the demonstrations of will and the acts of bargaining that are crucial to great power relationships

—these depend on the full resources and institutions of the nation. It is the level of intensity, the degree to which the policy of deterrence involves the country as a whole, and the consequences of failure which are unique in the current context of history.

The Limits of International Organization

The function of military power can be defined from two perspectives. From the viewpoint of the individual nation-state, military power is the ultimate means of protecting the nation's security and interests. From the perspective of the international system, force is the ultimate means of resolving conflicts between nations which cannot be settled through adjustment or compromise. There has been a continual search throughout history to find mechanisms which would compel nations to settle differences without using military force. Except for the Roman Empire at the height of its strength, no nation has achieved effective world hegemony which would permit it to impose a system of regulations for the resolution of international conflicts. Certainly, on some occasions, informal pressures, like those of the medieval church, operated as a modified form of international regulation. But in modern history the nation-state has been the supreme political unit to which men entrust their loyalties, their interests, and their safety. In most recent times the efforts to control international disputes have thus been exerted through the development of voluntary international organizations within which member nations agree on certain rules by which to govern their behavior in interstate relations. Indeed, the establishment of such an organization was a stated aim of the allies in World War II and led in 1945 to the creation of the United Nations.[1]

1. For a review of the wartime planning for the UN, see Harley Notter, *Postwar Foreign Policy Preparation, 1939-1945* (Washington, 1949).

The United States emerged from the war as the greatest military power in the world with sole possession of atomic weapons. Its goal was not world hegemony but the development of an international system of political, economic, and military cooperation, based on the support of the major powers and concentrated in the agencies and organs of the United Nations. The requirement of great power concurrence, guaranteed through the right of veto in the Security Council over important issues, was no more than recognition of the facts of international political life. But if the veto was the price to be paid to insure the inclusion of the United States and the Soviet Union in the UN, it was also an instrument for their protection. Through the veto any of the great powers could thwart a move to construct an international system which it considered to be disadvantageous to its interests, no matter what the wishes of other nations.

The military system anticipated in the UN Charter was made of several parts. Under the Charter, all members renounce aggression but reserve the right of self-defense. A state that exercises this right also is obliged to report its action to the Security Council which has exclusive authority in matters involving threats to the peace. In contrast to the League of Nations, in which *general* unanimity in the Council was necessary, the Security Council can act on a majority vote provided this includes the concurrence of all of its permanent members. At the same time, all members are obliged to support measures decided upon by the Council.

Actual experience has never really followed the Charter's model. In the Korean conflict in 1950, the Security Council acted in the absence of one of its permanent members, the Soviet Union, and in the Suez crisis of 1956, the UN proceeded to establish an Emergency Force under a resolution in the General Assembly after a similar proposal was vetoed in the Council by the powers that had precipitated the action, Britain and France. Only in the case of the Congo, in the terrible period of dissension and instability following the Belgian withdrawal in mid-1960, did the

UN establish a military effort in accordance with the authorization of the Security Council.[2]

But in the Congo special circumstances prevailed. The crisis did not involve the direct interests of the two major powers, although as a matter of principle both France and Britain, also permanent members of the Council, abstained on the basic resolution authorizing military intervention. What held the main Congo resolutions together were their anti-colonialist aims, the new importance of Afro-Asian states in UN affairs, and the priority that the anti-colonialist objective held over any East-West disagreement. Yet even if the Congo affair was an example of Security Council action, it did not conform to an important working assumption of the Charter: that the greatest threat to peace came from inter-state conflict. Despite its international implications, the Congo was essentially an internal affair, involving the relation of provincial governments to central authority and the problem of legal succession.

The Congo case illustrates how, in the evolution of the UN, the organization has become an important means of seeking peaceful change in the transition of states from colonial to independent status. Indeed, as later Congolese history demonstrates, UN action can fill a power void that could otherwise attract the major powers and provide a catalyst for conflict. At the same time, the major powers have not necessarily lost or forfeited their political interests in these areas, but have rather had to pursue their objectives through the UN. In doing so, their freedom of action is often reduced and they are subject to inhibitions forced by organizational procedures and the pressures of world opinion. They can, however, use this situation to their advantage by using the

2. For general works on UN peace-keeping forces, see Lincoln Bloomfield, *International Military Forces* (Boston, 1964), and Inis Claude, "The UN and the Use of Force," *International Conciliation,* No. 532 (March 1961). For specific case studies, see Leland M. Goodrich, *Korea* (New York, 1956); Gabriella Rosner, *The United Nations Emergency Force* (New York, 1963); Arthur Lee Burns and Nina Heathcote, *Peace-Keeping by U.N. Forces* (New York, 1963).

setting of the UN to seek a general consensus for their position.[3]

While the charter had originally called for a kind of world trusteeship by the great powers, it also established a plan for developing the military means through which the Security Council could enforce its decisions. The Council was to have a military staff to plan and direct operations and, through a series of treaties, was to be provided with military contingents that would be kept in readiness by member nations. Here again, experience has differed from the Charter. The military staff, made up of officers from the great powers, soon split sharply over plans for the provision and deployment of forces. The committee continued to meet for years, but its sessions became increasingly ritualistic and sterile.[4] Troops to support UN action were, in fact, raised in an ad hoc fashion. Under the special conditions in Korea, the United States became the agent for the UN and provided not only the command structure but by far the largest number of non-Korean forces. Other conditions prevailed in the Suez and Congo cases, in which troops were provided wholly by non-aligned nations and were employed by the Secretary General, acting under the appropriate resolution of the Assembly or Council. This method of raising and deploying UN forces was deliberately designed to prevent the entry of military groups from the great powers into the zone of instability.

The Cold War has thus had a major effect on these two parts of the military system provided for by the Charter: the authority of the Security Council, and the provision of military means to enforce decisions of the Council. It also has had an effect on the indispensable corollary of the development of a UN system of

3. For a broad view of the effect of the UN on American foreign policy, see Richard N. Gardner, *In Pursuit of World Order* (New York, 1964); also Lincoln Bloomfield, *The United Nations and U.S. Foreign Policy* (Boston, 1960).

4. See Leland M. Goodrich and Anne P. Simons, *The United Nations and the Maintenance of International Peace and Security,* (Washington, 1955).

enforcement: the dismemberment of national military establishments through progressive regulation and limitation on armaments. In effect, the Charter provided a blueprint for the development of an international system of conflict resolution in which nations would be deprived of military means and would have to learn to use nonviolent instruments of statecraft to pursue their objectives. The goals of arms control and disarmament have, however, been no less elusive than the achievement of an effective system of international enforcement.[5]

The crux of the dispute between the United States and the Soviet Union in the field of arms control and disarmament has long been the problem of inspection. In the early Baruch Plan of 1946, the United States proposed the international control of atomic energy but stipulated that it would not give up its atomic weapons until an effective system of international inspection had been achieved. As reasonable as this may have seemed from an American viewpoint, the proposals were rejected by the Soviet Union. The Russians refused to accept what would have been a permanent position of nuclear inferiority by permitting the Americans to maintain their atomic weapons and the means of their production. The Soviet Union thus responded by advocating the immediate elimination of all atomic weapons which, at the time, were exclusively American.

In the years between 1946 and the signing of the limited nuclear test-ban treaty in the summer of 1963, negotiations on arms control and disarmament followed an uneven pattern. The early talks practically dissolved in the years of tension that preceded and followed the Korean conflict. By the mid-1950's, however, the Soviet atomic breakthrough and possession by both major powers of the more destructive hydrogen bomb, as well as increasingly effective long-range delivery systems, led to initiatives in the area of surprise attack.

5. See Bernhard G. Bechhoefer, *Postwar Negotiations for Arms Control* (Washington, 1961).

As any reduction of armaments became impossible because of the inspection issue, the United States proposed that a control system be developed which would inhibit either side from launching a surprise first strike. Such an agreement might minimize the threat, if not the means, of aggression. But here, too, the complex problem of international inspection and exchange of security information could not be solved. The internal secrecy essential to the Soviet system would be breached by necessary exposure. Moreover, the threat of first strike was an important factor in the deterrent relationship between the two powers. For even though the United States had continually pledged not to use military force except in self-defense or in response to an attack upon one of its allies, neither it nor the Soviet Union gave up the right to use nuclear weapons first, or to escalate a limited conflict to the strategic level by undertaking a direct attack on the homeland of the other. Indeed, it was this ability to threaten escalation, in terms of both weapons and geographic area, that would be a main incentive for halting a conflict at a limited level of violence.

By the late 1950's the negotiations on the elimination of nuclear testing seemed to have the greatest chance for success.[6] In the summer of 1958 a technical conference of scientists concluded a tentative agreement on a test ban that required only minimal inspection sites for purposes of detection. Within months, however, the technical agreement was brought into question when a new series of American tests demonstrated the difficulties of detecting underground blasts. Not only was it impossible to distinguish between natural and man-made explosions, but it was also possible to "muffle" an explosion so that the seismic reading of its intensity would be considerably diminished.

6. For a review of political and technical developments of nuclear test-ban negotiations from 1958 to 1960, see William J. Gehron, "Geneva Conference on the Discontinuance of Nuclear Weapon Tests," Department of State, *Bulletin*, XLIII, No. 1109 (September 26, 1960), 482 ff.

The meaning of these two findings was that a relatively large underground nuclear test might be monitored only as a minor earthquake. In the face of these disclosures and what, under the continual pressures of the Cold War, had become a mutual distrust of intentions, the United States announced that it could not proceed with the 1958 technical agreement unless provision was made for additional on-site inspections in case of underground blasts. This the Soviets refused, though the test-ban talks continued, even through the period of new tests by both powers in 1961. These new tests, first by the Soviets and then by the Americans, broke the informal moratorium that had existed since 1959. A most significant feature of the series was the detonation of a gigantic sixty-megaton bomb by the Soviets, a blast that, it was estimated, could be increased to one hundred megatons with no further testing.

Despite these setbacks there were good reasons why the nuclear test-ban negotiations were continued. Tests in the atmosphere had measurably increased the amount of radioactive fallout which, while generally remaining within tolerable limits, could reach deadly proportions. While the effect of this radioactivity was highly disputed by scientists, they all agreed that additional pollution of the air was dangerous. The consequences of further testing thus presented a peril to the whole world and, apart from any human misgivings on the part of Soviet and American leaders themselves, there were political and popular pressures for a cessation of nuclear explosions. Continuance of the talks became an important response to this growing sentiment, and the performance of the participants was judged, especially by neutralist nations, as a barometer of their interest in achieving a peaceful world. The test-ban negotiations were thus part of the Cold War maneuvering for political support.[7]

7. For a critique of disarmament negotiations from the viewpoint of their political value, see John W. Spanier and Joseph L. Nogee, *The Politics of Disarmament* (New York, 1962).

But a more obvious motive, in the long run, was to limit the number of nations that might develop the wherewithal to produce atomic weapons.[8] The proliferation of nuclear weapons was actually begun in the early 1960's when France under General Charles de Gaulle exploded an atomic device in the Sahara and joined the "nuclear club." The possibility of an increasing membership posed problems for both the Soviet Union and the United States. In general terms, the two powers jeopardized loss of control over the use of violence in international conflicts. Even a crude and relatively small atomic stockpile in the hands of a minor power under irresponsible leadership carried sufficient destruction potential to be wielded as a formidable blackmail instrument against the major powers, let alone other states. There was also the fear of a "catalytic"war, a war started by a nuclear explosion from an unknown source to which both super-powers felt obliged to respond for fear it was the opening blow in an offensive launched by its opponent.

Most ominous of all was the vision of nuclear weapons in the hands of the Communist Chinese. The schism between the Chinese and Russians, which has long historical roots, had become increasingly severe since Khrushchev's denunciation of Stalin's rule at the Twentieth Party Congress in 1956. Out of the struggle, the Soviet leadership emerged with an admitted awareness of the perils of war in the nuclear age and a willingness to adjust communist strategy to emphasize nonviolent means of political and economic competition. The Chinese, on the other hand, sounded more aggressive and were particularly critical that the Russians did not take advantage of the superiority the communist side had gained by the Soviets being the first to launch a vehicle into space.

8. See Richard N. Rosecrance, ed., *The Dispersion of Nuclear Weapons* (New York, 1964); also Leonard Beaton and John Maddox, *The Spread of Nuclear Weapons* (New York, 1962).

For the Chinese, the Soviet space achievements in 1957 marked a decided shift in the world balance which should have been followed up by a deliberate exploitation of revolutionary forces throughout the emerging nations of the southern hemispheres.[9]

By the early 1960's the estimates on how soon the Chinese would have atomic weapons ranged from three to ten years. Much depended on the assistance the Chinese received from the Russians who, it became more and more clear, were reluctant to share nuclear leadership with their allies. Indeed, the Russians' denial of nuclear aid seems to have become one of the most serious sources of conflict between the two communist leaderships. The seriousness of the split was emphasized during the summer of 1963 when, in the midst of a heated exchange of notes on ideological differences with the Chinese, Khrushchev suddenly announced his readiness to sign a treaty forbidding nuclear tests in outer space, the atmosphere, and underwater—the three environments in which the detection of explosions was possible through national monitoring systems and did not require international inspection. Such a pact had been proposed by the Americans and British a year earlier but rejected by the Soviets. It clearly did not solve the inspection issue which was avoided by excluding underground testing from the agreement. But no less significantly, the treaty indicated the readiness of the Russians to defy the Chinese, who denounced the pact. Nor did the Chinese success in exploding an atomic device a year later, in 1964, compensate for their having been deprived of support in building a nuclear capability. Indeed, their antagonism may well have been intensified by having achieved success on their own.

The limited nuclear test ban was a minimal step in arms control

9. There is a large literature on the Sino-Soviet dispute. See Donald S. Zagoria, *The Sino-Soviet Conflict* (Princeton, 1962); Richard Lowenthal, *World Communism* (New York, 1964); and Zbigniew K. Brzezinski, *The Soviet Bloc,* revised edition (New York, 1961).

and disarmament. It did not halt the Chinese advance, but neither did the Chinese bomb upset its significance. It was a response to changes in military technology and world political alignments, even if not to the aspirations set down in the UN Charter. For the real fact is that there is no international system for settling conflicts and enforcing decisions, though the UN has become increasingly useful in adapting its structure to the needs of conciliation and pacification. The test-ban treaty of 1963 did not mark the beginning of the abandonment of force as a requirement of policy by the nations of the world. Military power remains essential to world involvement, and the United States, like all major states, must develop plans and programs through which force is related to the political objectives of foreign policy. Thus far these plans and programs have been shaped around the strategic doctrine of deterrence. But as a guide for the development of American military power, deterrence has become an increasingly complex concept in response to the changing forces of world politics.

The Development of Military Policy

Immediately after World War II, American military policy was torn between the conflicting and often confusing motives of American society and its political leadership. The war had been fought with the experience of the First World War very much in mind. Citizens were asked to become soldiers with the full expectation that, when the fighting was over, there would again be a return to "normalcy." Exactly what normalcy meant was not clear, but it certainly included rapid demobilization as soon as the emergency ended. This is what had happened before and this is what would happen again. But now, after the "unconditional surrender" of the enemy, the United States did not intend again to isolate itself from the world; this was another lesson of the inter-war period. Indeed, for President Roosevelt and his political aides the construction of a new world system was as important a commitment as the destruction of the fascist powers.[10]

The first objective was, however, dependent upon the second. Thus the military requirement of defeating the enemy took absolute precedence over all else, though the plans for developing a United Nations Organization went forward vigorously. Moreover, every effort was made to develop the kind of domestic support that would carry the United States into the UN and avoid a setback like the defeat President Wilson had suffered in 1919, when the Senate had rejected the Covenant of the League of Nations. Congressional leaders were brought into direct and continuous relationship with State Department staff working on the development of the UN. In order to develop broad public support, the President continually emphasized that the war itself was being fought by *the United Nations* and, by doing so, encouraged the image of a world organization that would prevent further wars when it was formally established after victory was gained. Indeed, it was undoubtedly this promise which, while understandably important as a prod to the American public, led to so much popular disillusionment about the UN when the organization struggled, often in vain, under the trials of early development and the withering influence of the Cold War.

Besides the problems of winning the war and establishing the UN, there emerged another issue: increasing difficulties in relations with the Soviet Union. At the wartime summit conferences, the President and Prime Minister Churchill found themselves confronted with an increasingly recalcitrant and hard-headed Stalin, while reports from Ambassador Harriman in Moscow warned that communist ambitions to propagate its ideology had not changed

10. Harley Notter, *op. cit.;* also Robert E. Sherwood, *Roosevelt and Hopkins* (New York, 1948), esp. Part V.

despite the wartime alliance with the democracies.[11] There is no real evidence that President Roosevelt was not fully aware of the problems to be faced in dealing with the Russians, or that he was hoodwinked into agreeing to Soviet demands. The truth is undoubtedly less conspiratorial and more straightforward. Americans, and the President no less so, were intent on the objective of unconditional surrender. The President wanted to win the war and the Russians were essential to his aim. He wanted to build a world organization and it was important that the Soviet Union be a member. Once the war was won, the UN would provide a mechanism and system within which to deal with Russian ambitions, and the President, perhaps naively, felt that he could handle the Soviets in this context. But for the time being first things came first: the war, the UN, and then the problem of communist expansionism.

In 1945 and 1946 the formulation of postwar military policy was thus carried on amidst these conflicting motives: to proceed with the demobilization of the wartime forces; to prepare to meet commitments under the UN Charter and in settlement of the war's victory; and to provide contingencies to deal with potential Soviet expansionism. Even under the pressures for demobilization, the United States was obliged to maintain the largest peacetime military force in its history in order to meet its commitments. The question was: What system should be adopted to develop and maintain such a force?

The broad policy alternatives fell into two major categories. The first was a traditional army plan that had always been defeated by a combination of anti-militarism and indifference: to develop a system of peacetime Universal Military Training (UMT) that would provide the United States with a potentially

11. Robert Sherwood, *op. cit.* For an important note on Harriman's views, see Harry S. Truman, *Memoirs,* Vol. I, *Year of Decision* (New York, 1955), 70-72.

ready force without the necessity of a large standing army.[12] The second solution was more radical and relied on technological advances made during the war: to harness American air power to the atomic bomb and provide the United States with a formidable weapon of destruction with which to maintain American influence in the world.[13]

UMT was in the American tradition. It was based on the concept of a citizen army which reflected the historical distrust of military centralization and professionalism and appealed to the crusading kind of patriotism that rouses a democratic people to arms. Nonetheless, politically, UMT was unpopular. It meant foisting direct responsibilities and burdens upon hundreds of thousands of citizens soon after the end of war and the promise of relief from military obligation. It also aroused the familiar unpopularity with military life which veterans carried out of the armed services—unpopularity stemming from the waste, the chafing command system, and the meaninglessness of war aims and orders for the solitary soldier isolated from the great sweep of war. It is a great paradox that for all the adoration of military heroes and the splendid response to patriotic histrionics, military life itself remains such an unpopular existence for most Americans.

There was, on the other hand, much in favor of basing American military posture on air power and the atomic bomb. In the midst of the devastation under which both ally and enemy lay at the end of the war, these weapons were symbols of America's position as the strongest power in the world, indeed of American omnipotence. They were also the weapons that, in the popular mind at any rate, had brought victory; for the widely screened images of triumph were German cities blasted by strategic bomb-

12. *Universal Military Training,* Hearings, Committee on Military Affairs, House of Representatives, 79th Cong., 1st Sess.

13. For an excellent general review of the development of the doctrine of air power, see Bernard Brodie, *Strategy in the Missile Age* (Princeton, 1959).

ing and Hiroshima and Nagasaki smoldering under the first atomic bombs exploded in anger. Air-atomic power, moreover, was the instrument of "total victory" and "unconditional surrender," which were conceived to be the normal objectives of war. The cost of air-atomic power, finally, was less visible than UMT. The basic requirements were technological, and the manpower needs could be met without the imposition of an unpopular conscription. The air force had emerged from the war as the most glamorous of the services, with all the thrill and promise of advancement necessary to attract young Americans. The most tangible needs were for research and development, but here there were valuable by-products as funds thus allocated would be plowed back into the economy and would assist in converting from a wartime to a peacetime economy.

American military strategy was, in fact, based on a primary reliance on air-atomic power from the end of the war until the early 1960's. Throughout these years the overriding assumption was always the need to be prepared for a world-war kind of conflict with the Soviet Union. Less compelling demands were met with ad hoc measures but no basic change in policy. The manpower requirements of keeping occupation forces in Europe and Japan in the late forties, and later of manning alliance systems in these same areas, were filled through a continuation of the wartime selective service system, renewed periodically by Congress. UMT was defeated first in 1947 and again after the Korean conflict when the unexpected need for ground forces in that war gave new impetus to exploring the possibilities for training the citizenry in arms.

The defeat of UMT after Korea was closely related to the "new look" inaugurated by the Eisenhower administration in 1953. The "new look" was not really new but rather an intensification of the priority of air-atomic power. The mottos of the new look came to be the threat of "massive retaliation" made by Secretary of State John Foster Dulles, and the promise of "more bang for a buck" made by Secretary of Defense Charles Wilson. If the new look was a shift, it was not from what had been American military policy, but from the doubts that had come to develop about that policy since about 1949.[14]

The inter-service rivalries that characterized defense organization in the late forties were more than just incidents of bureaucratic infighting; they were also disputes over strategic policy. Out of the National Security Act of 1947, the air force had emerged as an independent service, freed from subordination under the army and in possession of the main instruments of the air-atomic strategy. As the air force sought to maintain this position of preeminence, and the army turned to pick up the pieces after the first loss on UMT, the navy was likely to be caught in the middle, left with no important strategic mission. This downgrading of the navy seemed to be confirmed when, in 1949, in the heat of the annual budget-cutting campaign that had gone on each year since the end of the war, Secretary of Defense Louis Johnson suddenly stopped allocations for the construction of the navy's prize, a supercarrier that could haul aircraft capable of carrying atomic weapons.

The navy revolted. Navy Secretary John Sullivan, who had not been previously informed of Johnson's decision, resigned. The navy-officer hierarchy organized a counter-attack group, under then Captain Arleigh Burke, which focused its attention on the air force and looked for redress from allies in Congress. The "revolt of the admirals" was on. Under the guise of what began as a congressional investigation of air force procurement methods, the navy was given the opportunity to vent its wrath, and the outburst took the form of public criticism of prevailing military doctrine. Navy spokesmen warned of the dangers of what was essentially a single-weapon strategy and were particularly critical of the

14. See the case study on the "new look" by Glenn Snyder, in Schilling, Hammond, and Snyder, *Strategies, Budgets and Defense Politics* (New York, 1962).

adequacy of the new air force bomber, the B-36. They questioned the usefulness of the air-atomic system to deal with such ambiguous threats to the peace as Soviet pressures in Turkey and Greece and instability in the Middle East. They even raised the issue of morality and painted ugly pictures of the results of strategic bombing with atomic weapons.[15]

The immediate effects of the navy's outburst and the congressional hearings that followed were substantially nil. Neither the President nor Congress was willing to undertake a more expensive defense program. It was not a matter of substituting an aircraft carrier for an air force wing, but of *adding to* air force requirements to meet the demands of the navy, and probably the army as well. Such a move was contrary to the prevailing spirit and seemed utterly needless to those who were psychologically convinced that, if it came, the next war would be fought almost wholly from the air and would be directed against the Soviet Union itself. This spirit persisted not only against the navy attack, but also against the increasing concern in the planning echelons of the State Department that American military capability was neither large enough nor varied enough to support the full range of the nation's commitments. These doubts, expressed mainly by George Kennan, then planning chief for State, led in early 1950 to a National Security Council study, NSC 68, which specifically called for larger conventional forces to fight limited wars.[16] NSC 68 had hardly appeared when the Korean conflict broke out and the United States found itself in the middle of a limited war with inadequate and poorly trained troops.

Criticism of the air-atomic strategy had also been involved in the controversy over the hydrogen bomb that began in late 1949 when the Soviets exploded their first atomic device. Work on the

15. *Unification and Strategy,* Hearings, Committee on Armed Services, House of Representatives, 81st Cong., 1st Sess.

16. For the story of NSC 68, see the essay by Paul Y. Hammond, in Schilling, Hammond, and Snyder, *op. cit.*

more powerful hydrogen bomb had been virtually halted in 1945 after the success of the A-bomb and the early decision to seek international control of atomic energy. With the collapse of disarmament talks and the announcement of the Soviet explosion, the drive to proceed with the H-bomb was again initiated. In a debate that was largely limited to the scientific community and the highest levels of government, two factions emerged. One, led by Edward Teller, urged an all-out effort on the H-bomb to insure American superiority in the arms race. The second, led by Robert Oppenheimer, cautioned against an intensification of big-weapon competition and proposed increased experimentation to develop small, low-yield atomic weapons which could be employed with discrimination and would provide multiple-weapons systems to meet a variety of conflict situations. Late in 1949 President Truman ordered work on the H-bomb to proceed. But the proposals to develop a diversified atomic arsenal were not rejected. Under Project Vista in 1951 and 1952, for example, a group of scientists at the California Institute of Technology submitted a study of the possibilities for the development and use of low-yield atomic devices; and indeed such new weapons systems actually became operational by the late 1950's.[17]

The Eisenhower administration that took office in 1953 did not wholly reject these doubts about the emphasis on air-atomic power. The administration was, however, pledged to two overriding objectives: to bring the national budget into balance in the face of soaring defense expenditures that followed the outbreak of the Korean conflict; and to get the United States out of the Korean War and avoid getting involved in similar conflicts in which no decisive solution could be pursued. These two objectives

17. The H-bomb debate can be followed in the transcript of the Oppenheimer hearings, *In the Matter of J. Robert Oppenheimer,* Atomic Energy Commission (1954); see also Warner R. Schilling, "The H-Bomb Decision: How to Decide Without Actually Choosing," *Political Science Quarterly,* LXXVI (March 1961), 24-46.

were, of course, related. Once the immediate aim of ending the Korean War was achieved in 1953, it became necessary to avoid future "Koreas" while developing a military establishment that was kept within conservative budget limits. The way to do this, according to Secretary Dulles, was to project the strategy of air-atomic power to its full conclusion, and to lay to rest any doubts about the American will to respond to challenge. The Soviets were thus warned that the United States would respond to threats to its interests and to the peace of the world by exerting military pressures at times and places of its own choosing. No longer would the United States react to Soviet initiative or be forced to accept the battleground chosen by the communists. The ability to take the initiative away from the Soviets, and thereby to strengthen the policy of deterrence, would flow from the so-called doctrine of "massive retaliation." [18]

The Dulles doctrine was full of ambiguities. Under what conditions would massive retaliation be threatened? Could local provocation in Berlin or on the off-shore Chinese islands lead to a thermonuclear attack on Moscow with few or no intermediate steps? Even more questionable, was a thermonuclear attack a rational response to communist guerrilla activity in Southeast Asia? There is no doubt that a strategy of deterrence requires a degree of ambiguity—an element of surprise, of the unknown—to be effective. But Secretary Dulles operated under the weakness of having only one means—air-atomic power—to respond to a variety of situations. Thus, no matter how ambiguously it might be stated, the United States could support a threat only through the use of atomic power. It could well be asked whether, in an open society in which rationality is encouraged and there is a demand for political accountability, massive retaliation would, in fact, be a response to any but the most direct and provocative

18. Secretary Dulles first articulated the doctrine of "massive retaliation" in a speech on January 12, 1954; see *New York Times*, January 13, 1954.

of communist actions. In this context, Dulles' doctrine lacked credibility.[19]

Massive retaliation was, however, only one element in the Dulles strategy. A second, and conceivably as important an element, was the insistence that threats which merited less than a nuclear response would have to be met by local forces, largely manned by nations in the area of danger. This was the implication behind General Eisenhower's pre-election evaluation of the Korean War when he said: "If there must be a war, let it be Asians against Asians, with our support on the side of freedom." It was also the basis for the drive to develop a series of defense treaties, bilateral and regional, around the world and to use American economic aid as a means of supporting local military forces needed to combat communist pressures.[20]

The Dulles strategy was thus based on a division of labor. The United States would provide the ultimate threat to communist aggression through its air-atomic power, while other nations, tied to the United States through defense treaties and military and economic assistance programs, would provide the conventional forces needed to meet local threats and pressures. The division of labor proved, however, to be unworkable. For one thing, there was no viable military capability in most of the "grey areas" in Southeast Asia and the Middle East, and no expectation that such a capability could be built. Few of the developing nations, moreover, preferred to accept this alternative to communist absorption. Except for those states under severe pressure—South Korea, the Nationalist Chinese on Formosa, and South Vietnam—they sought to play a more independent role. Indeed, some—and the most important like India and Egypt—sought a position of neutralism

19. For an early critique of the Dulles doctrine, see William W. Kaufman, ed., *Military Policy and National Security* (Princeton, 1956), 12 ff.

20. For a study for the application of this strategy to the Korean case, see Gene M. Lyons, *Military Policy and Economic Aid* (Columbus, 1961).

which would enable them to deal with the East-West conflict in terms of their own independent development rather than the strategic requirements of the great powers.

But the ultimate blow to the doctrine of massive retaliation came with the realization, in late 1957, that the Soviet Union possessed an intercontinental missile capability that made the United States itself vulnerable to direct attack. The American military advantage, critical to the Dulles doctrine, had been based on the world-wide network of the Strategic Air Command that could, from a number of positions, strike at the heart of the Soviet Union. Until the late 1950's there was no such threat to the United States itself. The margin of maneuverability in this protected position was destroyed with the launching of the first Soviet sputnik in the fall of 1957. The superiority of the United States in the arms race now began to give way to a strategic balance between the two super-powers, as the Soviets moved to turn their potential into operational power.

The American response to the new strategic balance took several directions in the late 1950's and early 1960's. The first move was to fill in the gaps in American military strength in order to provide a broader range of capabilities, particularly for limited and internal wars. Not only were the force levels of the army increased until they reached just under one million by 1963, but military transportation facilities were expanded to provide means for airlifting large contingents of troops into danger zones. These two goals of increased power and mobility were dramatically demonstrated in the fall of 1963 when, in a trial run, troops in the strategic reserve based in the United States were flown to Europe and deployed into fighting positions during a steady three-day period of non-stop flights.[21] Under wartime conditions, circumstances of confusion, tension, and enemy action would certainly make such a transfer of forces more difficult. Nonetheless, the exercise was an impressive demonstration of the new ability of

21. *New York Times,* October 23, 1963.

the United States to bolster the limited-war capacity of the NATO alliance in case of a Soviet threat to Europe, and to provide a viable alternative to the use of nuclear weapons.

In 1961 the Kennedy administration also took steps to develop special forces trained for guerrilla-type operations. These forces were directed against ambiguous threats to stability that arise from insurgent efforts to unseat governments supported by the United States. In the 1960's the case of South Vietnam provided an almost classic area of application for counter-insurgency operations. Threatened by rebels who were aided by the communist regime in North Vietnam, the Saigon government was a slender reed—but a reed nonetheless—on which much of the general security of Southeast Asia rested. The Eisenhower dictum of "Asians against Asians, with our support on the side of freedom" would have been disastrously ineffective in meeting the challenge. The Saigon government (in any of its forms) hardly represented "freedom"—only the best alternative in a difficult and dangerous situation. But beyond this acceptance of reality, the South Vietnamese, for good and logical reasons, lacked not only the means but the will to fight unless they were sustained from outside. American assistance was thus extended beyond equipment and training to actual participation in combat operations in advisory and logistic support of South Vietnamese forces.

The development of limited-war and counter-insurgency forces broadened the range of American options and thus added credibility to the doctrine of deterrence in a way that had not been possible in Dulles' day. The major deterrent nevertheless remained the ultimate threat of strategic nuclear power, and it was this power that was now directly vulnerable to attack as a result of the Soviet ICBM capability. A first strike by the Soviets might so cripple U.S. strategic forces that effective retaliation would be prohibited. A new requirement thus had to be met—to protect the American retaliatory capability, not only the vehicles and warheads but the whole system of command and control from the

President down to aircraft and missile commanders. Again, this protection was the result of intensified efforts in the late 1950's and early 1960's.

These efforts included new research and development in weapons systems, new methods of sheltering, and new tactical concepts. Advances in rocket fuels provided increased power that was also safer and quicker to ignite than earlier fuels, and thus more effective for missiles that had to be launched from concrete silos in which they were protected from all but a direct hit. Concrete "hardening" also provided protection for air installations and most importantly for the network of complex communications systems through which command and control was achieved. But beyond "hardening," the retaliatory force was protected through increased mobility—on the theory that a moving target is harder to find and hit than a stationary one. Strategic Air Command bombers were not only kept on a round-the-clock alert, but by 1962-63 a certain number were continually air-borne, ready to move toward targets should the bombers on the ground be destroyed. Finally, the navy's nuclear-powered submarine was pushed into production and, once operational, provided a weapon that could stay in motion at sea for almost a year without coming into port; which could approach enemy shores with minimum possibility of detection; and which carried sixteen Polaris missiles capable of sending nuclear warheads 2,500 miles with good accuracy.

The diversification of American military capability and the protection of retaliatory forces were, in effect, unilateral responses by the United States to the more tenuous balance of power that followed the Soviet ICBM capability. There was, however, another response which was essentially bilateral and which involved joint efforts by the Americans and the Soviets to keep the balance as stable as possible. There was, on the American side, for example, growing speculation that if the retaliatory capacity of both sides was effectively protected, the incentive for first strike would be greatly reduced since the probability of knocking out a major part of the enemy's power would be extremely low. Mutual invulnerability thus provided the kind of protection against surprise attack which it would be impossible to negotiate into a treaty. At the same time, the mutual concern for stability in the light of the consequences of miscalculation and the uncertainties of revolutionary forces in the world was an incentive for both powers to explore the feasibility of other control mechanisms. Not only was the nuclear test-ban treaty a consequence of these explorations, but perhaps more significant (though less spectacular) was the installation of a "hot line" between Washington and Moscow to permit instantaneous and continual communication in case of emergency. Such communication was essential not only to the control of conflict but to the effectiveness of deterrence. It was important to avoid precipitous action through a miscalculation of intentions; but it was also important to have a means of telling the other side when the chips were down.

Limited war, counter-insurgency, invulnerable strategic forces, arms control measures—all of these are components in a general strategy that is considerably different from the single-factor air-atomic strategy that had dominated American military doctrine since 1945.[22] It is no longer assumed that the next war will be a World War II plus nuclear weapons and missiles. Indeed, a basic objective is to avoid this kind of conflict, not only by deterring aggression through threat of unacceptable retaliation but by agreement with the Soviet Union on controlling unstable conditions that could lead to general war. At the same time, there is a preparedness—and presumably a willingness—to fight wars at lower levels of violence if American political interests can be protected in no other way.

The requirements of this more complex military policy generate a stream of conflicting pressures on American society. The re-

22. For a general review of the development of this strategy after 1961, see William Kaufman, *The McNamara Strategy* (New York, 1964).

quirements of deterrence involve an annual budget of some $50 billion a year; armed forces stationed throughout the world; a vast network of research, development, and training facilities; a determination to use military power if necessary, and a national will to support such a decision. At the same time, the forces developed by these requirements must be controlled in order to insure rationality and to avert catastrophe. Any decision to use military power must be calculated against the political objectives to be gained or lost. Yet the size of the military establishment and the national frustration and impatience with limited achievements in reaching political goals create pressures for using military power in a less calculating way. At the same time, the dilemma of military power is related to the dual vision with which we must view the Soviet Union. We are forced to look at the Soviet Union as an enemy in order to justify the maintenance of such an enormous military establishment; but we must see the Soviets as a partner in terms of the political necessity of cooperating in order to avoid a war in which the means of destruction could virtually eliminate any chance of gaining meaningful political objectives.

The requirements of military policy and the limits of military power thus tug at American society in two often opposing directions. This is an entirely new experience for the United States, whose earlier sorties into the complexities of military policy were on an "all-or-nothing" basis. The major objective of our huge military resources is not necessarily to "win" any victories. It is to deter potential international conflict, to pursue political goals through more lasting though less decisive means than military force, and to gain the time to develop an international system, through deliberate arrangements and through political evolution, in which the present risks and dangers of war can be averted.

The Making of Military Policy

The requirements of a national security policy based on a combination of deterrence and arms control are four: (1) the development and maintenance of an effective deterrent capability; (2) decision-making procedures that are at once responsive to the complexities of contemporary world politics and to the demands of the democratic process; (3) open communications with the Soviet Union in order to avoid accidents and miscalculation of intentions; and (4) a strength of will on the part of American leaders and the people to act decisively when necessary and to resist acting too quickly when it is risky to do so.

These requirements have had important effects upon the organization of the American government. They have necessitated a centralization and amalgamation of authority in the Executive Branch of the federal government and particularly strengthened the power of the Executive Office of the President. The President, as commander-in-chief of the armed forces and chief negotiator and representative in foreign affairs, is in effect the ultimate source of authority in national security affairs. It is, for example, the President alone who can issue orders for the use of nuclear weapons. This power gives the President, together with his staff and immediate advisers, tremendous leverage in the political process through which policy and strategy are developed.[23]

In comparison, the power of Congress has steadily declined. The power of Congress to declare war, for example, has for all intents and purposes been abrogated by the changing nature of warfare. In the Korean conflict, American troops went into battle as a police action in response to a recommendation of the UN Security Council. There was no congressional declaration of war. In the Berlin Blockade of 1948-49, and in subsequent crises related to the question of access to Berlin, it has been the President,

23. See Richard E. Neustadt, *Presidential Power* (New York, 1960).

as commander-in-chief, who has made the basic decisions, decisions that had to be supported by a willingness to go to war in order to be effective.

In the Far Eastern incident of 1955, moreover, the Congress, by joint resolution, actually gave President Eisenhower prior approval to use armed force to resist efforts by the Chinese Communists to take the off-shore islands of Quemoy and Matsu; the only condition was that he first determine that such an invasion would jeopardize the security of Formosa.[24] In point of fact, the joint resolution did not give the President authority he did not already possess, both through his position as head of the armed forces and under the bilateral defense treaty with the Nationalist Chinese. But in responding to President Eisenhower's request for unequivocal support for his executive actions in the Formosan Straits—a request no doubt prompted by a desire to avoid a repetition of the method of entrance into the Korean War, in which Congress did not participate at all—Congress acknowledged the primary and dominating role of the President in issues of war and peace.

This is not to suggest that Congress plays no role whatsoever in matters of defense. No President can ignore Congress. Not only does Congress exercise powers of oversight and appropriations, but congressional support gives a sense of popular concurrence to presidential action. Congressional support is also essential to the President's domestic programs, and he is unlikely to jeopardize it by a head-on conflict on security issues if he can avoid it. At the same time, any President is certain to respect the need for preserving congressional prerogatives under the American system of government. In this respect the treaty power continues to give the Senate an important policy-making role in cases where the

24. Similar congressional action was taken in support of the presidential position in the Middle East in 1957, during the Cuban missile crisis in 1962, and during the Tonkin Gulf incident in 1964. See Report No. 1329, Committee on Foreign Relations, U.S. Senate, 88th Cong., 2nd Sess., 8.

President feels forced or inclined to use this route to conclude international agreements. It is of course true that the President has frequently used the method of executive agreement to come to terms with other nations, a method which does not require Senate approval. But the choice of the treaty route is open to him if he wishes to emphasize the domestic support he has, or if he wishes to pay respect to the constitutional position of the Senate in foreign affairs.

Within these bounds there are obvious restrictions on the role of Congress in defense affairs because of the complexity and size of the issues, the technical nature of so many of the problems, and the numerous other demands on a legislator's time. The influence of Congress in the area of defense is, in many respects, more the result of an intervention into the executive process of policy making than an exercise of its own prerogatives. Congress has become a court of appeal for those in the Executive Branch whose positions are overruled within the executive hierarchy. This has been particularly true of the military departments who have found congressional committees a useful arena in which to battle (or re-battle) their case, either in competition with sister services or against the increasing civilian authority that has developed in the Department of Defense. In the B-36 controversy, for example, the navy was able to bring its argument for new aircraft carriers to Congress after Secretary Johnson's decision to discontinue the program. Similarly, in the early 1960's the air force, through forceful presentation to the Armed Services Committees in both houses, was able to push the development—at least to the building of prototypes—of a manned supersonic bomber despite the opposition of the Secretary of Defense. In both cases Congress was presented with an opportunity to review not only the particular decisions with regard to the choice of weapons systems but the broad strategic implications which these choices involved.

The review of decisions that are matters of controversy within the Executive Branch is thus an important method of exerting congressional influence. It requires, however, a high level of liaison between the bureaucracy and Capitol Hill, and a kind of "open door" policy by legislators. But it is a method which is encouraged by the annual appropriations process and which directs the attention of Congressmen and Senators to those items, out of the vast and complicated array of items in an annual budget of $50 billion, which are vulnerable to questioning and investigation. In contrast, the annual review of foreign and defense policy is a process in which Congress essentially learns what is going on and to which it can contribute little.[25]

Within the Executive Branch, the same problems of size and complexity which have made Congress' role so difficult have led to increasing centralization. Under the National Security Act of 1947, a national defense establishment was established as a policy-making body with limited powers of coordination over the three military departments, army, navy, and air force. Amendments to the original act and general operating experience have greatly expanded this limited authority. Almost complete decision-making power now rests at the level of the Secretary of Defense and is exercised in a variety of ways: through central budgetary controls and through the authority to transfer research programs and weapons systems from one service to another; through the establishment of such centralized functional agencies as the Defense Intelligence Agency and the Defense Supply Agency; and through the development of unified commands reporting to the Secretary and the Joint Chiefs of Staff and maintaining integrated control and training over units from all three services.

This tendency toward centralization has left the services secondary to the Defense Department in all but one major area:

25. For meaningful analyses of the role of Congress, see Samuel P. Huntington, *The Common Defense* (New York, 1961), 123 ff.; also Roger Hilsman, "Congressional-Executive Relations and the Foreign Policy Consensus," *American Political Science Review*, LII, No. 3 (September 1958), 725 ff.

recruitment and promotion of personnel. This power, while residual, is not inconsequential; so long as an officer's career depends on his own service, he is most likely to follow that service's views no matter where the basis of authority in other matters is to be found. Service loyalty has thus not been substantially changed in the shift toward centralized authority. Indeed, it might have intensified as the services have sought to maintain their integrity in the face of depleting authority and to use the few independent powers they have retained.

The increase in civilian authority in the defense establishment is more than an extension of the traditional concept of civilian control of the military.[26] It is that to a certain extent, but more correctly the increased role of civilians comes from changes in the nature of warfare. The importance of weapons technology has forced the military to become increasingly dependent on civilian scientists and engineers, not only for the design and development of new weapons systems and detection devices but for their use as well. At the same time, the changing nature of weapons does not permit the military to rely wholly on previous combat experience as a guide to future wars. No one has had experience using hydrogen bombs, tactical atomic weapons, and long-range missiles. The battleground of the future is highly theoretical and the problems of troop formation, requirements, and the rest cannot be anticipated on the basis of classical military history alone; there is also much to be learned from calculated extension of the known capabilities of new weapons and the probable response of an opponent.

But the civilian role in military affairs is, above all, enhanced by the objectives of defense policy. The relationships that flow from a policy of deterrence and arms control are essentially psychological and political. The development, deployment, and use of the defense establishment must be delicately related to political objectives. The mechanisms for insuring this relationship are

26. Gene M. Lyons, "The New Civil-Military Relations," *American Political Science Review,* LV, No. 1 (March 1961), 53 ff.

several. The formal method is the National Security Council, established in 1947 as an advisory board of cabinet-level officers to make recommendations to the President. As a corporate body, the Council is subject to the wishes of the President. The President has the responsibility for policy and the Council is available to him, but he is under no obligation to call the Council into session before deciding on any major policy matter. Of the Presidents since 1947, General Eisenhower used the Council more systematically than the others, developing a military staff-like system within the Council structure.

Within the Defense Department, the Secretary has his own political advisers, mainly concentrated in the office of the Assistant Secretary for International Security Affairs. In the State Department, military affairs are the concern of all bureaus, though there is special emphasis in the Policy Planning Council and in the Bureau of Politico-Military Affairs, the former established in 1948 and the latter in 1961. At the White House level, the President's Special Assistant for National Security Affairs not only provides the secretariat for the National Security Council but is the contact point between the President and the departments—a strategic position from which he can often match the influence of the Secretaries in the formulation of policy. Also in the White House, the Special Assistant for Science and Technology provides a second center of influence in national security affairs, as presidential adviser and as leader and coordinator for the scientific community in its role and relationship with the government.

The new demands on civilians for policy and operational involvement in military problems have precipitated a new professionalism in national security affairs, which is manifested in a number of ways.[27] There has, especially since the mid-1950's, been an increasing insistence that major political appointments in the fields of foreign affairs and defense be based on experience

27. For a full discussion of the new professionalism, see Gene M. Lyons and Louis Morton, *Schools for Strategy* (New York, 1965).

and special qualifications, with other criteria of political, regional, or ethnic background being subordinate. While this tendency had been followed earlier in foreign affairs, it was late coming to the defense establishement where the needed expertise was concentrated in the career military. But with the shift in specialist requirements in the Pentagon, greater care has been given to appointments. The last Eisenhower Secretary of Defense, Thomas Gates, for example, had served as Deputy Secretary, Assistant Secretary, and Secretary of the Navy immediately before his appointment, and had also had experience in the defense field during World War II and in the immediate years after the war. The Secretary of Defense in the Kennedy administration, Robert McNamara, brought special competence in the area of operations research, proven ability in large-scale management, and earlier experience in applying systematic analysis to military problems while on air force duty during and after World War II.

This insistence on competence and experience, evident at other political levels in the Defense Department, is in many respects related to the rationalization, or "intellectualization," of the policy process, for which the military was greatly responsible. This rationalization has origins in several sources. It rests, first, on the application of techniques of operations research to military operations during World War II. Both the British and the Americans found that by projecting weapons capabilities and by carefully observing response behavior, it was possible to develop more effective firing methods, evasive tactics, or other more efficient methods of operations. This consciously rational method of determining the better "use" of weapons was reinforced by expanded scientific efforts in the postwar period to produce better weapons. These two trends—better weapons and their better use—were then institutionalized in the non-profit, scientifically oriented, university-like corporations set up by the military departments (and later by the Secretary of Defense) to bring this new kind of expertise into the defense establishment. While the most successful and glamorous of these groups is the RAND Corporation set up by the air force, others, such as the army's Research Analysis Corporation, the navy's Operations Evaluation Group, and the Institute of Defense Analyses, have also made important contributions to rationalizing the policy process.

This tendency toward rationalization, based on weapons, their uses, and their costs, was joined by a second intellectual change: a more dynamic and realistic approach to the whole field of international politics and foreign policy. In place of legalistic, goal-setting tendencies in the study of world affairs, there grew up in the postwar period a new school of realism which gave greater emphasis to the role of military power, but more importantly, to the necessity of translating military strength into political objectives. Grounded in the history of the inter-war years, the wartime experiences, and a more concentrated concern with contemporary politics, the new realism found its most articulate expression in the writings of Hans Morgenthau and George Kennan.[28] Even for those who opposed its premises, it forced a more rigorous methodology on all writers and teachers in the field, and its effects, through education, scholarship, public debate, and the changing requirements of policy makers, had, by the 1960's, given a new depth to thinking about international politics. At the same time, other advances in international studies had produced specialists in different areas of the world—Latin America, Africa, the Middle East, the Far East—in which American commitments were growing, and greater sophistication and skill in dealing with the complex interplay of political, economic, social, psychological, and military factors that are involved in national security issues.

The new expertise in defense and diplomacy poses a number of problems. There is, first of all, the real problem of bringing expertise to bear on policy in an effective way. When the issue is

28. For examples: Hans J. Morgenthau, *Politics Among Nations,* 3rd edition (New York, 1960); and George F. Kennan, *American Diplomacy, 1900-1950* (Chicago, 1961).

highly technological, there is necessarily a heavy reliance on the specialist. When the issue is less limited, more open to judgment, less susceptible to an absolute determination, a willingness to hear the expert may depend on the value that is attached to quality and depth in analysis and interpretation. However highly rationalized the policy process may become, the ultimate decisions are in the hands of the President, and his will and style dominate. While the "experts"—civilian and military—may limit the alternatives of choice, their role in making a choice depends on the President's giving them their place in the decision-making hierarchy.

This is not to say that a President—or his chief advisers—is free to ignore expert advice. He does so only at his own risk. Beyond the obvious need to take specialized knowledge into account, there is a political motive: this same advice can be made available to Congress or the press and used to demand accountability for executive action. At the same time there is nothing "monolithic" about expert advice. Experts may differ, not only when the problems are essentially political but when they are highly technological as well. There is never only one way to attack a problem in military research and development, for example. After several stages of experimentation and testing, the factors of feasibility and efficiency may become so clear that the best solution becomes indisputable. But until that point, decisions involving time, money, and considerable effort usually must be made, and there is literally no alternative to depending upon the knowledgeable judgment of chosen experts.

The rationalization of the policy process in national security affairs thus gives tremendous power to experts in government; but it does not mean that we are moving toward government by elite. Indeed, the open nature of presidential elections, the reliance of Congressmen on parochial interests, the vital role of pressure groups in the legislative process, and the susceptibility of public opinion to mass communications, all these features of American political life serve as restrictions on complete rationalization. Even further, they may act as direct influences on policy, to restrain or provoke policy change in the face of contrary expert opinion. A basic shift in American policy toward Communist China, for example, is as much dependent on factors of domestic politics as on calculated estimates of the future of the communist bloc. Similarly, a President might easily find it necessary, because of internal pressures, to respond more openly and directly to communist adventurism than a studied analysis of the national interest dictates.

These limits on rationalization may be looked at from two points of view. They suggest that through the complex interplay of American political forces a "general will" of the people is an influence in national security policy, at least in its tone and broad dimensions. This, one might say, is a "good thing." From another perspective, however, this "democratizing" influence may be more dangerous than satisfying. In so far as the "general will" on such matters as defense and diplomacy can be determined, it is likely to be expressed in less complicated terms than the actual situation merits. At the same time, the ambiguity of dealing with the Soviet Union as both enemy and partner; the problem of determining where the objectives of international communism become subordinate to the demands of Russian or Chinese national interest; the frustration of not being able to identify the "payoff" from foreign aid, military assistance, and diplomatic support; and the impatience at being forced, time and again, to explain that we are not an aggressive people—these kinds of pressures can lead to a sense of impatience to which both the President and Congress may feel obliged to respond—whether or not such a response is warranted by "external" factors.

In this kind of situation, the response of Congress is likely to be fragmented and divided, and more apt to reflect opinion than to shape it. It is the President who must balance the "feeling" of the country with the demands of his own responsibility and, if necessary, become the teacher of the people if he finds that there is resistance to what he must do. For here, as in other respects, we are left with the increasingly important role of the President as the major impact of the Cold War on the American political system. The roles of Congress and public opinion and pressure groups remain operative but highly dependent on presidential initiative. While expert advice is at a high premium, the effectiveness of the knowledgeable specialist is also tied to a responsiveness by the President. There are clearly pressures on the President to rely on expert advice: the very nature of national security issues, the importance of science and technology, the complexity of political and military factors, the need for long-range perspective, the accumulation of expertise that is available, the expectation that more and better knowledge provides a firmer basis for decisions.

But in the final analysis it is the President who must choose. He may be restrained by what he feels the country will support and how far Congress will be willing to go. His power to change the temper and direction of public opinion is not unlimited. It is nevertheless extraordinarily potent—the information he alone possesses, the monopoly he can have of communications media, the responsibility he is expected to assume, the leadership and unity only he can give. For we are living in a political system that is dominated by the presidency. This domination is not wholly the product of the Cold War. It comes from the continuing experience of dealing with crises and challenges since the Great Depression of the early 1930's. But today it is largely carried forward and expanded by the necessity of coping with problems of war and peace.

The Economic and Social Impact

The requirements of a policy of deterrence with arms control affect more than the political structure of the country. They affect the economic structure no less directly and, by their pervasiveness, have a significant impact on social patterns as well. Indeed, the high dependence of many sectors of the economy on defense spending is an open invitation to a "devil" theory of international politics. The concern with "munitions-makers" who spark international rivalries and conflicts in order to profit from war has been a familiar theme in American history. It is a seductive explanation for a complicated subject, since it offers a single-factor analysis and reduces dilemmas to a convenient choice between good and evil.

The Cold War is too complex to be explained in such oversimplified terms. The political influence of economic interests dependent on defense spending is, at the same time, too important to be ignored. Its importance was underscored by President Eisenhower in his Farewell Address to the nation. Speaking after eight years as President, Eisenhower warned against "the acquisition of unwarranted influence, whether sought or unsought, by the military-industrial complex" and cautioned that "only an alert and knowledgeable citizenry can compel the proper meshing of the huge industrial and military machinery of defense with our peaceful methods and goals, so that security and liberty may prosper together."

The position of the defense industries in the economy is, in the first instance, a matter of record. Since the Korean War defense spending has accounted for some 10 per cent of the gross national product. This percentage, moreover, relates only to direct purchases of goods and services under major national security programs and does not include other expenditures which are generated in communities by the injection of defense spending. At the same time there has been a particularly heavy concentration of defense effort in certain key industries. By 1960, for example, 93.7 per cent of those employed in the aircraft industry were engaged in defense work; in ship and boatbuilding the figure was 60.7 per cent; in electric components and accessories 38 per cent; in instruments

20.1 per cent; primary metals, 13.3 per cent; and fabricated metals 7.9 per cent.[29] There is also a geographic concentration which has both economic and political significance. In states where 10 per cent or more of employment is directly attributable to defense contracts, and where the indirect effect is almost as high, shifts or reductions in requirements can cause major catastrophes and lead to extreme economic suffering.

Certainly it would have been impossible for the United States to build an effective deterrent posture without the creation of a large, defense-oriented industrial complex. In the process, however, the defense industries have developed a vitality and momentum of their own and are not simply the creatures of the Pentagon. There is as much initiative from outside as inside Washington about the ways and means of spending defense money. At a technical level, innovations in weapons systems are as likely to come out of the work of prime military contractors as any other single source. This is especially evident when one remembers that three-quarters of the annual federal program for research and development (which approached $15 billion by 1965) is carried on outside government agencies, and 80 per cent of this is under contract with private, profit-seeking firms.[30]

Further, companies with heavy investments in particular weapons systems are bound, in all candor, to look critically at changes in the projection of strategic requirements or at disarmament proposals that will reduce their operations. Their criticism may be based on technological considerations or, equally, on military

29. United States Arms Control and Disarmament Agency, *The Economic and Social Consequences of Disarmament,* Part II (Washington, 1962), 39. These figures remained generally consistent into the 1960's; see *Convertibility of Space and Defense Resources to Civilian Needs,* Vol. 2 of Selected Readings in Employment and Manpower, Committee on Labor and Public Welfare, U.S. Senate, 88th Cong., 2nd Sess., 588-596.

30. "Report to the President on Government Contracting for Research and Development," reprinted in *Systems Development and Management,* Part 1, Hearings, Committee on Government Operations, House of Representatives, 87th Cong., 1st Sess., 191.

or political predilections. There is a benefit to be gained from opposition to shifts or reductions even if it is ultimately rooted in self-interest; it serves the purpose of subjecting proposed changes to critical scrutiny. But it can also generate tremendous political and psychological pressures. The real issue is the extent to which industrially based pressures make it difficult or even impossible for the President and his advisers to evaluate the national interest in cold objectivity, or for the country to accept a decision once it is made. Indeed, this pressure undoubtedly led President Eisenhower to show the concern he did with the "military-industrial complex."

But pressures can be generated from the communities in which defense industries are located, as well as by the industries themselves. Such communities become vulnerable to shifts in government spending, and politicians and labor leaders will thus join the industries in resisting changes that might mean less work. At the same time, communities in which there is little defense work actively seek military contracts when employment drops as a result of factors that have nothing to do with defense adjustments. The Cold War has put enormous resources in the hand of the federal government to meet the needs of economic stability and growth and to cushion the worst effects of economic change. The competition for these resources is played out at a high political level. In the struggle, the broad public interest can be badly confused with the private interests of particular economic, political, or regional groups.

The situation in South Bend, Indiana, in early 1964 is an illustration of the critical role defense spending can play in the economy of a community. It is particularly instructive, since the immediate cause of severe unemployment in South Bend was not a reduction in military contracts but the decision of the Studebaker Corporation to transfer its main manufacturing center to Canada to achieve lower operating costs. The Studebaker move left some seven thousand jobless and produced difficult secondary effects in the South Bend area. At the time of its move, Studebaker had an outstanding contract with the army to produce trucks. At the request of the two Indiana Senators and the Congressman from the district, the Defense Department agreed to halt renegotiation of the truck contract until the legislators had an opportunity to make arrangements to keep the work in South Bend. The legislators soon completed negotiations and announced that Kaiser Jeep Corporation would move into South Bend and take over the army truck contract. While this one operation absorbed only part of the labor force let out by the Studebaker move, it provided an initial break, gave a sense of encouragement to the region, and offered a basis for expansion.[31]

The South Bend case is, in many respects, a harbinger of the kind of industry-labor-government workings that will be necessary to bring communities that are heavily dependent on defense contracts through periods of change resulting from shifts in the military budget. There has been considerable speculation in recent years, for example, about the economic and social consequences of disarmament. Most studies have been highly technical and assume that there are more than sufficient needs in the United States to absorb the productive capacity that would be freed by a substantial reduction in defense spending. But as a report of the U.S. Arms Control and Disarmament Agency in 1962 added: "Advance planning and sensible policies at all levels of government will be essential to the maintenance of overall economic activity in the face of the progressive elimination of defense demand." At the same time, there will be special problems of transition (like the problem in South Bend), and here: "concerted effort on the part of government . . . and of business and labor, to bring to bear numerous available instruments and, if necessary,

31. *New York Times,* February 25, 1964.

to create additional ones, can reduce to a minimum any hardship and waste in the adjustment process . . ." [32]

Transitional arrangements, necessitated either by a reduction in armaments programs or by changes in the distribution of contracts, could range from temporary relief through the distribution of government surplus food to the reallocation of resources to meet other national objectives, such as the elimination of slums or the construction of new schools and hospitals. In either case—and in the number of alternatives between—government's role in the economy is considerably different from the traditional view, even though it has origins in the past. The "pump-priming" techniques of the New Deal and the objectives of the Employment Act of 1946 both serve as a basis for continuing government action to insure economic stability and growth. A long period of Cold War defense budgets could, however, give the government a more permanent role in the economic life of the nation than ever before. Not only will there be pressures for government to help absorb the costs of defense reduction, but beyond this the Cold War—and the full sweep of political and social forces that have accompanied it—has raised social needs to a high level of national consciousness. Whether the Cold War subsides into a "manageable" coexistence, intensifies, or fades away, it will be difficult to leave the struggle against poverty, the demands for more education, and the blight of the sprawling urban areas to the complete interplay of self-generated private interests without some kind of government-originated social planning.

But beyond its general economic impact, government defense spending has come to play a special role in economic growth as a result of large amounts spent for advanced research and development. A certain part of military research and development is probably not transferable to the civilian economy; but much of

32. United Nations Arms Control and Disarmament Agency, *op. cit.* See also Kenneth Boulding and Emile Benoit, eds., *Disarmament and the Economy* (New York, 1963).

it is, and indeed a good deal of the economic growth attributable to technological innovation in recent years can be traced to the technical demands of military requirements. The use of computers may be taken as an example. The development of electronic data processing has not only provided an essential tool for technological progress but has had important implications for communications, management, and education. In reviewing the impact of the "computer revolution" on industry, *Business Week* noted that "every large intercontinental ballistic missile has the equivalent of a computer on board. Every Polaris submarine carries the equivalent of several large-scale computers, and every Minuteman missile silo has a computer to check the condition of the missile—and of the computer inside the missile." The report then suggested the significance of these systems for industrial growth:

> The government is directly or indirectly paying the cost of the development of these computers—and for the capital equipment to manufacture them. It has to do this because the military is, at present, the only customer for such advanced circuitry at such high development cost. But by the time the military demand is filled, the commercial base will exist to turn out such computers at relatively low cost.[33]

A reduction in the military research and development budget would not leave a complete vacuum in government spending for research, even if it were sharply cut back. Much research in atomic energy and the space program has both military and nonmilitary applications, and while a reduction in Cold War tensions might make it more difficult to get congressional approval for current levels of expenditure, government-supported research will continue to be necessary to meet national objectives in both these fields. It will also be necessary to provide the pre-investment base to make technological exploitation feasible and profitable in other areas, a process already demonstrated by the need for government support for the development of a supersonic airliner. The same is

33. "New Tool, New World," *Business Week,* February 29, 1964, 80.

no less true in such fields as health, agriculture, and meteorology, which have been traditional areas of government interest but which have been greatly extended through new opportunities for research and development provided by today's technology, and through the tremendous drive which the Cold War has given to research as a national objective and "good." The result of all these relations is that, under the impact of the Cold War, the United States has built a national research base which cannot be maintained and extended by private industry and which will be essential to the continued strength of the country. There is, one might say, no turning back. The question is no longer whether or not government, and particularly the federal government, should intervene into the economy, but rather how rationally and responsibly government programs can be developed and coordinated with activities in the private sector.[34]

The role of government in economic stability and growth and in research and development has been extended in another and related area under the impact of the Cold War: education and manpower training. Like the development of the American economy itself, manpower resources to meet national objectives had traditionally been left to the interplay of personal preferences and opportunities. The one major exception to this has been, understandably, in the military. The establishment of the military and naval acadamies, the programs of the Reserve Officers Training Corps, and schools for advanced military training and education comprise a total system for the provision of military leadership. In a less complete but no less significant way, the government, through the Land Grant Act of 1862, provided the basis for the establishment of colleges for the training of technical skills needed for agricultural and industrial growth. The development of the

34. For a statement of problems involved in the long-term role of government in research and development, see *Federal Research and Development Programs,* First Progress Report, Select Committee on Government Research, House of Representatives, 88th Cong., 2nd Sess.

huge state university systems, carried on by the states after initial federal action, has far exceeded the immediate objectives of the original act. But in this development there lies a precedent for a more rational method of determining and satisfying national manpower requirements than the country has generally followed in the past.

The immediate demands of the Cold War have been essentially scientific and technological, and the education of scientists and engineers has been accelerated and expanded both through direct action and through the support of research. Large research grants from government agencies to universities stimulate teaching in a variety of ways: they provide facilities for instruction, attract teachers by the opportunities for new investigation, and offer prestige and power to scientists, thus giving incentives to young men and women to seek careers in fields that are well supported. But research also absorbs the attention and interest of scientists to such an extent that teaching is in danger of being neglected or left to those least able to excite and stimulate students.

The need for direct action to provide more scientists and engineers was dramatized when the Soviet Union became the first nation to send a man-made satellite into space in 1957. The Soviet feat was particularly shocking since it was a major success of technology, a field in which the United States claimed preeminence. The Russian sputnik set off a series of organizational and intellectual changes in the United States. At the level of government, the President appointed a special adviser for science and technology, the Defense Department created a more centralized authority for research and engineering, a separate civilian-controlled space agency was established, and both houses of Congress established new standing committees to deal with legislation in the fields of science and technology. Almost immediately the total government-supported research and development budget was increased until it approached the $15 billion mark. At the same time, the National Defense Education Act of 1958 became the first major federal program in higher education since the Land Grant Act of 1862. Under the NDEA, a system of loans and scholarships was set up to provide new opportunities for both undergraduate and advanced education in fields of national concern, particularly science, engineering, and language training.

The impact of the Soviet sputnik on American education went much deeper, however. It set in motion a national inquiry into education that went far beyond the immediate problem and involved every local school board in the country.[35] Professional scientific societies undertook special studies on the teaching of mathematics, physics, and biology in high schools and, through these efforts, began to provide better textbooks and teaching techniques. New demands were put on secondary schoolteachers for better preparation to cope with new methods, and the advanced standing of students who were taught under the new systems tended to raise the level of work they were capable of once they entered college. The pressures for more science then set off counter-pressures for more history and literature, for as much attention to the humanities and social sciences as to the physical sciences. From this point the national debate moved from the narrow focus of science and technology to the broader issue of how to overcome the inhibiting obstacles of insufficient financing, poor facilities, and too few well-trained teachers.

Inevitably, the national debate on education became greatly preoccupied with the particularly desperate plight of the underprivileged, of whom the Negroes, in the North and the South, comprise a heavy proportion. What had been a response to a specific challenge in the Cold War became enmeshed with the

35. Probably the most important inquiry was carried out by James B. Conant with the support of the Carnegie Corporation of New York; see the following books that came out of Dr. Conant's work: *The American High School Today* (New York, 1959); *Slums and Suburbs* (New York, 1961); *The Education of American Teachers* (New York, 1963); and *Shaping Educational Policy* (New York, 1964).

most tortuous internal problem the United States faces. The fight for civil rights by Negroes had already been greatly affected by the Cold War. Their participation in the Second World War had initially acted as a catalyst for many Negroes to demand equal rights from a country that asked them to fight and risk their lives. The maintenance of large active forces after the war led to the desegregation of the armed forces in 1948; and later this led, in turn, to desegregation of housing, schools, clubs, stores, and churches on military posts, and pressures for desegregation of all such facilities in the areas surrounding military installations, even in the deep South.[36] In the world arena, the emergence of the nations of black Africa into independence and the internationalization of the struggle for human rights further fed the fires of dissatisfaction. All these pressures had grown by the time the great debate on education began in the late 1950's. By the early 1960's, after initial action had been taken at many levels—federal, state, and local—the nation's attention was turned toward the problem that seemed to defy normal remedies: the problem of educating the poor—and the problem of the poor was largely a problem of color.

The impact of the Cold War on economic stability and growth, on scientific research and development, on educational programs, and even on the civil rights movement is but an indication of its pervasiveness. The Cold War is clearly a national experience of great intensity, and it is only natural that it affects other major issues in the society. What is really important is to understand not just how these relationships came about, but what they mean.

The Cold War has generated tremendous power and resources that can be used to deal with the internal problems of American life, as well as to meet the strategic requirements of international involvement. Will there be pressures to continue the Cold War just to maintain a base and justification for this power and these

36. As an example, see United States Commission on Civil Rights, *Family Housing and the Negro Serviceman* (Washington, 1963).

resources, or will it be possible to develop a consensus around other national purposes should the reasons for the Cold War change, or even begin to disappear? The point is not that the Cold War is *going* to disappear tomorrow. It is rather that the Cold War is an understandable but nonetheless unhealthy basis on which to rely solely for a consensus on how to meet economic and social problems. If everything must be justified in terms of the Cold War—scientific research, aid to education, economic growth —and if in no other way is it possible to gain the votes, power, or influence to deal with these issues, then there will be tremendous pressures in the society to resist any change to the basic structure of the Cold War. Under such circumstances, the radical right is not the only source of irrationality. Pressures that make it difficult for a President to make hard and realistic decisions in matters of national security can rise out of less radical sources, if the society is so conditioned that it is ultimately necessary to invoke the Cold War to support every important political action.

The Future of the Cold War

The Cold War has changed since the late 1940's. The strategic balance between the United States and the Soviet Union has reached a cautious stage of stability, new power has emerged out of reconstructed Europe and communized China, and self-propelling forces have been released in the developing nations of the southern hemisphere. The two super-powers remain pre-eminent in the military force they control, in the resources they possess, and in the influence they can ultimately bring to bear on any matter which touches their vital interests. But the world is no longer polarized, even though the United States and the USSR remain in basic disagreement over ultimate goals. Under the umbrella of thermonuclear stalemate, there is room for initiative by lesser powers that cannot be controlled by either the United States or the Soviet Union. Military force, and particularly nuclear force, per se, is not always pertinent or relevant to conflict and instability. What is relevant is political influence, and the utility of military power can most often be measured by the degree to which it can be translated into political terms.

Short of disaster or withdrawal, the foreseeable future is more likely than not to resemble the recent past: continued struggle, continued frustration, periodic crises, and, hopefully, continuing opportunities to stabilize international relations, at least to the extent of avoiding conflict among the great powers through mistake or miscalculation. Most Americans accept the Cold War as a fact of life and will probably continue to do so. But whether they will be content with limited success (and tolerant of limited failure), and whether they will accept the hazards of the Cold War because they assume that thermonuclear war simply *cannot* happen, are more difficult questions. A good deal depends on how they look at the state of world politics.

The Cold War as a crusade against communism is one way to look at the world. But it is a dangerous way. Certainly anti-communism is a cohesive force for a diffuse, fragmented society, and has served this purpose in the past. But it is also a force that can blind us to changes in the communist bloc, oversimplify the diversity that exists in the world, and limit alternatives for action. It is not without reason that the violent anti-communism of the radical right reached its highest peaks of popular support after difficult international setbacks: the rise of McCarthyism after the fall of China to communism and the outbreak of the Korean War; and the ascendancy of the John Birch Society and schools of anti-communism after the Soviet sputnik and the subsequent loss of American invulnerability and prestige. The loss of relative power becomes difficult to accept in a world in which Americans have become accustomed to invincibility. What is forgotten, or disregarded, is that there are forces over which we have limited control in a world in which we are intrinsically involved.

Should the Cold War continue, there will be increased and

cumulative frustration, especially if there is no other real basis for consensus in the society than the struggle against communism. Without ignoring the basic antagonism between the ideas of freedom and those of totalitarian communism, there would seem to be a real need to find stronger roots for American policy. The possibilities exist: in the international institution-building process in which the United States has been engaged since 1945; in the extension of the American ideal throughout American society; in the adaptation of American economic and social structures to the new science and technology; and in the unique leadership that the United States can offer to nations in a stage of revolutionary transition. It may be too much to expect people to identify their personal interests with these goals. But it is not too much to ask of a nation's leaders, for this would seem to be their responsibility. How well they rise to their obligation will mark the difference between success and failure in meeting the challenge of the Cold War while preserving the essence of the democratic process.

5

COMMON MARKETS AND THE AMERICAN ECONOMY

MEREDITH O. CLEMENT

WHAT is most strikingly different about our present economic situation is not the extent of American involvement in world trade, but the impact of the American economy on world markets because of its size, its capacity for expansion, and its internal energies.

If, more than we have perhaps acknowledged, there are historical precedents and experience for dealing with contemporary problems, there are nonetheless distinct characteristics of the world economic structure within which we now operate. The present period is marked by three vital and forceful tendencies: (1) the competition between two of the most highly industrialized sectors of the world economy, the Soviet Union and the United States; (2) the drive toward industrialization by those nations recently granted political independence but still economically dependent; and (3) the incentive for nations to form regional blocs for purposes of economic growth and development.

Regional economic integration, the special focus of this essay, may be all things to all men. In the Soviet-dominated sector it is a means of consolidating Russia's hold over Eastern Europe, a move resisted first by Yugoslavia and more recently by Poland and Rumania. For the emergent nations of Asia, Africa, and Latin America, it is often as much an act of political opposition to the industrialized nations as it is a rational union of economic potential. In Europe, where regional integration has advanced furthest, it is a response to the need for a new market, a method of achieving political balance within Europe, and a means of asserting European strength in the face of the end of empire and the shift of world political power to the U.S. and the USSR.

As a form of international organization, regional economic integration is not new. The history of customs unions in the nineteenth and twentieth centuries is, to a certain extent, precedent for what is now happening. But today the move toward economic union is more intense, more ambitious, and more widespread. In Western Europe, moreover, it involves powerful economies, which together have an important effect on the structure of the world economy and thus on the environment within which the American economy operates. How drastic might the impact of European regional integration actually be? Is the prospect more apparent than real? Does the American economy possess the dynamism and resilience to adjust without serious or protracted injury?

These are vital questions and their answers are necessarily problematic and complex. Nevertheless, the future of the American economy is, to a significant degree, contingent upon these answers. Moreover, it is clear that the effectiveness of America's international influence, no less than the vitality of its internal economy, is being challenged by the trend toward common markets. The task of this essay is to suggest the nature of this challenge and the alternatives open to the United States.*

* The help and advice of Mrs. Richard Sterling and the substantive suggestions of my colleague, Richard L. Pfister, have been of great service. The author alone, of course, is responsible for the arguments and conclusions of the essay.

Stimuli to Regional Economic Integration

As a structural solution for political and economic problems, regionalism has emerged as a response to postwar realities, rather than as a fulfillment of international planning. In the final stages of World War II, policy makers had turned their thoughts to insuring the peace and quite naturally concentrated most of their efforts on the structure of the postwar international community. While this structure was being mapped out, the war itself and its immediate causes were preying on the minds of all. Possibly of equal concern was the spectre of renewed depression, such as the world had experienced in the thirties when chaotic international monetary conditions accompanied a catastrophic drop in world production and trade and a near collapse of long-term foreign lending. The impotence of the League of Nations, without United States participation, was a vivid memory. In retrospect it was obvious that the opportunities opened by the Allied victory in 1918 had at best been amateurishly mishandled and at worst had aggravated interwar difficulties. If it was within human competence in 1944 to avoid the more serious mistakes of the past three decades, there was every incentive to do so.

Allied statesmen, bureaucrats, and scholars thus set about to prepare the postwar world. In 1944 and 1945 they drew up exciting proposals, out of which emerged several international institutions, political and economic. In the economic sphere, a modified laissez faire was the pattern: the International Monetary Fund and the International Bank for Reconstruction and Development were created to support international mechanisms to revive international trade and capital transactions. An International Trade Organization was also planned to promote free, non-discriminatory trade on a multilateral basis.[1] The whole scheme mirrored the

1. As it happened, unforeseen hurdles prevented the implementation of the I.T.O. The General Agreement on Tariffs and Trade, negotiated as its replacement, became the locus of attempts to reformulate tariffs and commercial policies.

Western (especially American) orientation of its chief architects and was based on a diffused power structure and on the cooperation of a number of major nations of relatively equal political and economic influence.

This pattern clearly miscalculated the extent of devastation that Europe had suffered and the possibility of an American-Soviet power confrontation. But the miscalculations were soon evident. They showed up under the persistence of American and Soviet hostility in the settlement of postwar affairs and the ever-weakening position of Europe in 1946 and 1947. Out of both these realities, "bloc politics" emerged. On the one side the Soviet Union consolidated its stand in Eastern Europe between 1945 and 1948. On the other side, the United States, in establishing its Marshall Plan in 1947, asked for a concerted economic response from the countries of Western Europe. Based on the experience of its own large tariff-free internal economy, the motives of the United States were twofold: to avert future dissension in Europe and to present a united front to the Soviet-dominated bloc in the East. Some Europeans were partisans of the "European movement" and, in this respect, receptive to American initiatives for their own sake. But others, particularly the French, saw European integration as a means of containing Germany during and after its reconstruction, and thus ridding Europe of the vestiges of "Prussianism."

As regionalism took shape on both sides of the "iron curtain" in Europe, another force revealed itself moving in the same direction. The first throes of the "revolution of rising expectations," a reaction to years of economic exploitation and political servitude, signaled the disintegration of long-existing and long-accommodated colonial empires. In consequence, not only were the number of sovereign states multiplied several fold, but the trading and governing ties that had held groups of nations together in somewhat cohesive units were loosened, unleashing a tide of international political maneuvering and realignment on a global scale. To a certain extent, close relations continued within groups like the British Commonwealth and the French Community. But the new nations also regrouped themselves into bargaining units independent of the former mother countries; they were now brought together by common interests of geography and economic and political status.

Coupled with these developments was a revolution in manufacturing and agricultural techniques, especially in the United States. The enormous benefits to be derived from production on a large scale and in long, continuous runs had been known for years. Indeed, from one point of view the economic fruits of the Industrial Revolution, which benefited the agricultural sector as well, can be explained in terms of the progressive adoption of mass-production methods which mechanization made feasible. It was widely acknowledged that the United States was the model of this process; this, rather than the superabundance of productive factors, was responsible for the the long-standing economic superiority of American goods in world markets.

But the productivity revolution did not consist of a simple extension of this process. Its main basis was to be found, rather, in the application of scientific—not mechanical—discoveries which were, again as in the case of mechanical innovations, only economically profitable with a further expansion of the productive unit. No longer would a moderate size commodity market, such as those provided even by the larger Western European countries, suffice to achieve the appreciable economies of large-scale production. In the postwar era, with its emphasis on scientific progress, the tremendous advantages of large-scale production were driven home with a vengeance.

The requirements of large-scale production were particularly relevant in Western Europe where statesmen, since the late 1940's, had begun to examine regionalism as a reasonably permanent goal. In the end, the solution to their economic and political difficulties was reckoned by men like Jean Monnet to be some form of political unification. But it was also persuasively argued that Western Europeans were not yet prepared to throw off their national identities; cultural characteristics were too diverse, national interests were discordant, and external advantages were not strong enough to overpower these centrifugal elements. In 1954 French veto of the European Defense Community confirmed these arguments. At least for the time being, Western European political unification was beyond reach.

This did not, however, deter these same statesmen from accepting political consolidation as an ultimate target. If it was for the moment impracticable, then some other multi-national goal, one that was attainable in the not too distant future and which would put Western Europe firmly on the path to unification, would have to suffice. Economic integration was hit upon as such a goal. Hopefully, economic integration would fuse the divisive national sentiments and, by enhancing European economic specialization and interdependence, create a common economic interest which would quickly spill over into the political sphere. But it would do more.

It would also (and if this was of second priority it was nevertheless significant) permit the European economy to recover some of the ground it had been losing to the United States and the Soviet Union because its markets were so highly fragmented that large-scale production would have been an economic waste. In the immediate postwar years the shortage of productive capacity and the requirements for recovery in Western Europe combined to generate a mountainous balance-of-payments deficit—the so-called "dollar shortage"—and there was little immediate hope of relief. But once the task of reconstruction was accomplished, integration would serve two purposes: if successful it would provide the means whereby Western Europe could again become an economic power capable of making its own way in the world; and it would be the starting wedge of the movement for full political unification of Western Europe.

Needless to say, even economic integration presented substantial obstacles with highly political repercussions. Removal of internal barriers to trade, such as tariffs and quotas, might be ineffective without common excise tax programs. Independent monetary and fiscal policies might be incompatible with free trade. National transportation policies must be carefully coordinated. Problems of this sort are not negligible. Nevertheless, an auspicious start was made in February, 1953, by the establishment of the European Coal and Steel Community. This was an attempt to coordinate the utilization of the coal, steel, scrap, and iron ore resources of France, Germany, Italy, and the Benelux countries in order to provide a rational distribution of productive facilities at the lowest possible unit costs. Although the ECSC had its share of intractable problems, its moderate initial successes were encouraging. So much so that they prompted an integration planning conference at Messina in the late spring of 1955 which culminated in the foundation of the European Economic Community, embracing the same nations as the ECSC. The formation of the European Free Trade Association, a response by those nations that found the EEC treaty unacceptable, soon followed.[2]

The sharp political split may have provided a ready environment for the European integration movement, but there has been no such compelling force at work in the more recent and halting integration movements in the underdeveloped regions.[3] Like the European Free Trade Area, these movements are partially eco-

2. EFTA encompasses Austria, Denmark, Great Britain, Norway, Portugal, Sweden, and Switzerland.

3. The fledgling regional schemes in underdeveloped areas include: the Latin American Free Trade Association (Argentina, Brazil, Chile, Colombia, Ecuador, Mexico, Paraguay, Peru, and Uruguay); the Central American Common Market (El Salvador, Guatemala, Honduras, Costa Rica, and Nicaragua); l'Organisation Afro-Malgache de Coopération Economique, with two sub-groupings; and the East African Common Market (Kenya, Tanganyika, and Uganda). More rudimentary organizations exist in the Near East and Southeast Asia. See S. Dell, *Trade Blocs and Common Markets* (New York, 1963), Chap. 7.

nomic responses to the potential closing off of continental European markets. But the major incentive to regionalism comes from the need to gain greater efficiency through joint development projects and to achieve the stronger bargaining position in world markets that could come through communal action. In terms of overall economic structure, the developing nations must overcome two perpetual weaknesses: the tendency of foreign investment capital to sustain the existing, feeble economic structure by concentrating on industries which extract resources and on plantation agriculture, rather than on industrial development; and their dependence on shifting export prices for the raw materials and tropical agricultural commodities from which they earn foreign exchange. If the development of these retarded economies is to proceed without frustrating slowdowns—even reversals—they must have access to foreign markets and reasonably stable prices for their products.

Countries producing raw materials are especially sensitive to these problems, having suffered acute misery during the depression of the thirties when their export prices plummeted. Then, too, the long-run barter terms of trade (which, for these purposes, may be defined as the volume of imports that can be acquired in international markets with a given volume of exports), although interrupted by a brief, dramatic improvement during World War II and again during the Korean action, are believed by leaders in the new nations to be progressively deteriorating.[4] Through time the underdeveloped countries will have to increase productivity simply to maintain imports for their development programs and

4. Recently researchers have questioned the validity of this belief. See, for example, Theodore Morgan, "The Long-Run Terms of Trade between Agriculture and Manufacturing," *Economic Development and Cultural Change* (October 1959), and Robert E. Lipsey, *Price and Quantity Trends in the Foreign Trade of the United States* (Princeton, 1963), Chaps. 1 and 2. Nevertheless, spokesmen for the underdeveloped areas do not appear to be convinced by this evidence and, it goes almost without saying, their actions are based on their beliefs, however unsubstantiated these may be.

modest standards of living. These issues are accentuated in the minds of leaders in the aspiring nations by several vague, but no less convincing, theoretical arguments that an international economy based upon free, non-discriminatory, multilateral trade is responsible for an ever widening discrepancy between the living standards of the "have" and the "have not" nations. They are thus convinced that special and extraordinary measures must be taken if their countries are to develop viable economies.

Both Western Europeans and the peoples of the underdeveloped nations chose economic integration as a salient part of the solution to their quite different problems, a fact which testifies to the many-sided potentialities of integration. It may be a means to cultural uniformity and political consolidation. It may improve productivity and economic welfare by a more rational allocation of productive resources. It may help to provide more stable commodity and factor markets. And, above all, it may be a source of more powerful bargaining strength, in international economics and politics, than the sum of that wielded by the component countries acting independently.

Consequences for the United States

The possible ramifications of regional economic integration have impelled a sober reappraisal of American political and economic strategy. There is little doubt that the posture of the United States in international politics will undergo significant changes. Until an ultimate form of political association among the EEC countries takes shape, until de Gaulle's conception of continental Western Europe as a "third force" in world politics is either accepted or rejected by these countries, until the relation of Britain and other countries to the Common Market is determined with finality, until the nuclear weapons policy of the EEC countries is clearly defined, until other crucial issues are definitely decided upon, the political position of the United States vis-à-vis

Western Europe will be in a state of continuous flux. Moreover, regionalism in the underdeveloped areas, even in Latin America, being at a truly formative stage, will have consequences still more difficult to anticipate. The global strategy of the United States must be flexible enough to accommodate a variety of possible outcomes of the several movements toward regional integration.

There is nothing new in this. Transformation of the international structure has always fostered mutations of international strategies. But the economic integration movement will be a truly prolific source of such vital structural changes. For the present at least, it would be perilous to base American global political strategy on any status quo. None is relevant.

The economic consequences of regional integration are also difficult to fathom. Many decisions of economic significance remain to be made. The denouement of EEC deliberations on agricultural policy; the provisions and enforcement of anti-trust laws and patent and trademark rights; a common procedure for meeting European balance-of-international-payments difficulties; the extent and nature of centralized economic direction, and so on, must all be worked out. The evolution of regionalism in the less developed areas is even more problematical. Yet it is already apparent that the impact of common markets upon the United States economy will not be an unmixed blessing. Undoubtedly the response of the American economy will be an appreciable reallocation of factors of production, especially as between agriculture and manufacturing but also within manufacturing itself. This will cause some change in the occupational composition of the labor force, but perhaps not so great a change as is commonly supposed. Barring the re-emergence of trade restrictions in Western Europe, there need not be any significant reduction in the level of employment and rate of utilization of American productive facilities. The *rate* of growth of the American economy will almost certainly be affected, however.

Adjustments such as these are occurring continuously in a

market-oriented economy. A change in consumer tastes, development of new production techniques, alterations in the supplies of labor or capital must all be accommodated by reallocation of resources. International regional integration will simply compound and complicate these adjustments.

The certain prospect that common markets would magnify the "normal" market-force adjustments was not taken casually in this country. Neither was it viewed with alarm, however, until the United States suffered a very substantial deficit in its balance of international payments, accompanied by a startling depletion of the United States gold reserve and a rapid accumulation of short-term dollar liabilities to foreigners. After several years of relatively modest deficits—in the neighborhood of $1.5 billion—and an unanticipated and substantial payments surplus due to the Suez Crisis of 1956, United States receipts on foreign account in 1958 fell short of payments by $3.5 billion. In 1959 and 1960 the shortfall grew by $200 and $350 million respectively, after which the situation improved (although 1963 again witnessed a relatively poor balance). As a result of these payments deficits, United States gold holdings fell from a total of almost $23 billion in 1957 to less than $16 billion by 1964, while short-term dollar liabilities to foreigners rose from less than $16 billion to more than $26 billion.

This payments deficit and depletion of net reserves was due to a complex of phenomena. Loss of export competitiveness, a relatively abrupt change in international taste patterns, high foreign defense and aid commitments, a resurgence of private investment abroad, a loss of confidence in the stability of the dollar—all of these have been cited. But the fact that the deficit became substantial in 1958, the first year of EEC operations, colored much of the subsequent popular debate over the international payments problem.

This deficit situation, more than any other economic influence, has made government officials acutely aware of the costs of failing to adjust to the movement toward regionalism abroad. More is at stake than employment levels, rates of return on investment, the pace of economic growth, and the standard of living in the United States. The dollar is a major bulwark of the international monetary system; should its position be imperiled, as it will if the sizable deficit in the United States' balance of payments is prolonged, the world monetary system could also suffer irreparable damage. Monetary collapse could precipitate a rapid disintegration of the world multilateral trading network, so laboriously re-created in the postwar period. The finely articulated structure of international specialization, made possible by widespread international transactions, would also break up. Since a high degree of economic specialization and high per capita incomes seem to go hand-in-hand, it is apparent that a great deal hinges upon the kinds of economic pressures that regional integration will bring to bear upon the United States' balance of payments and, especially, upon the United States' ability to withstand and adjust to them.

We see that common markets will exert major pressures upon the volume and type of United States exports and imports. Another salient effect, particularly for the growth rate of the American economy, is the likely change in the relative attractiveness of domestic and foreign investment opportunities. Both of these phenomena—direct foreign trade balance effects and relative investment effects—have widespread ramifications. Aside from the obvious impact on growth rate and resource allocation, and hence upon overall American economic efficiency, the level of economic activity of the United States and its balance-of-payments position are directly involved. The precise *nature* of the causal relationships among these economic variables is not difficult to understand. But to *quantify* these relationships with the precision required for important policy decisions is an awesome task. It is sufficient here simply to assess the prospects involved.

The Impact on American Exports

The Rome Treaty of the EEC calls for the gradual elimination of tariff duties levied on goods manufactured within the EEC, and the adoption of uniform tariffs on the imports of manufactured goods originating in non-member countries. The format of the European Free Trade Association is essentially identical, although participating countries are permitted to retain their individual tariff identities vis-à-vis non-member nations. Even if the external tariff is no higher than it was prior to integration, a common market creates an immediate advantage for intra-market sellers. Members' demands for goods that were formerly supplied by exporters in non-member countries will, after the rearrangement of tariffs, be directed toward suppliers in other member countries. The advantage given to member country suppliers may thus be substantial.[5] The barrier that a customs union throws up before the rest of the world is not insurmountable, but its effectiveness will cause *trade displacement*. Put simply, tariff adjustments tend to substitute the exports of member countries for the exports of non-member countries.

In the case of the EEC this basis for trade displacement is particularly significant for industrial goods. It is expected that Common Market manufacturers will face intensified competition behind the uniform external tariff wall. The extent of this competition will depend largely upon the attitudes and policies of the EEC with respect to cartels and other monopolistic tendencies. The tariff wall itself will, of course, continue to block non-member producers out of this struggle, as did the separate national tariff schedules in the past; but provided a reasonably vigorous antitrust policy is adopted, the elimination of import duties within

5. The advantage is generally considered to be related to the production cost differentials between low-cost producers within and without the customs area, relative to the height of the tariff on goods coming from the outside.

the EEC will mean that only the lowest cost producers within the Common Market will survive. This internal competitive struggle, by forcing the closing of high-cost factories and by rewarding successful development of new techniques and new products, will be a major benefit to the members of the community. The heightened competition will be resisted by national groups, to be sure; but in the final analysis, European resources will be used more effectively with a probable commensurate increase in European incomes. To the extent that the economies of other nations adjust themselves to the new situation, world productive effort will likewise be more efficient and the volume of trade will rise.

Both the lower costs of production enforced by competition within the EEC, and the higher external tariff applied to imports into the Common Market, will give manufacturers in the community appreciably higher protection than they enjoyed when each nation was empowered to set separate tariff rates. One estimate, admittedly crude, is that the new conditions will provide much greater protection for some 75 per cent of the varieties of manufactured articles produced in the EEC countries. In contrast, EEC tariff schedules will reduce protection for only about one-sixth of the manufactured items.[6] Even here, moreover, a continuation of import quotas and other non-tariff types of restrictions will dilute the influence which is otherwise beneficial to non-member exporters.

Only about one-eighth of American exports of manufactures goes to EEC countries, so the heightened tariff protection afforded by the EEC may not seem too significant. But United States exports of manufactures to the EEC are concentrated in a relatively few categories—machinery, chemicals, and aircraft stand out—and in these categories a substantial reduction in tariff duties would be necessary before Americans could again compete in Western Europe on the same basis as before 1958. It would

6. W. S. Salant, *et al., The United States Balance of Payments in 1968* (Washington, 1963), pp. 101-103.

appear that the EEC tariff schedule was designed specifically to reduce European dependence on the United States. In any event, the trade displacement effects of the EEC upon United States exports of manufactures will certainly be sufficient to aggravate an already difficult balance of payments problem. For some commodities, notably agricultural machinery, chemicals, machine tools, and motor vehicles, the results may well be critical.

American exports of raw materials will, with a few important exceptions, be less adversely affected by the trade displacement effects of the customs union. The heavy dependence of European industrial production on imported crude materials has made manufacturers peculiarly sensitive to the costs of these materials. Generally, this "cost orientation" has acted as a constraint upon tariff protection for European raw materials producers. Prior to integration, tariffs on most industrial raw materials were either low or non-existent, and the common EEC external tariff schedule reflects this condition. Thus European producers of raw materials have been given no appreciable advantage over non-member producers and, except for probable difficulties for exporters of petroleum products and aluminum, American raw materials exports are unlikely to suffer appreciably.

In contrast to raw materials, American agricultural commodities will be hard pressed to find markets in EEC countries. If the current trend persists, EEC agricultural measures are likely to result in complicated tariff duties and agricultural price supports. The ultimate effect of EEC agricultural policy is likely to be the preservation of as much of the Common Market demand as is necessary to absorb the entire EEC agricultural output. Only if there is an excess of demand over supply of agricultural commodities within the EEC as a whole is there likely to be a market for the farm output of non-member countries.

Moreover, the operation of the EEC will diminish the prospect of there being periods of excess agricultural demand. In the last few decades there has been a thoroughgoing renovation of agricultural techniques which is only now making appreciable headway in Western Europe. Rising agricultural output in Europe is the likely result. In addition, given the political influence of farm blocs, the common price support levels to be installed by the EEC will probably approach those of the highest-supporting country prior to the adoption of uniform supports. A general increase in support prices will provide further impetus to agricultural production in the remaining EEC countries. And again, since intra-EEC trade in goods will be virtually free, an agricultural surplus in a particular commodity in one country will not necessarily call for controlling production so long as the Common Market as a whole does not have a surfeit of that commodity. Only when the combined EEC countries are self-sufficient in the whole spectrum of currently produced agricultural commodities will there be incentive, provided by competition from non-member producers, to limit production.

Thus, again if only the trade displacement possibilities are considered, United States agricultural exports to the Common Market, representing about 35 per cent of United States dollar sales of farm products abroad, have a dim future.[7] Of course, not all agricultural products will be equally affected. Unless the EEC admits several new countries to associate membership, American tobacco and cotton growers will be subjected to little if any adversity. But there seems to be almost no hope of bargaining effective reductions in EEC agricultural protection. In view of the probability that as incomes rise throughout Western Europe the demand for agricultural commodities will lag behind—being relatively displaced by manufactured goods and services in the expenditure pattern of consumers—EEC markets for United States agricultural exports are not apt to expand rapidly.

Even so, the United States, because of its relatively favorable mix of farm products, is less likely to be strained by Common Market agricultural policies than most agricultural countries. It

7. When *total* exports of American agricultural products—including exports for payment in local currencies under P.L. 480—is used as the basis, the share falls to about 23 per cent.

is true that American agricultural production generally competes with, rather than complements, that of the EEC and EFTA countries. But other temperate zone agricultural countries are even less fortunate, particularly if their products have to buck EFTA and EEC competition without favorable concessions. European and non-American temperate zone agricultural commodities can easily be substituted, one for the other. Moreover, the Common Market's external tariff schedule grants a preferential status to a number of underdeveloped countries, particularly in Africa.[8] The existence of this gap in the EEC tariff wall suggests that non-preferred countries exporting tropical agricultural products will undergo serious privations. Non-member producers of cocoa, coffee, sugar, and some tropical fruits—that is, the Latin American countries—will bear the full brunt of "overseas territories loopholes" in the EEC tariff schedule.

In a similar vein, there is not likely to be any noticeable easing of the long-standing Western European discrimination against Asian industrial products. Much of this discrimination is directed against Japan, the only industrialized nation outside of Europe and North America. Being deficient in most industrial raw materials and far from self-sufficient in food production, Japan will undoubtedly feel severe payments pressures which will compel the Japanese to institute a comprehensive austerity program or to attempt to expand their exports to other world markets. If the latter alternative is pursued, the major Japanese export effort must be in the Western Hemisphere, where markets are sufficiently absorptive to provide a sizable new demand for the kinds of manufactured goods in which Japan finds its comparative advantage.

This line of argument suggests that, in addition to the *direct*

8. Preferential tariffs were extended to associate members of the EEC. These are the countries which at the time of the Rome treaty were dependent territories of France and Belgium, Madagascar, and certain overseas territories of Italy and the Netherlands. The associate members are, therefore, located predominantly in Africa. A list of these countries is in J. J. Van der Lee, "Community Economic Relations with Associated African States and Other Countries," *The Annals* (July 1963), 24.

displacement of American goods from Western European markets as a consequence of tariff manipulation, there is also likely to be an appreciable *indirect* impact on American exports to non-European areas. In the first instance, if the underdeveloped nations undergo substantial cuts in their export earnings, United States exports to them will dwindle. Since Western Europe is a larger purchaser of commodities from the underdeveloped countries than the United States, there is little doubt that their export earnings will be adversely affected. The group of Latin American countries, a particularly important customer of the United States, will perhaps be hardest hit. If this is the case, American exports to the underdeveloped areas can be sustained only by an appreciable surge of foreign lending to these areas or by increases in outright grants.

In the second instance, industrial or developed countries whose exports are directly and negatively influenced by European integration will make a concerted effort to recoup their losses by an export drive in non-European countries—to the probable detriment of American exporters. Should the export drive be frustrated, balance-of-payments pressures outside of Western Europe may build to such an extent that quick-acting counter-measures, mainly designed to reduce imports (including those from the United States) will be implemented. In any event, the *indirect* consequences of the trade displacement suffered by non-member countries, tending to reduce American exports, will compound the direct displacement of American goods from European markets. European economic integration is, then, the source of a pervasive depressant force on American exports.

The Creation of New Trade

EEC and EFTA successes may, nonetheless, create potentially powerful countervailing pressures, tending to increase United States exports. Indeed, there is close agreement among analysts of integration that new trading opportunities caused by rapidly rising income levels in Western Europe will more than offset trade losses the U.S. might suffer. The result should be a widespread increase in the exports of the United States and of non-member countries in general. There can be little doubt of this consequence of rising Western European incomes over the long run, provided of course that non-member countries' economies are responsive to the signals of the marketplace.

There is also room for skepticism, however. Underdeveloped countries have long been at a disadvantage because of an inability to adapt to economic change; indeed, regionalism is one way in which these nations can meet this deficiency. Moreover, the present state of the international financial system requires that governments adopt short-run planning horizons. Waiting for balance of payments and internal adjustments to work themselves out is a luxury that even the United States has difficulty affording. Exports to Western Europe will probably expand, but any expansion will be substantially less than the growth of intra-European trade.

Trade creation depends to a great extent upon the character of internal economic adjustment within the EEC and EFTA, and the ability of other countries to maintain competitive prices. One of the major elements of the EEC—and here, of course, it differs from EFTA—is its intent to rationalize the use of productive resources.[9] As integration progresses not only will intra-EEC traffic in goods be unfettered but the movement of factors of production will also be unrestricted. Unless factors of production outside of Europe can respond similarly to relative price pressures, or unless factor movements in the EEC are unresponsive to market pressures, a relative increase in the adaptability of the Common Market countries is inevitable. This will mean that,

9. The process of rationalization is difficult to define simply. It is perhaps best thought of as a reallocation of productive factors within the rationalizing region, so as to reflect cost and demand conditions in the relevant market on the assumption that these conditions are known with certainty. Rationalization would be a reflection of the decisions of an omniscient, omnipotent economic planner.

compared to recent performance, the EEC countries will react much more readily to simple alterations in supply and demand conditions and to dynamic technological and product innovations. Historical precedent strongly suggests that, in this event, EEC exports to non-member nations should expand even if imports increase. Thus, even though there may well be growth in American exports to the Common Market, this export expansion could be overshadowed by an increase of imports from Europe. On balance, a further deterioration in America's balance-of-payments position is possible.

Nonetheless, rising Western European incomes are fundamentally a prime mover of American export expansion. For one thing, if Europe should suffer a substantial recession, there would be a revival of protectionism as part of the defensive response to the reduction in output and income; but rising incomes would allay the demands of protectionists. For another, to the degree that Western European integration stimulates income growth, it will also stimulate exports from the United States and other non-member countries. This relationship is so certain as to be a fundamental "law" of economic analysis.

Yet this seemingly simple relationship is not without its complications. Income expansion is generally accompanied by an expansion of productive capacity and real output. If the increase in Western European output were similar to that which occurred in the postwar period prior to integration, the growth of European imports (and hence of American and other non-member countries' exports) would be greatly accelerated.[10] In the not too distant past, additional European income was largely expended on goods produced abroad, and prior to the mid-fifties substantially upon goods made in the United States. But these years were unusual and their pattern need not prevail in the future. In the immediate

10. Other necessary assumptions for the conclusion to be valid are that consumer tastes must not change and the distribution of income must remain unaltered.

postwar years Europeans were preoccupied with rehabilitation and recovery, and the United States was virtually the sole source of supply of badly needed goods. During the Korean War, Western Europe, like the United States, undertook a massive stockpiling program.

Even more to the point, however, is that the current rapid growth of European production is in part a result of the incentive which the customs union tariff differential gives to intraregional trade. The fact that some output expansion is the direct consequence of tariff changes suggests that some of the increase in productive facilities will be of the import-replacing variety. If import replacement occurs on a significant scale, an increasing share of internal European demand will be supplied by intraregional productive plants. Thus, while American exports will still be aided by income expansion in Western Europe, the relationship is not likely to be as strong as it once was.

Nor is this the only complexity. The rate at which the integrated region can expand productive facilities is also a crucial issue. On the one hand, if productive facilities rest idle—if there is substantial unemployment—then import replacement possibilities are enhanced and the relationship between Western European income growth and expansion in non-member country exports is weakened. On the other hand, if the economic expansion of Western Europe were to start from a condition of full employment, productive facilities (in general, as well as of the import-replacement type) could not be augmented as readily. Some of the increased incomes would spill over into demand for the exports of non-member countries, including the United States. Moreover, the drive to expand European productive capacity may be so intense that some of the new facilities must be supplied from sources outside the integrated area. Thus, when rapid income growth occurs during a period of substantially full employment, expansion of imports into the integrated regions will be larger than otherwise.

The rate at which productive capacity is used has yet another pertinent effect. It was argued above that United States exports will meet heightened competition in markets outside of Western Europe as non-member countries try to sustain the level of their exports in the face of trade diversion in Western Europe. The activities of Western European producers themselves in these outside markets must not be overlooked.

For some time the United States economy has operated at less than full capacity. In contrast, Western Europe, in the main, has been able to maintain full employment of its resources. The fact that there is little or no unutilized economic capacity does not seem to have affected Western Europe's power to export, contrary to what might be argued on theoretical grounds. Nevertheless, American producers have secured an advantage in that they can promise and make immediate delivery of goods, whereas Western European exporters are frequently unable to fill orders without appreciable delays, thereby reducing the attractiveness of their products. At the same time, the pressures of internal demand in the EEC and EFTA countries are pushing up the prices of Western European goods relative to American export prices. The loss of price competitiveness which some United States products have been sustaining until quite recently is being reversed.

From this line of reasoning it becomes clear that the rate of economic growth and cyclical conditions in Western Europe are of vital significance for the United States. Should the growth rate in Western Europe be maintained at its present high level it is likely that American producers will be able to expand their exports to outside markets and to Western Europe. The adverse consequences of trade displacement on exports will be more than compensated by the expansion of export markets. Conversely, if the Western European growth rate should slow down, or if the Western European economy should enter a recession while the United States does not, American exporters will find it increasingly difficult to sell in foreign markets.

Thus if the United States is to achieve and maintain a fully employed economy it is almost mandatory that Western Europe do so as well. As the Western European market becomes more completely integrated—more monolithic—so that it responds to cyclical conditions as a single unit, it is extremely doubtful that the United States economy could remain at a high level of operation when Europe is depressed. Europe no longer "catches pneumonia when the United States sneezes." Indeed, the direction of contagion might well be reversed.

The Impact on American Imports

The foregoing discussion provides some insight into the position of American imports. Here again, as in the case of exports, quantitative evaluation is a hazardous undertaking, but certain qualitative generalizations are feasible.

There are several reasons for supposing that American imports of agricultural commodities will not be appreciably altered because of integration. The United States is, of course, not entirely self-sufficient in agricultural products, its largest single item of import being coffee. By and large, any serious deficiencies are to be found in the products of tropical countries. In kind, Western European production is largely similar to American farm production. But the political power of the American farm bloc suggests that even were European producers able to meet the prices of American goods in the United States, the challenge would be effectively eliminated by protective legislation.

Western Europeans are not likely to be able to supply agricultural commodities at competitive prices, however. Agricultural products are relatively bulky compared to their value, and these types of goods, unlike manufactured items, have difficulty absorbing high transportation costs. Furthermore, increased protection of European agricultural producers under the EEC will not stimulate cost reduction. Even though the economies of large-scale operations are available and the size of agricultural production units is increased, the consequent cost reduction would have little economic relevance in the United States. The agricultural policy of the Common Market, by maintaining rather high internal prices, is designed to provide Europe with a relatively self-sufficient agricultural sector. Even if these high domestic prices generated an exportable surplus, and its export to the United States was substantially subsidized, import controls would prevent its entry into the American market. Thus a number of factors preclude the possibility that Americans will expand their imports of European agricultural products.

Similarly, Western European integration will not noticeably affect imports of industrial raw materials into the United States. Since, with rare exceptions, Western Europe has relatively few important raw materials available to exchange in world markets, any across-the-board reduction in materials production costs is likely to be reflected in the prices of European manufactured goods. Industrial raw materials will thus not become increasingly available for export. It is true that Western Europe's demand for crude materials will grow as its industrial capacity expands. So will that of the United States. Perhaps technological developments will permit the two industrial sectors to economize on the use of raw materials, but this process will occur independently of the movement toward economic integration. In any event, demand growth, juxtaposed to a rather limited flexibility of raw materials production, should exert an upward pressure on the prices of these commodities in world markets. Whether or not the response of raw materials users to this price pressure will result in an increase or decrease in expenditures on raw materials imports depends upon technical considerations. It is probable, however, that an increase in prices of industrial raw materials will intensify the search for domestic substitutes and the development of natural resource-saving techniques and products. As this economizing process works itself out, an unpredictable change in the commodity composition of United States imports will certainly take place. The postwar period has witnessed a rapid transition of this kind. Yet, based upon American experience, a good bet is that these factors will cancel out and that the aggregate percentage share of raw materials imports into the United States will remain relatively steady.

In analyzing the effects of European integration upon American imports of manufactures, the economic factors cited so far must be given freer play. Manufacturing protectionism is less deeply entrenched than protection for agriculture in both Europe and America. Additionally, one of the desirable consequences of the EEC will be the rationalization of European industrial production that increased factor mobility will facilitate. As tariff barriers to internal trade disappear, the competitive struggle will insure that, if productive capacity so permits, Western European manufacturing output will be available to outsiders at prices as competitive as possible.

Whether the reallocation of resources during integration will induce a substantial realignment of relative prices—the key signals in a market-oriented economy—is not altogether clear. Relative price adjustments favoring European producers, and hence tending to cause expansion of United States imports, will depend upon the existence of two conditions. As manufacturing is rationalized the resource reallocation must bring about appreciable economies in resource usage. Only then will the real costs of production in Western Europe fall. But this is not sufficient to bring about reductions in money costs. Economies of scale must be exploited, to be sure, but internal demand pressures must not be so great that the potential real cost savings evaporate in an increase in costs of production. Thus, provided that economies can be gained in large-scale production and internal demand prevented from becoming excessive, the Common Market will improve the competitive position of European manufactures in the American market.

Until now, Western European governments have been relatively effective in restraining inflationary pressures. As it becomes more difficult to expand productive capacity, however, and as labor markets become tighter, successful containment of inflationary forces is less certain. Perhaps as time passes consumers themselves will be more reluctant to forgo present consumption, so that total demand will be augmented by growing consumer purchase as well. Some offset to the price reductions permitted by large-scale economies and increased efficiency is a likely result.

Moreover, it is not altogether true that the large-scale production possible in an integrated Western Europe will yield substantial cost reductions. Certainly in some industries, although not in basic ones, enlargement of the internal market will make it possible to achieve significant cost savings. And as the current scientific revolution has its impact on European production techniques, economies of large-scale operations may open up more universally. But there is no good reason to suppose that technological innovation will be more beneficial to European than to American producers. If European productive resources are to be combined more efficiently, it will be because of increased competition—the elimination of less efficient producers—within manufacturing Europe.

That an intense competitive struggle among European manufacturers will take place is a foregone conclusion. Indeed, this is one element of the sacrifice which Europeans *seem* willing to make in order to improve their economic lot. European producers may not yet have felt the sting of increased competition because member countries' tariff rates are still high enough, even after a 50 per cent reduction, to afford appreciable protection. Nonetheless, it seems likely that in the foreseeable future European manufactured goods will gain a slight competitive edge over American goods in United States markets. Provided that European demand itself does not absorb the entire output of European manufacturing, a small increase in American imports of manufactured goods can be expected.

The Impact on Foreign Investment

One way to meet the problem of export displacement is to seek to reduce the level of the Common Market's external tariff barrier through intergovernmental negotiations. The "rounds" of tariff bargaining under the authority granted to the President by the traditional Reciprocal Trade Agreements Act were not, however, up to the task of meeting a common bargaining unit, the EEC. The Trade Expansion Act of 1962 was a new approach, giving the President greater bargaining latitude. It was undoubtedly a significant step, but its effectiveness cannot yet be judged; actual negotiations under its authority have still to be assessed. More important, however, Trade Expansion Act tariff bargaining need not be on a commodity-by-commodity basis, as has been the practice heretofore. Consequently, United States negotiators will not be able to pinpoint reciprocal tariff reductions so as to minimize the damage to American producers of import-competing goods. Any agreements will also create their own peculiar countermoves. Domestic repercussions, especially among import-competing industries, must be weighed in the balance. The net result of tariff bargaining is difficult to gauge, but a reasonable prospect is that American exporters will not be entirely successful in gaining access to Western Europe to the same extent as before economic integration.

The American business community may also overcome export displacement by establishing bases of operations behind the European tariff wall through direct foreign investment, either by erecting new or by purchasing existing productive facilities. Increasing market demand acts as a stimulus to American investment abroad, as does the potentially higher economic growth rate in Western Europe.

These factors are certainly a cause of the remarkable revival of American investment in Western Europe since the mid-1950's. From an average of less than $100 million per annum in 1950-55, American investment in Western Europe is now running in excess of $1 billion per year, and by far the greatest proportion of this increase is in direct investments. It cannot be established, however, that integration alone, and anticipation of it, is solely responsible for the surge of American foreign investment. It is not, for example, an adequate explanation of the startling rise in purchases of foreign securities, rather than operating plants per se, by American investors. Furthermore, several other relevant forces were at work. Stable exchange rates and the re-establishment of non-resident convertibility of Western European currencies in December, 1958, have acted as a fillip to United States foreign investment there. The concern of investors for the remittance of returns on their investment and repatriation of their capital lost much of its urgency. Moreover, the easing of tension in Europe, the decreasing possibility of war, and European support of "centrist" governments are equally reasons for the increased rate of American investment in Europe.

The expanded outflow of funds from the United States means that the American balance of international payments will tend to be in deficit unless exports can be increased relative to imports. Yet the formation of a successful customs union predisposes trade movements of the opposite sort. A strong impression exists, then, that integration in Western Europe is largely responsible for the serious balance-of-payments problems of the United States in the last half-decade.

There are, quite naturally, other elements in the American position which compound these difficulties. The competitive position of American products in world markets has until recently been declining, even discounting the effects of integration. There are also the vast sums spent abroad by the American government for economic aid to underdeveloped areas and in support of an overseas defense posture. These commitments are of course considered vital to the continued well-being of the United States. While a few people of extreme persuasions would question their advisability, efforts to curtail significantly either of these programs are not likely to succeed. Yet it has been repeatedly argued to some effect that since the United States payments deficit is partly attributable to Western Europe's economic renaissance, Europeans should shoulder some of the burden of American foreign commitments, particularly those which consume exceptional amounts of American foreign exchange earnings and which are of mutual interest.

Thus there are grounds for being pessimistic about our balance of payments in the near future; but in the longer run the situation is likely to change. The vigor of the forces tending to increase the American capital outflow is not likely to diminish; but neither is it likely to be strengthened. Economic expansion in the EEC and EFTA areas, or increases in their membership by the inclusion of other nations, would provide added inducements for American foreign investment. By way of contrast, however, the further liberalization of world trade on a relatively multilateral basis, even coexistent with proliferating regional groupings, and the possible lowering of external tariff rates in common market areas, increase the attractiveness of domestic investment. Furthermore, the added incentives to acquire capital holdings within the integrated regions are not necessarily cumulative. As one group of experts has reasoned:

> The factors which induced international investors to withdraw funds from the United States and to invest them in other countries for the purpose of reaching a new portfolio balance

> probably will not change. However, the reaction of international capital movements to these factors will change. The flow of funds needed to reach a new portfolio balance in which some European assets are held for the first time is greater than the flow required to maintain such a balance. Outflow of funds from the United States due to this factor will tend to be less in the future.[11]

It must also be remembered that foreign investment will, after a period of maturation, provide a counterflow of funds as earnings are brought home. There are conflicting estimates of the size and timing of this return, but all agree that it will in the long run be substantial.

Economic growth rates are also likely to change in response to international capital flows. In an economic system isolated from the rest of the world, where no international investment is allowed, a country's rate of investment—a prime determinant of the growth rate—is limited to the amount of saving it can generate domestically. While frequently a country may try to save more than it wants to absorb in capital formation, it is impossible to invest in excess of its saving. Where international investment is permitted, however, the domestic saving limit on investment breaks down. Provided that a country or region receives investment funds from abroad, it may enjoy capital formation in greater amounts than the saving it is able to provide from its own efforts. Conversely, the country supplying capital will be able to undertake less domestic investment than its rate of saving would otherwise warrant. Of course, differential rates of capital formation are not the only determinants of differential rates of economic growth. Changes in supplies of other factors of production and the rate of technological advance are obviously relevant. Yet capital is especially crucial to the growth process. It is a necessary productive factor in an advanced economy and the means by which technological ad-

11. Salant, *et al., op. cit.,* 125.

vances find their way into the productive processes. Increases in productivity of the economy would be inconsequential without capital formation. Thus investment has always been singled out for special attention by students of economic growth.

The fact that regional integration will tend to attract investment capital because of high profits implies a more rapid rate of economic growth for the integrated region and a retardation of growth in the area losing funds. Initially, integration will itself be an indirect cause of faster growth. Still there is a tempering factor. If it can be assumed that the availability of technological improvements is the same for all countries and that capital movements are relatively unrestricted (which seems reasonable for the North Atlantic economies), diminishing returns to investment will soon even out the productivity of newly formed capital facilities. After this adjustment is completed, relative growth rates will once again be set, by and large, by a country's capacity to save. Integration per se, however, does not seem to promote an increase in the propensity to save. Consequently, while the increase in the standard of living of the integrated area may well be permanent, the boost given to the economic growth rate by regional integration is a transitory condition. European incomes will undergo a permanent increase relative to American income levels, but there is no objective reason to believe that integration itself will necessarily eliminate the income gap.

A final characteristic of the post-integration pattern of foreign investment must be noted. For some time at least, because of shortages in European productive capacity, deficient European investment capital, the rationalization of European industrial activity, and the competitive struggle, new investment in the EEC and EFTA areas will normally have brighter profit prospects than net capital formation in other countries. This is one source of attraction that Western Europe holds for foreign investors, and other factors serve to reinforce this attraction. American investors are no more prone to this added inducement to invest in Western Europe than others. But Americans are the only major source of investment funds outside of Europe. The underdeveloped areas, and by long-standing tradition especially Latin America, are substantially dependent upon the United States capital market. Yet the inducements to invest in an integrated Europe are so strong, and the fear of nationalization of foreign-owned facilities by underdeveloped countries is so great, that American investment in the economically backward areas has fallen off precipitously in the last few years. In the world outside of Europe, American direct investment has been more than halved since the founding of the Common Market, and portfolio investment has fallen by about one-third. Total foreign investment by Americans has not been reduced, but it has been redirected toward Western Europe and, unfortunately, away from the more needy countries.

Why is this unfortunate? If capital formation is a vital component of growth in advanced economies, it is even more critical for underdeveloped ones. In these areas the great bulk of the populace lives at levels barely above subsistence. Domestic saving is so small and capital needs are so great that foreign investment funds often mean the difference between success and failure of development plans. All too frequently they mean the difference between life and death for many thousands of people. Yet investors are motivated by profits—not altruism—and even though investment yields are high in the underdeveloped regions, Western European integration offers the prospect of greater returns.

The resulting change in the geographic pattern of foreign investment, imbalanced as it is toward the advanced economies, may be of mortal consequence for some developmental programs. The pressures on the underdeveloped areas to redress this imbalance, by political or economic means, are difficult to overestimate. The demands of these areas will be particularly focused on the United States; they will be incessant, powerful, and perhaps conflicting and exorbitant. It is important, however, that the United States government, if it is to continue to exert leadership in today's world, respond sympathetically to the legitimate needs of the developing nations.

The Fundamental Challenge of Integration

The general features of the economic effects of regional integration upon the United States are now clear. The momentum of the common market movement will carry it forward for some time to come. In the near future, the balance of payments of the United States will remain more adverse than otherwise, as American exports are displaced and American imports are expanded because of heightened international price competition. The increased outflow of investment funds is a compounding factor. These short-run consequences of integration will cause internal dislocations and hardships as the working of the price system, somewhat sluggishly, induces adjustments in production and in the allocation of productive resources. Adjustments of one sort or another cannot be avoided. Moreover, for political and military reasons, the trend toward integration cannot be reversed by the United States, even if it were economically advantageous to attempt a reversal. But it is possible to try to channel the integration movement in desirable directions and to arrange a suitable response in the United States. These are the strategic policy avenues open to the United States.

As these short-run economic effects of integration unfold, there will no doubt be a hue and cry for a general withdrawal from the world community or, alternatively, for relief for damaged parties in the United States. The government cannot allow these demands to go unheeded. As one acute observer has put it, there must be a "mechanism for cushioning the impact of change on particular sectors of the economy. This is to make free enterprise *more* enterprising, because one of the main efforts of enterprise is using or abusing the government apparatus to prevent the necessity of change." [12] This kind of enterprise must be counteracted. Means must be available and instruments devised that will effectively combat the forces pushing the United States and other regions of the world toward isolationism and autarkic independence. Measures for enhancing the economic vitality of the underdeveloped areas must also be found. These general courses of action alone seem consistent with the United States position of world leadership.

In part the American response has been to try to shape the policies of economically integrated regions into as close an approximation of free trade as possible. This no doubt explains the vigorous backing given the United Kingdom in its attempt to join the Common Market, even though this would probably have brought greater short-run economic hardships to Americans. It also accounts for the passage of the relatively liberal Trade Expansion Act in 1962, when previous efforts to increase the President's tariff bargaining authority had never achieved resounding success. Likewise, it probably explains the administration's decision, against reasonable advice, to insist that agricultural commodities as well as manufactured goods be considered together in negotiations under the General Agreement on Tariffs and Trade. Other economic and political maneuvers all point to the same thing: the United States government is most reluctant to reverse the American-sponsored movement toward a free and multilateral world economy, nor is it willing to see a reduction in American political involvement in world affairs.

The other part of the American policy response is largely domestic. While the short-run consequences of economic integra-

12. H. G. Johnson, "Where the World Is Going," *Canada, The Commonwealth, and the Common Market,* ed. by W. B. Cunningham (Montreal, 1962), 132. It is to the point here to recall the "dislocation relief" provision of the Trade Expansion Act.

tion cannot help but injure the American economy, the long-run effects may be highly beneficial. This depends in part upon efforts to bring about a permanent reduction in the external tariffs of the common market areas and upon a commensurate reduction in America's own tariff protection. But equally important, and certainly more within the control of Americans, the longer-term gains from regional integration depend also upon the capability of the American economy to adjust to the external disturbance. Measures must be taken to increase the mobility of American resources so that relative price movements quickly initiate the proper sort of reallocation response. These measures are much easier to devise than to implement. They tend, moreover, to require positive action by the federal government. But to the extent that full resource utilization can be re-established and maintained in the United States, these inevitable adjustments will be less onerous. In short, the internal response to common markets will take directions that in any case will be highly desirable—toward full employment of all resources and toward a more efficient price mechanism. Successes along these lines will determine the extent to which Americans will realize the potential fruits of economic integration abroad.

The challenge of common markets to Americans is, then, truly elemental. As it is true that "economic isolation and political leadership are wholly incompatible" [13] and that freer trade and multilateralism are jeopardized by regional economic integration, a fundamental decision is inescapable. The many by-products of that decision cannot help but penetrate to the foundations of American social, political, and economic life.

13. The words are President Kennedy's. See *The Congressional Record* (January 25, 1962), 904.

BIBLIOGRAPHICAL NOTE

The literature, both critical and popular, on regional economic integration is voluminous. Perhaps the better of the comprehensive economics treatises are B. Balassa, *The Theory of Economic Integration* (Homewood, Ill., 1961), and R. Sannwald and J. Stohler, *Economic Integration: Theoretical Assumptions and Consequences of European Unification* (Princeton, 1959), both written for a professional audience. For the general reader, Emile Benoit, *Europe at Sixes and Sevens: The Common Market, The Free Trade Association, and the United States* (New York, 1961); P. Uri, *Partnership for Progress: A Program for Transatlantic Action* (New York, 1963); and Committee for Economic Development, *The European Common Market and Its Meaning to the United States* (New York, 1959) seem most useful. L. N. Lindberg, *The Political Dynamics of European Economic Integration* (Stanford, 1963) is a fine, up-to-date politico-administrative study of the EEC. Attention should also be directed to the series of essays edited by C. G. Haines, *European Integration* (Baltimore, 1957); U. W. Kitzinger, *The Challenge of the Common Market* (Oxford, 1961); the more wide-ranging work by S. Dell, *Trade Blocs and Common Markets* (New York, 1963); and "The New Europe: Implications for the United States," *The Annals* (July, 1963), an issue devoted entirely to a discussion of the progress and effects of regional integration. A valuable explanation of the performance and problems of predecessor European economic unions is the trilogy of studies by J. E. Meade, H. H. Leisner, and S. J. Wells, *Case Studies in European Economic Union: The Mechanics of Integration* (Oxford, 1962). No monographic studies on the regional economic movements in Africa exist, but the provocative essay of T. Balogh, "Africa and the Common Market," *Journal of Common Market Studies,* I, No. 1, raises a number of crucial issues. On Latin American integration, the papers by R. F. Mikesell and V. L. Urquidi in *Latin American Issues: Essays and Comments,* ed. by A. O. Hirschman (New York, 1961), and the monograph by V. L. Urquidi, *Free Trade and Economic Integration in Latin America* (Berkeley, 1962), are notable. Finally, *Economic Consequences of the Size of Nations,* ed. by E. A. G. Robinson (New York, 1960), and W. S. Salant, *et al., The United States Balance of Payments in 1968* (Washington, 1963) are brilliantly suggestive of the purely economic impact of regional economic integration. The discussion in the second half of this essay relies heavily upon the latter study.

There are, possibly, a number of ideas and points made in the text of this essay requiring documentation. Postwar planning in the early and mid-1940's can be studied in H. A. Notter, *Postwar Foreign Policy Preparation, 1939-1945* (Washington, 1949), and the first chapter of E. Strauss, *Common Sense About the Common Market: Germany and Britain in Post-War Europe* (London, 1958). On the role of the Marshall Plan in fostering integration in Western Europe, refer to H. S. Ellis, *The Economics of Freedom: The Progress and Future of Aid in Europe* (New York, 1950), and J. M. Jones, *The Fifteen Weeks (February 21-June 5, 1947)* (New York, 1955). For a discussion of the broad economic forces to which regional integration was partly a response, see W. Diebold, Jr., "The Process of European Integration," *Current History* (March, 1962); and P. A. Forthomme, "Some Complexities of European Integration," and K. Deutsch, "Towards Western European Integration: An Interim Assessment," both in the *Journal of International Affairs,* No. 1 (1962). Roadblocks to political unification in Western Europe are the focus of the contributions by S. K. Padover, D. Lerner, and T. V. Kalijarvi in the issue of *The Annals,* previously cited. A. Etzioni, "European Unification and Perspectives on Sovereignty," *Daedalus* (Summer, 1963), deals explicitly with the problems confronting economic integration as a means to achieving political unification.

The possible contributions of economic integration to the development of the underdeveloped regions are the subject matter of the works by R. F. Mikesell and V. L. Urquidi noted above. A valuable essay, because of its explicit concern for the impact of European integration on the growth prospects of the underdeveloped areas, is Douglas F. Dowd, "America and the World Economy: Second Thoughts on the Common Market," *Yale Review* (Winter, 1964). Arguments, by eminent authorities, that free, multilateral trade may lead to a widening difference in the living standards of developed and underdeveloped nations will be found in Gunnar Myrdal, *An International Economy: Problems and Prospects* (New York, 1956); H. W. Singer, "The Distribution of Gains Between Investing and Borrowing Countries," *American Economic Review* (May, 1950); and R. Prebisch in United Nations, Economic Commission for Latin America, *The Economic Development of Latin America and Its Principal Problems* (New York, 1950).

The ways in which the United States is likely to have to redirect its resources in adjusting to regional integration abroad are sketched in the study cited above by W. S. Salant, *et al.,* especially Chapter 4. That the required reallocation of labor may not be too taxing is suggested by O. R. Reischer in *Trade Adjustment in Theory and Practice,* U.S. Congress, Joint Economic Committee, 87th Cong., 1st Sess., 1961, 9-11. The role of the dollar in the international financial system and the potential hazards facing this system are cogently presented by R. Triffin, *Gold and the Dollar Crisis: The Future of Convertibility* (New Haven, 1960). R. N. Cooper, "The Competitive Position of the United States," in *The Dollar in Crisis,* ed. by S. E. Harris (New York, 1961), is a short, comprehensive account of the underlying reasons for the past and prospective balance-of-payment behavior of the United States. Major provisions and the implications of the United States Trade Expansion Act are discussed in the chapter by W. B. Kelly, Jr., "The 1962 Trade Legislation," in D. D. Humphrey, *The United States and the Common Market: A Background Study* (New York, 1962).

T. Scitovsky, *Economic Theory and Western European Integration* (Stanford, 1958), is one authority who believes in the importance and efficacy of an intensified competitive struggle in the EEC countries. This theme also runs through the compendium edited by E. A. G. Robinson, cited before. That a substantial reduction in manufacturing costs may not be achieved by the expansion of producing facilities consequent to integration in Western Europe is noted particularly by G. Marcy and T. Scitovsky in their contributions to the Robinson volume. The argument in this essay that integration will provide a temporary fillip, rather than a sustained boost, to the rate of economic growth, is questioned in Part II of B. Balassa's treatise mentioned above. J. O. Coppock, *North Atlantic Policy—The Agricultural Gap* (New York, 1963), Chapters 1, 2, and 11, provides a non-technical discussion of integration and government policy toward agriculture.

6

DEVELOPMENT AND INTERNATIONAL POLITICS

KALMAN H. SILVERT

THE troubling news that Communist China had detonated its first atomic explosion evoked widespread comment that it was also the first underdeveloped country to join the Nuclear Club. This statement explains more about atomic bombs than about modernization. Being underdeveloped does not describe a universal grey wash of poverty. In many cases, it also signifies more than a small plutocracy converting the energy of the unwashed into means for maintaining the elite in oriental splendor. There are many differing ways in which societies fail to be modern and many different styles of adjustment among the economic, social, and political ingredients of underdevelopment—or what may more aptly be called partial development. To return to a military example to underscore this point, an extensive atomic armory matched to long-range delivery systems makes the Soviet Union a first-rate military power; but its gross national product per capita still defines it as only intermediately developed.

When dealing with the emergent nations, the search for a pure definition of modernization is meaningless unless the great differences in societies are considered. France, to use an example of a country almost invariably assumed to be the prototype of early political development, shows a recent history of instability and personalistic leadership—sophisticated and grand as it may be—which is much closer to the political patterns of Argentina than many observers dare to let themselves think. The search for the quintessence of modernism might lead us even to cast doubt upon the modernism of the United States, entangled as it is in the agonies of a rather old-fashioned crisis, the integration of an ethnic minority into the fabric of national community. These definitional problems will plague us so long as we attempt to impose simple measures on complex situations. China's bomb is an evidence of development, just as France's political crises and America's racial agonies are of underdevelopment. No single criterion, taken by itself, can respond to the diversity of the mixtures of traditionalism and modernism, of backwardness and advance that we can expect to find everywhere. The study of political modernization is then in goodly part the analysis of these mixtures, of the differing accommodations to advancement and retardation that each changing society makes.

The contrariness of the processes of human change has often been noted. The folklore of specialists in development is based on two common axioms, only partially facetious. The first is that all development is asynchronous—out of phase, out of timing, warped and twisted. The second is that some of the problems of underdevelopment can be solved only by more development. These rules of thumb suggest that modernization everywhere must be a painful and destructive, as well as constructive, process, and that seemingly vicious circles must constantly arise to plague the policy maker.

To say that development does not proceed evenly raises questions not only of theory but of planning strategy. Scores of national leaders, in trying to program the growth of their countries, must make almost daily decisions as to whether to devote scarce resources to economic development, social reform, education, or any of the other numerous areas of obvious need. How these decisions of priority are to be made, how technical determinations are to fit ideological preferences, and where the greatest impact can be made, are matters not at all clear.

For example, some specialists insist that development flows automatically from economic advance. Others argue that economic development is not sufficient, that a people must also be organized socially to work with vigor and dedication, to be willing to sacrifice today for a better tomorrow, and to see that the fruits of production are so distributed as to make for a pluralistic and open society. Still others emphasize that the entire process depends on education and that no social progress can be made without the prior development of skills and talent. American foreign assistance policy has experimented with all three of these ways to break into the growth process efficiently. But no firm theory has yet emerged save for a stubborn faith in industrialism as the producer of modern societies and a less certain conviction that action must be taken on several fronts at the same time.

The second axiom, that some problems of underdevelopment can only be solved by more development, flows easily from the above questions of the strategy of growth. How can a country educate its citizens if it has not a taxable surplus? How can it have a taxable surplus if its citizens are so poorly trained that they are forced to live at subsistence? How can an illiterate populace support a development-minded government in the first place?

As difficult as these questions of strategy may be, the first step toward their resolution lies in knowing that vicious circles can be broken by international cooperation, and that strategies of development are being devised through the cooperative efforts of thousands of statesmen and physical and social scientists in both developed and underdeveloped countries. Before the modern period a hunger cycle in India had to run its terrible course before arrest; the weakened peasants produced less and less until so many died that what food remained for the survivors permitted a slow rebuilding of the economy and the populace. Now hunger cycles are halted by massive grain shipments from abroad, and the limits of indigenous resources no longer make death and suffering inevitable.

The knowledge that the advanced nations of the world can consciously and programmatically assist in the internal processes of change in the less privileged lands is a new factor in world events. The restlessness of the backward is not in itself sufficient to explain the emerging pattern of what are increasingly intercontinental as well as international relations. Instead, we must add the *effective awareness* of the relationship, which has come not only with vastly more expanded and intimate communications but with those revolutionary changes which the advanced states themselves are experiencing. The technological revolutions in industry and agriculture in the United States have produced domestic market surpluses as well as internal problems of employment and distribution; *internationally they have also widened the economic distance between the rich and the poor at the same time they have opened the possibilities for closer human relationships.* What appears to be an economic paradox may well be the basis for political rapport.

Let us examine this point in some detail. It is statistically undeniable that the advanced nations are enriching themselves much more rapidly than the retarded ones. For example, taking Latin America's increases in production together with the population expansion, we find that in approximately two hundred years—at present rates of growth—the per capita income of those twenty republics will finally be more or less equal to that of the United States today. In more general terms, an economist has recently written:

> The most basic and alarming feature of the underdevelopment problem is the fact that in the non-communist area the gap between the developed and the less developed countries is,

generally speaking, increasing in terms of real income per head.

> It has been increasing if we make comparisons over a relatively long period, say the last fifty years . . . over the last half century there has been little change in real income per head in most of Asia, traditionally the home of half the world's population. We all know that, by contrast, real income per capita has risen considerably in the West, especially in the United States, Western Europe, and a few high-income countries elsewhere such as Canada, Australia, and the white portion of South Africa.[1]

The statistics cited by this author show that between 1913 and 1957 the per capita national income of North America (excluding Mexico) rose from $917 to $1,868, while the same figures for Southeast Asia, for example, went from $65 to $67, for China from $50 to $61, for the Soviet Union from $100 to $463.

The enormity of the modernization task in merely economic terms is strongly suggested even by these few figures. Nevertheless, the very degree of development of the modern states introduces a new resource. That such words as "overdeveloped," "affluent," and "super-power" have come into the vocabulary of political economy suggests that the slow grinding of economic mills can be speeded up, that the harshness of the old iron laws of economics can be mitigated by new powers, if not new rules. These words also suggest that certain nations can export accumulated capital to other economically retarded ones. Thus the already low levels of consumption in many emergent countries need not necessarily be further depressed to force the savings needed for capital investment. Speed and a reduction of suffering can be simultaneously achieved.

Other factors also contribute to the uniqueness of the contemporary situation. The emergence of fifty-one new states from Asia and Africa since the conclusion of World War II has complicated the workings of international agencies, changed normal patterns of diplomacy, and threatens to transform the world power balance.

1. Jan Tinbergen, *Shaping the World Economy* (New York, 1962), 8.

At the same time the persisting Cold War, and especially its ideological dimension, have forced the major powers to woo the underdeveloped, not for the purpose of coveting their present power but to influence their future style of life and their allegiance. As the hundred countries of the underdeveloped universe begin to form their future institutions, the major powers have become vitally interested in the shape those institutions will take. More so than ever before, then, international politics is also intimately and vitally domestic politics.

The necessity to generate a fresh understanding of these events has been felt throughout American society from the halls of government to those of the universities, from the office of the ward heeler to the stumps of candidates discussing foreign aid and atomic war with their constituents. Just as the United States will never be the same because the world has changed so drastically in the last two generations, so the converse is also valid. Unhappily for simplicity, even the mere fact of change has changed: the velocity of social events is now so high as almost certainly to work a qualitative difference on the processes of social change. The stakes in the process of modernization are towering, and the excitement of the matter entrancing to the imagination.

> It is not mere rhetoric to speak of this attempted Great Ascent [the modernization process] as the first real act of world history. Certainly in size and scope it towers over any previous enterprise of man. For over one hundred nations, economic development means the chance to become a national entity, to live in the chronicle of recorded events. For over two billion human beings, it means something at once humbler and infinitely more important: the chance to become a personal entity, simply to live. . . .
>
> The Great Ascent is not merely a struggle against poverty. The process which we call economic development is also, and in the long run primarily, a process through which the social, political, and economic institutions of the future are being shaped for the great majority of mankind. On the outcome of this enormous act will depend the character of the civilization of

the world for many generations to come, not only in the poor and struggling nations, but in the rich and privileged ones as well.[2]

New Structure of International Power

The most obvious concern forced on the United States by the underdeveloped countries involves the structure of international relations, especially as it affects national security problems posed by the Cold War. It is frequently repeated that the United States is a status quo power in respect to the international system, and that the Soviet Union and many of the developing nations are revolutionary in their desire to find their place in global politics. This analysis leaves much to be desired. Specifically, it does not relate international happenings to domestic change and national ideologies where, at least in the underdeveloped world, the primary transformations are taking place. What, for instance, are the newly available techniques for change and resistance to change? How do these techniques fit into the power structures of the nations concerned? And, as governed by ideology and worries about "image," which techniques for the accomplishment of which ends are the several states prepared to use? The increased activity of Latin America, Asia, and Africa in the world imposes certain inhibitions on the major powers at the same time it opens new avenues of political action. Needless to say, the adjustment to new restrictions and freedoms is by no means concluded and has been a major source of contention in the making of American foreign policy.

A leading American student of international relations recently wrote, "The United States has at its disposal the greatest concentration of material power existing in the world today . . . it is the most powerful nation on earth. Yet the government of that most powerful nation is incapable of making the actions of even the weakest of foreign governments conform to its desires." The writer continues:

2. Robert L. Heilbroner, *The Great Ascent* (New York, 1963), 9-10.

> Some of these people [of the weak nations] have become active participants in the process of emancipation, and they now have governments that govern in their name and with their support. Thus, a strong nation intervening with military force may not accomplish its task by removing the government or even conquering the country. It may also have to subdue the population at large, which may take up arms against it. While these possibilities do not rule out the use of force, they make a powerful nation think twice before resorting to it.[3]

The examples of this difficulty in swaying the course of events in the modernizing countries are many, and include more than the obvious cases. The compromise solution in Korea, the supreme discouragement of the long French and American involvement in Vietnam, and the persistence in power of the Castro government in Cuba against intense American resistance are by no means the only illustrations of this dilemma of contemporary politics. They are the most dramatic, of course, for the three cases threatened that direct confrontation between forces of the United States and the Soviet Union which all Cold War diplomacy has been designed to avert. At a second level of crisis, where such confrontation has been a more remote possibility, the Congo and the Middle East and other areas also reveal not the mystical intransigence of events, but rather a qualitative shift in the nature of the elements of competition being brought to bear on world affairs.

Even at a third level, where long-term political relations are relatively free of immediate East-West crisis implications, agonizing difficulties have been encountered. Massive economic and political support did not prevent the Frondizi government of Argentina from falling; nor did the investment of major prestige commitments by the United States in support of democratic Latin American governments stop military *coups* from taking place in the Dominican Republic, Ecuador, Peru, Guatemala, Argentina, and Bolivia in the space of two years. Certainly these cases do not prove that *objective* American power is being lessened. In com-

3. Hans J. Morgenthau, "The Impotence of American Power," *Commentary* (November 1963), 384, 385.

pany with one or two other nations, we have the ability to destroy the world. Instead, it may well be that the *nature* of power and its relative *balance* are changing, and that what is required is full recognition of what it now takes to achieve desired ends.

One of the most obvious innovations worked by recent shifts in the international scene is the oft-remarked matter of "image," of the public relations consequences of the extensive communications systems lacing together the new publics that are on the scene. We are often told that American race relations should be improved if the "colored world" is not to lose faith in the United States as leader of the free world. Certain diplomatic and military actions unquestionably have been modified out of respect for the "looks" of things. Before the Bay of Pigs invasion of Cuba, for example, American diplomatic spokesmen carefully explained the matter to other Latin American governments in order to blunt charges of imperialistic intervention and to prepare them for possible internal reaction; the United States thus enlisted their neutrality if not their active support. If "image-building" has not actually changed policy (which cannot be firmly demonstrated), it certainly has modified the manner in which decisions are announced and carried out. Let us also note that the basic purpose of "image-building" is not alone to gather support for specific policies, but to create predictability in international affairs and promote the stabilizing effects of bloc power.

A second and closely related aspect of the relationship between power and its application is given institutional form in the United Nations. Increasingly, the General Assembly and such specialized agencies as UNESCO and FAO have become forums for continuing debate among the stable as well as emerging political blocs. If the United Nations has not been able to effect collective security measures where great-power sovereignty has been involved, it has provided the setting for continuing diplomacy, for the constant necessity to reason, bargain, and pressure for given measures. The breaking up of all the old colonial empires except for that of Portugal has been the single most important factor in changing the complexion of the UN. Only fifty-one members inaugurated the organization in January, 1946. By mid-1965 membership will have risen to 115, and the General Assembly facilities are being enlarged to include an eventual membership of 126.[4] This influx of new states has not only given a neutralist complexion to the UN but has also—and probably more importantly—introduced into the international arena the generation of national interests significantly different from those of the major powers. The expression of desires for rapid modernization, and the preoccupation with domestic politics such hopes reflect, have been attractive to all underdeveloped nations, and not only to those just coming into their sovereign own. The result has been to shake up traditional spheres of influence among such old but underdeveloped nations as Afghanistan, Iran, Liberia, and the Latin American states.

The third effect on international power of the aspirations of the underdeveloped nations, then, is to introduce a new set of interests which in themselves are changing old balances and prodding the established powers to new policies and techniques. In the most general of terms, the developing nations are not primarily concerned with the Cold War, East-West competition, or even such fundamental ideological worries as whether they should choose democratic or authoritarian devices for their polities. Instead they are almost monomaniacally concerned with rapid economic development and sovereignty.

The different bases of interest between the United States and the developing nations is perhaps best illustrated by the Cuban question. The United States interpreted a communized Cuba as a threat above all else to national security, then as an economic and ideological defeat, and lastly as a nuisance in the conduct of foreign policy. In contrast, during the early phases of the Castro regime the other Latin American governments saw the island as an experiment in development. Then slowly a perception of Castro

4. Thomas J. Hamilton, "A Crowded House," *New York Times,* November 1, 1964.

Cuba as an ideological and legal problem began to emerge. Only very late, at the time of the missile crisis of October, 1962, when nuclear war threatened, did Cuba become a basic security matter for these governments as well as for the United States. In consequence, at that almost ultimate stage of the game, for the first time the nations of the Organization of American States acted as a unified and unanimous bloc—a manifestation which has since not been repeated. This difference in priorities between the United States and its allies among the emergent nations is characteristic of the tug-and-pull of priorities in such other troublesome spots as South Vietnam, the neutralist nations of the Near East, and even in such seemingly stalwart allies as Pakistan.

The last important way in which the power balance has shifted is perhaps crudest—the use of overt military force. Modern automatic weaponry, much of it World War II surplus, has been widely distributed throughout the underdeveloped world, clandestinely and privately as well as through military aid programs. The appeals of nationalism amplified through the techniques of modern communications have provided reasonably able and sometimes extremely dedicated soldiery to use the weapons. The result has been to raise the cost of "policing" operations in such situations as the Congo and to make an Algerian war for independence such an enormous drain on French resources. Certainly the coming to independence of many former colonies has been hurried because of this simple military factor.

Meanwhile, inside the industrialized nations other substantive changes have been occurring which directly affect the way in which power is used in international affairs. In the subjective realm, there is some reason for the cautious argument that the use of force per se is coming under greater and greater question. Major segments of public opinion throughout the developed world are dedicated to the proposition that the use of coercive power in international relations should be an ultimate resource, that short of self-defense the peaceful conciliation of international dispute should be the rule. Certainly the still fresh horrors of totalitarianism in Europe and the mass annihilations of World War II have shaped some of these attitudes. Whatever may be the cautionary factors, there is no doubt that the full capabilities of modern military technology have not been unleashed in some part because of *moral* inhibition as well as fear of reputational damage. The mere mention of the possibility of using atomic devices for defoliation in Vietnam brought widespread negative reaction in the United States and abroad during the Johnson-Goldwater presidential campaign of 1964. No matter the pressure for a military solution to the Cuban problem, no responsible person has suggested the use even of conventional mass aerial bombardment, let alone atomic warfare.

The decision to limit the types of arms to be used in "brush-fire operations" can have massive political consequences. The case of Cuba is again appropriate here, for the arms provided the Castro government by the Iron Curtain bloc are important only relative to the self-imposed power restrictions of the United States. If responsible estimates of American casualties in a conventional attack on Cuba range upward from 100,000, and if the U.S. does not feel itself free (for internal as well as external reasons) to use its full arsenal, then any Cuban-American armed hostilities must take on the characteristics of what would have been full international war only a short generation ago. This example underscores significant changes in the nature of power balances. It is not merely that power ratios have changed (the nuclear countries are relatively *more* powerful than ever, as well as absolutely so), but rather that the very *nature* of force has changed with the ability to blot out total cultures. To assume that value systems are not accommodating to this new fact, to assume that the hand of the U.S. is stayed only by fear of damage to its "image," is to presume a conscienceless people—and also to fail to understand at least one reason why preventive war against the USSR was abjured, and why the world has so far survived the Cold War with such relatively limited military consequences.

Another impact on American domestic politics of the new shape of underdevelopment may be seen in the rapidly increasing politicization of the Negro population. The Black Muslim movement, whose ideological inspiration from abroad is obvious, provides us only with the readiest example. Many commentators have speculated that the feeling of greater confidence permeating the American Negro community is buttressed by the emergence of new nations south of the Sahara, whose troubled early national histories are given wide coverage in the Negro press. Ethnic minorities other than the Negroes have been culturally supported in their integration by a pride in their pasts which they can reinvest in their new nation. The American Negro, stripped of native language and culture and constantly informed of his "inherent" inferiority, cannot but feel a racial vindication with the creation of Negro cultures wrapped into the pseudo-modern structure of the sovereign nation-state. In turn, the eruption of the Negro into American national political life cannot but have consequences on relations with the entire world, developed as well as underdeveloped.

The use of American power to contain the communist nations has traditionally been justified not alone as crude self-defense but also as a policy to allow the internal dynamics of those nations to push them toward more open societies. At the same time, the major governmental spokesmen of containment have argued a *moral responsibility* in becoming self-appointed policeman to the world. This duty has been constantly to better American society to serve as an example of the possibilities inherent in democracy for fruitful human dignity. As George F. Kennan, a major architect of containment, put it:

> Any message we may try to bring to others will be effective only if it is in accord with what we are to ourselves, and if this is something sufficiently impressive to compel the respect and confidence of a world which, despite all its material difficulties, is

still more ready to recognize and respect spiritual distinction than material opulence.[5]

Self-interest and responsibility have sprung together in the American attempt to evolve new policies to meet the restlessness of the developing world. The budgetary effect of economic and military aid programs is mild compared to the impact that the process of development has had on patterns of American diplomacy and the preoccupations of the American intellectual community. Foreign aid programs are, however, a way to begin to comprehend the breadth of the problems posed by the emergent nations and the depth of their impact on American life. This is no less true in the light of contemporary rethinking of the political and economic usefulness of foreign aid as an instrument of national policy.

Foreign Aid as Modernizing Technique

Assistance to foreign countries has become a standard part of the repertory of international relations since the last war. It is not that capital and technical expertise did not flow in international channels before 1945, but rather that the effort itself has become a self-conscious part of governmental programming, and the massiveness of the endeavor is balanced only by the urgency of the need. The United States is by no means the only one of the developed nations to incorporate assistance programs into the conduct of its foreign relations. Indeed, four other states devote

PERCENTAGE OF GROSS NATIONAL PRODUCT DEVOTED TO AID PROGRAMS AMONG MAJOR POWERS

France	2.4%
United Kingdom	1.3
Netherlands	1.2
Federal Republic of Germany	1.0
United States	0.9
Italy	0.9
Japan	0.6

[Source: *Chronique Sociale de France,* Nos. 4-5, June 30, 1964, 222.]

5. *American Diplomacy: 1900-1950* (Chicago, 1951), 154.

a higher percentage of their gross national products to such programs than does the U.S.

Because of the high income level of the U.S., this intermediate percentage figure can be converted into the highest absolute figure. Total American aid between 1954 and 1959, for example, was $7,476,000,000, as compared to that of France (still spectacularly high for that country's economy) of $4,117,000,000. The following table gives the real numbers for the activities of the major donor nations.

BILATERAL ECONOMIC AID TO NEWLY DEVELOPING COUNTRIES
1954–1960
(in millions)

	Grants	Net Loans	Total
Total	[$10,352]	[$3,199]	[$13,551]
Australia	183	2	185
Belgium	10	56	66
Canada	207	37	244
France	2,982	1,135	4,117
Federal Republic of Germany [a]	5	71	76
Italy	42	119	161
Japan	179	—	179
Netherlands	105	14	119
New Zealand	26	1	27
Norway	4	—	4
Portugal	1	14	15
Sweden	2	—	2
United Kingdom	615	254	869
United States	5,991	1,485	7,476
Yugoslavia	—	11	11

Note: Years are fiscal years ending in year given.

a. 1959 only.

Source: Jan Tinbergen, *Shaping the World Economy* (New York, 1962). Ultimate sources: United Nations *Statistical Yearbook 1958* and *1960* (New York, 1959 and 1961).

In addition to bilateral assistance programs, the developing nations also have recourse to a large number of international bodies, most of them specialized agencies of the United Nations. The major organizations providing multilateral technical assistance are the Food and Agriculture Organization, the World Health Organization, the United Nations Educational, Scientific and Cultural Organization (UNESCO), United Nations Technical Assistance, the International Labour Organization, the International Civil Aviation Organization, the World Meteorological Association, the International Telecommunication Union, and the International Atomic Energy Agency. Multilateral capital assistance (as distinguished from the technical assistance agencies just listed) is provided by the International Bank for Reconstruction and Development, the International Finance Corporation, United Nations Special Fund, the International Development Association, the European Development Fund, and the Inter-American Development Bank.

How much capital flow would be "sufficient" to answer the needs of the emergent countries is, of course, a most debatable matter. Some estimates claim that little better than $5 billion annually for developmental purposes alone (excluding military assistance) could make the underdeveloped economies slowly self-sustaining. United Nations estimates are that $19 billion annually, almost four times the current rate of $5 billion, will be needed to double annual per capita income in the backward areas within thirty-five years. Some demographers, however, pessimistic about the explosive expansion of world population, estimate the need at over $60 billion annually to achieve a doubling of per capita income within the next thirty-five years. This wide disagreement reveals the roughness of the estimates being used, the vagueness of the criteria of sufficiency, and much doubt concerning the proper strategies of economic, social, and political development. Nevertheless it is clear that developmental moneys wisely used can have an amplified effect in stimulating development. An economist underscores the point that some capital is more useful than other capital for growth:

> . . . measured against the monumental problem of underdevelopment as a whole, the flow of foreign aid seems insignificant. The five billion dollars a year amout to no more than 2 or 3 per cent of the total output of the underdeveloped world, to less than 15 per cent of its total export earnings.
>
> Yet it is not small in relation to one still more critical figure —the amount of new capital which the underdeveloped nations manage to accumulate each year. *Foreign aid amounts to nearly 30 per cent of all capital formation in the underdeveloped world,* excluding only mainland China.[6]

Although foreign aid has enjoyed bipartisan support in Congress until recent years, the program has come under increasing annual fire from some liberal as well as conservative critics, and has frequently suffered from an uncertain defense by its advocates. Since 1962 the attacks on foreign aid have grown more weighty and widespread, centering not only upon questions of maladministration and waste but upon a growing doubt concerning the effectiveness of the instrument itself. The matter has become so beclouded with controversy and so subject to misinterpretation and misuse of facts that a rapid review of the rationale of American assistance programs is in order here.

The new American commitment to foreign aid was first enunciated as the famous fourth point of President Truman's Inaugural Address of January 20, 1949. He stated at that time:

> Fourth. We must embark on a bold new program for making the benefits of our scientific advances and industrial progress available for the improvement and growth of underdeveloped areas. . . .
>
> For the first time in history, humanity possesses the knowledge and the skill to relieve the suffering of these people [the underdeveloped "half of the world"]. . . .
>
> Greater production is the key to prosperity and peace. And

6. Heilbroner, *op. cit.,* 114. Italics in original.

> the key to greater production is a wider and more vigorous application of modern scientific and technical knowledge. . . .
> Democracy alone can supply the vitalizing force to stir the peoples of the world into triumphant action, not only against their human oppressors, but also against their ancient enemies —hunger, misery and despair.

Here is the core of the argument still used for the justification of assistance programs: the felt obligation to share; the argument that such sharing will be beneficial to the United States as well as to the recipient nations; the awareness of ideological threat from the communist bloc; and the simple faith that all ends can be reached by economic advance, "the key to prosperity and peace."

These views have since been expressed by all responsible executive officers. For example, Secretary of State John Foster Dulles, speaking before the Senate Foreign Relations Committee on January 19, 1959, stated:

> Unless and until the less developed areas reach the stage of self-sustaining economic growth, the world as a whole will suffer. For the inhabitants of those areas, an increasing rate of economic development has become an essential condition of free societies. The demand for economic and social betterment is now universal, and, if progress cannot be achieved in freedom, it will be sought by methods that jeopardize freedom.[7]

Dean Rusk, speaking before the Assembly of the United Church Women in Miami on October 11, 1961, continued the theme: "Whenever an underdeveloped country makes economic, social, and political progress, it expands the frontiers of freedom. Wherever we cooperate in breaking down the barriers of ignorance, poverty, disease, and despair, we further not only the well-being of mankind but our own security."

One of the major confusions in explaining foreign aid to the public, however, has stemmed from combining the immediate

7. Public Services Division, Bureau of Public Affairs, Department of State, Series S, No. 77.

problems of military defense with the long-term problem of assisting national communities which are self-consciously certain of their identities and their own ideological reasons for identification with the West. Of the $31,176,787,000 expended for aid between 1949 and the end of 1963, fully $26,026,741,000 went for what is called "Defense Support/Special/Supporting Assistance," or military aid.[8] Some $1,595,264,000 was expended for technical cooperation and development grants, $1,372,368,000 for development loans, and other amounts (including quotas paid into international assistance organizations) totaled $2,182,414,000.

This mingling of military with long-range developmental assistance, in which the lion's share has understandably gone to the former in this era of Cold War, has made for difficulties in rationalizing and explaining the programs at home and abroad. Some Latin American leaders, for example, complain to the United States that their entire continent and a half received less in combined assistance than Korea or Taiwan. American opponents of assistance, for their part, complain that funds are being given away, that military aid does not guarantee the loyalty of the soldier, and that recipients are often jealous and ungrateful. If, on the other hand, the various programs making up the total aid package were analyzed separately, public opinion could be formed more rationally.

In the most general—and perhaps most fundamental—sense, American military assistance has accomplished its limited purposes in most places by combining aid with a direct American presence. The Korean stalemate established a *status quo ante* and contained communist expansionism. The security of Taiwan falls in the same category. The rents in the containment package are primarily in Vietnam and in Cuba, and in the latter case the military aspects of pre-Castro relations were not of the first order

8. From Statistics and Reports Division of the Agency for International Development.

of importance. In another context, however, military assistance has sometimes led to unwanted domestic political consequences in the form of armed revolts and destruction of fragile civilian governments. The most notorious cases are in Latin America (Peru, Honduras, the Dominican Republic, and Bolivia, among others already mentioned), but South and Southeast Asia, in such lands as Pakistan and Iran, also show the strain on local events of armies supported by the United States.

The immediate effects of developmental and disaster aid, however, cannot be assessed in such contemporary frames of reference. The need to offer economic assistance is confused by the realization that development invariably brings in its wake political instability as nations seek to adjust their polities to changing economies and accompanying social shifts. After all, modernization is a total process. If it involves the creation of new cities, industries, governmental organizations, and educational systems, it also involves the creation of a new kind of person. This "modern" person, so to speak, must be relativistic in his thinking, pragmatic, and experimental. He must also have the capacity to be "empathic," to look across class lines and identify with unknown persons at a far physical remove who form with him part of the national community. The citizens of no country are uniformly modern in this sense, of course. But in the developing lands there are cases in which cave dwellers, nomads, isolated villagers, peasants and landlords, and sophisticated urbanites must seek to adjust their strikingly different modes of life at least on some basis of minimum compatibility.

As these problems of accommodation become apparent, the naive optimism of many leaders of the emergent world becomes deeply shaken. The easy formulae become traps. They soon find, for example, that partial industrialization commits their nations to the importation of raw and semi-elaborated materials to keep the new plants in operation. Then their balance-of-payments problems become acute, and they almost invariably see trade itself as a form of aid and attempt to stabilize the prices of their raw materials on world markets.

This seemingly obvious progression of events underscores the intricacy of development as a global problem, for the fixing of world price levels involves extremely thorny and delicate domestic questions as well as new theories of value and the marketplace. The stabilization of the supply of such commodities as wheat and coffee on world markets has a long history of experimentation, but such agreements have proved to be fragile reeds in moments of major surplus or of supply changes resulting from political upheaval. Still, the drive toward direct price stabilization (instead of indirect price stabilization through control of supply) is increasingly becoming a part of the foreign policy objectives of many underdeveloped lands. Mr. Raúl Prebisch, former head of the United Nations Economic Commission for Latin America, has stated the case for such stabilization:

> In 1950 the great industrial nations dedicated only about 0.3% of their total international income to expanding the resources of nations undergoing development. In 1962 this figure had increased to 0.7%.
>
> This figure, however, does not provide us with a sufficient motive for rejoicing since the deterioration of price relations has dissipated the positive effect of those financial resources to such a degree that if we deduct the losses caused by unfavorable price relations from the transference which the developing nations received in 1962, we find ourselves faced with a perplexing situation. The proportion of resources which the industrial nations transferred to the periphery of world economy in 1962 was still 0.3%—exactly the same figure which appeared in 1950.[9]

9. Speech on the occasion of the inauguration of the Geneva Conference on Commerce and Development as reported in *Cuadernos,* No. 85 (Mexico, June 1964), and cited here from *CIF Reports,* III, No. 10 (Mexico, September 16, 1964), 1.

That developmental assistance has become a useful and institutionalized part of American foreign relations is clear. To excise it from the American quiver of international resources seems impossible. Some of the more obvious questions having to do with developmental aid, however, can be summarized as follows:

1. How can the various types of American aid be made understandable to the American public? How can the *varying measures of effectiveness* for each type be made known and debated?

2. How closely should the granting of developmental assistance be linked to specific political occurrences? Should the criteria for the extension of development loans be conditioned by such emergencies as a budgetary deficit or a barracks revolt in a friendly nation?

3. Closely linked to the above point, the matter of the proper administrative relationship of the Agency for International Development to the State Department is still a matter for debate. How administratively independent should one be of the other, if at all?

4. How can the flow of private foreign capital be encouraged?

5. How can those other developed states which so far are doing little be incorporated into the general effort?

6. How can American governmental, foreign governmental, private, and international multilateral programs be coordinated effectively?

Even these questions, however, leave the basic incognita unrevealed. What is the nature of modernization? How does development occur? What is the order of events? How can outside assistance be used most effectively and efficiently? What is the *total* nature of outside influence? How much does ideology (as well as money and technical assistance) count in the process? It is partially in the answer to these questions that the eventual outcome of the ideological conflict between East and West depends. Also at stake is the degree to which the process of modernization may be long and bloody—or as short and as respectful of human life and dignity as possible.

Studies of the Underdeveloped World

The search for appropriate questions concerning development is becoming increasingly important in the major institutions of American society. Until World War II American universities did little systematic research into the underdeveloped areas. Asian studies centers were the major exception, some of them dating back even previous to the First World War, for to be a Sinologist was a recognized and prestigious profession. Egyptologists, too, were to be found. These occupational titles, however, strongly suggest the nature of their investigations: so few scholars were to be found in the several disciplines that those persons working in exotic areas were forced to be "area generalists," to cover the entire range of interests normally spanned by the array of university departments in the social and humanistic disciplines. Archaeologists and anthropologists were usually the central figures around whom foreign studies centers were built, and many of them succeeded in building invaluable museum collections. Individual students of literature and the arts also contributed their professional energies, as did a few historians, but political scientists, sociologists, social psychologists, and economists were rarities in these endeavors.

This neglect was the product not only of a lack of material resources. Much more important was the fact that today's feverish changes had not yet seized upon the developing areas, and that the social sciences, in particular, were conceptually and technically unprepared to tackle the dynamics of modernization. By the 1920's modern American sociology was just beginning to emerge from its social work and muckraking beginnings. The work of Durkheim, Mannheim, and Weber was not yet widely diffused and digested, and Parsons, Merton, and others of the contemporary American school were still to appear. Modern quantification was in its earliest stages, and of course the computer revolution was yet to occur. Economics had already received its push into macrocosmic approaches with the work of Keynes and his followers, but the econometricians had not yet bloomed and the discipline in general was ever deepening its belief in a set of general principles of universal application which still hobbles the work of some economists in cultures outside the modern continuum. The other social sciences were, with the exception of anthropology, not yet upon the trail which was to lead to their present profuse expansion.

World War II made clear to government and the great philanthropic foundations the widespread academic inadequacy in providing descriptive analyses as well as theoretical insights for the policy maker in government and business. The first efforts to broaden such knowledge were directed at proliferating the area studies approach in which the university community already had experience. A rapid expansion of language instruction, supported by the techniques learned during the war, was related to the growth of interdisciplinary area centers or committees in many universities. Then, as factual accumulations broadened and academicians of deeper specialization could emerge, "interdisciplinary committees" began to cede to "multidisciplinary committees," and such labels as "Sinologist," "Egyptologist," and "Latin Americanist" began to wear away. This first phase lasted more or less from 1946 to 1952, and then—without a drop in the number of area committees—the more specialized groupings grew. Naturally, these developments did not occur evenly. The Asian centers, the oldest of all, have continued to thrive and still lead the field in total numbers by far. African studies became modish in the mid-fifties, available resources drawing many scholars to that part of the world. The Latin American vogue began later, with the advent of Castro, and has continued unabated into the mid-sixties. Concomitantly, language instruction has also bloomed. "Where once French, German and Spanish were the only languages commonly taught in this country, the 153 graduate centers [of language and area studies programs] alone now offer over 155 languages, ranging from Afrikaans to Zulu. These figures are striking. Some 50 languages are available at the undergraduate level." [10]

The growth of language and area studies programs, and of the various kinds of research centers dedicated to international subjects, can be seen in the following tables:

GRADUATE LANGUAGE AND AREA STUDY PROGRAMS BY WORLD REGION

	1954	1956	1959	1962	1964
Africa	3	6	6	13	16
Asia	22	35	35	42	48
Latin America	11	19	19	29	30
Near East	7	12	13	18	18
Russia & Eastern Europe	16	21	19	34	34
Western Europe	5	6	5	8	8
Totals	62	81	96	136	153

Note: Totals refer to number of centers. This number is smaller than the language and area offerings.

Source: Department of State, External Research Staff, "Memorandum to Members of the Foreign Area Research Coordination Group (FAR)," September 14, 1964, 2.

10. Department of State, External Research Staff, "Memorandum to Members of the Foreign Area Research Coordination Group (FAR)," September 14, 1964, 2. The External Research Staff distributed a printed directory of all academic institutions involved in foreign studies at the end of 1964. For a perhaps more readily available but narrower source, see Association of American Colleges, *Non-Western Studies in the Liberal Arts College* (Washington, 1964), a Report of the Committee on International Understanding.

INTERNATIONAL AND GEOGRAPHIC AREA RESEARCH CENTERS
1964

International Research	No. of Centers	Geographic Area Research	No. of Centers
International Programs	34	General	2
Economic Growth	18	Africa	12
Political Development	7	American Republics	19
Socio-Cultural Change	6	Asia General	8
Agriculture	6	Middle East	5
Education	4	South Asia	8
Population	5	Southeast Asia	6
Totals	80		60

Source: Department of State, External Research Staff, "Memorandum to Members of the Foreign Area Research Coordination Group (FAR)," September 14, 1964, 3.

The same source estimates that there are some 850 *senior* researchers alone working in American universities in all aspects of foreign investigation. Certainly there must be many thousands of junior persons either in training or in the early stages of their professional careers. In 1964 the Social Science Research Council and the American Council of Learned Societies, jointly administering the Foreign Area Fellowship Program inherited from the Ford Foundation, made 229 research appointments. Forty were in the African Studies Program, eighty-three in the Asia and Near East Studies Program, thirty-five in the Latin American Studies Program, sixty-two in the Soviet and East European Studies Program, and only nine in the Western European Studies Program. These grants are given both to pre-doctoral and post-doctoral applicants.

This flourishing of interest and attention, supported by the Carnegie Corporation and the Rockefeller and Ford Foundations among many others, cannot immediately make up even quantitative deficiencies, of course. The nation is still drastically short of trained experts in many social science fields pertaining to Latin America, for example. It will also be readily understood that crash programs can manage to compress time only to a limited extent, that rather lengthy periods of maturation are required before persons working in underdeveloped lands acquire their area skills (language, a broad knowledge of the culture concerned, and so forth), root themselves deeply into the theory and methods of their disciplines, derive theories and research instruments appropriate for their areas, and then actually carry out their research and impart their knowledge through teaching and publication.

Part of the knowledge deficit, however, is being made up by scholars in the underdeveloped lands themselves. Here an even greater skewing of interest is taking place, with most academic inquiry being directed toward economic subjects, and anthropologists and sociologists following along. Very little political science or social psychology is undertaken, and historical work is still in the realm—by and large—of polemical studies designed to discover myths of the past which can serve in the contemporary task of nation-building.

The reason for the pre-eminence of economics is obvious. The common view, already referred to, that economic change is the basis for all other development flows into the mainstream of Marxist economic determinism, an attractive framework for many scholars in the underdeveloped world. In addition, economics appears the most exact and the least culture-bound of all the social sciences, and it satisfies an ideological wish: that the only phenomenon separating developed from underdeveloped persons is their level of economic advance; that other elements of culture are of equal worth, respectability, or validity. Latin Americans are often told by solicitous Americans (even by the late President Kennedy) that they have much of the material life to learn from us, but that we in turn can learn from them their cultural and spiritual richness. To what extent this statement is valid we shall address ourselves below, but for the moment the belief that economic advance is the cornerstone of all other development serves to explain the emphasis given this discipline in the underdeveloped world. International organizations have consecrated this view in such agencies as the UN Economic Commission for Latin America and its counterpart organizations in Africa and Asia.

The reasons for a strong interest in anthropology and sociology are almost as obvious as those explaining the growth of economic studies. Pre-literate cultures and the techniques for their modernization provide the grist for entirely academic as well as applied anthropologists. And where industrial urbanization is more advanced, as in some Islamic lands and Latin America, sociologists have sprung up to seek means to mitigate the costs of industrialization, just as in the United States. Almost all the social scientists of modern stripe working in the emergent nations have been trained either in Western Europe or the United States. They are increasingly sensitive to theoretical and methodological innovations, especially in the United States, and already are contributing significant work to the corpus of social studies.[11]

This broadly expanding interest in the problems of development

11. See, for example, the studies on urbanization edited under the sponsorship of UNESCO by Philip M. Hauser. Some of the titles of these important contributions to the comparative study of urban growth are *Urbanization in Latin America, Urbanization in Asia and the Far East,* and *Social Implications of Industrialization* and *Urbanization in Africa South of the Sahara,* all published by International Documents Service. These studies afford the most easily available introduction to the work of some of the best sociologists in the underdeveloped lands. As a continuing source of great importance, see the *International Social Science Journal,* and for the degree of academic involvement in broadly cross-cultural approaches, especially the issue entitled *Data in Comparative Research,* XVI, No. 1 (1964). The creation of an International Social Science Council and the expected establishment of such regional groups as a Latin American Social Science Council, as well as the growing importance of international disciplinary associations in the social sciences, all give evidence of the increasing self-study being undertaken among scholars outside the Western world.

is opening new intellectual ground for the American academic community and raising many problems of theory and method that are far from resolution. The fascination with comparative studies which has seized on persons in almost all social science disciplines is perhaps the major reflection of the necessity to order and integrate the vast new knowledge becoming available. Enormously difficult matters of academic freedom and the order of research have also arisen. A trained specialist turning to foreign fields usually does not care to concern himself with questions of a particular area or of a broadly "cultural" nature, but unless such information is available to him he may develop insufficient instruments of research and misinterpret his data. Conversely, very extended and synthetic studies suffer if there are no "hard" data concerning, for example, demography, land tenure systems, economic productivity, and even attitudes and values. The efficiency of order and the freedom of the inquirer to choose his own subjects is an inherent academic tension being aggravated during this period of scarcity and expansion in the study of development.

What of the quality of this new research into development problems? Certain major trends are clearly becoming visible which promise to affect fundamentally the theory and content of the social sciences and certain areas of the humanities. At the risk of simplifying, I should like to suggest some of the effects being felt immediately in certain disciplines.

Sociology and social psychology have until very recent years been highly parochial in their subject matter, limiting themselves almost entirely to American and Western European examples. Now we are witnessing a veritable explosion of these fields into the underdeveloped world and the rapid generation of all types of theories to explain the modernization process. Theorists are increasingly devoting themselves to the problems of change as such, and the sub-discipline of political sociology in particular is gaining new practitioners who find it easy to work with colleagues in the underdeveloped areas who themselves have an understandable drive toward mingling the institutional and social structural approach of the sociologist with the power questions raised by the political scientist. Comparative sociology is invading the subject matter of American courses on the family, social structure, urbanization, and other staples of the sociological diet. Sociology and social psychology will never again be the same.

Political scientists, who have long counted comparative government as a standard part of their discipline, have been engaged in a massive effort to enrich their theoretical and technical tools and to broaden comparative *government* into comparative *politics*. With extensive foundation assistance, and with the enthusiastic support of specialists in comparative government, political behavior, theory, and area studies, the literature has grown rapidly and with high quality. Within the space of a decade the discipline has generated enough materials and sufficiently distinct approaches to be able to engage in a fruitful Great Debate concerning the nature of political development and the most efficacious means and sites for its study. The eclectic and permissive nature of many of the discipline's leading scholars has served to fertilize this effort and to make ready room in major academic departments for this expansion.

The very strengths of economics, however, have somewhat impeded the efforts of those scholars seeking to take a fresh look at the problems of economic development. Many economists in the underdeveloped countries are "structuralists"—they presume that economic development depends in some measure on structural or institutional changes in their countries. The discipline in the United States and Europe, however, has long taken a given structure for granted and has made great analytical advances by emphasizing *functional* relations. Further, the divorce of the last century between economics and politics has been ratified in this one by the deep conviction of many economists that they can and should give only "pure" economic advice, and that political matters must not be considered in their recommendations. Many economists both at home and abroad, therefore, view other social factors as nuisances in their endeavors. As one renowned Mexican economist has put it:

> Theories about motivations and attitudes, and about the rational or irrational behavior of different sectors of society . . . are of little economic interest or urgency. The economist can easily name the social requirements for economic development but he expects the sociologist and other social scientists to indicate how to surmount the social and institutional obstacles to growth.[12]

This posture toward the discipline has made those economists who seek area competence and who employ an institutional approach somewhat suspect among their colleagues at large. The tendency has been combated by individuals who are devoting themselves more intensely to growth problems as such. In addition, the development of labor economics and the increasing emphasis given by certain researchers to education has served further to broaden the discipline and to make it more relevant to the questions being asked in the other social sciences.

Anthropologists, too, have begun to broaden their inquiries drastically. As the explosion of Western developmental techniques constantly erodes the available supply of pre-literate societies to be studied, anthropologists have followed migrants from the village to the city and have begun to apply their techniques and their questions to literate, historical, and even highly urbanized persons. The "culture of poverty" approach popularized for Mexico[13] is but one example of a tendency which has been enlarging since the opening of the debate concerning the nature of folk cultures and their relationship with the effectively national

12. Victor L. Urquidi, *The Challenge of Development in Latin America* (New York, 1964), 77.

13. See the work particularly of Oscar Lewis in his well-known studies, *Five Families: Mexican Case Studies in the Culture of Poverty* (New York, 1959); and *The Children of Sanchez: Autobiography of a Mexican Family* (New York, 1961).

communities rapidly being strengthened throughout the "third world."

This hurried listing could easily be extended to cover such fields as comparative religion, comparative literature, and so forth. For example, the effects of underdeveloped artistic culture have been profoundly felt at the popular level in the United States for a long time. Latin American and African music deeply affect popular musical tastes in the United States. Brazilian novels are translated and become best-sellers. No respectable Middle Bohemian home is complete without a Japanese lamp or print, and Persians are not the only ones who treat their rugs as a substitute for money in the bank.

These wholesale endeavors do not mark merely the ingestion of stimuli from abroad without further reaction and self-examination. The study of underdevelopment is necessarily also the study of development. And so it must be completely obvious that part of the task of studying the development of such countries as Afghanistan, Uganda, and Bolivia is also the study of the United States. If we merely wish to undertake a static analytical description of another country, the comparative element can of course be omitted; but if our task is the specific study of *political modernization,* then there is no escape from drawing a baseline referent from the already developed states—inadequately developed as they may be. I am not merely repeating in other words the bromide that the best way to study one's own country is to get out of it. I am suggesting, to the contrary, that the only way to study underdevelopment is to get inside *both* the modern and the emergent nations. This part of the task may well be what will make us focus on the domestic as well as the international problems of the United States.

It is in the area of intellectual growth, the expansion of aesthetic sensibilities, and an awareness of other "philosophies" of life that the explosion of the developing countries upon the consciousness of the developed may have its major impact. Without the awareness of the problems of development, the American academic community might not be growing as it is, asking the questions to which it is addressing itself, expanding its theoretical conceptions and its available data. Certainly these new efforts will be immediately reflected in an understanding of our own growth processes. Although this task will not be a simple one of transferring contemporary studies of development to a knowledge of our historical past, new focuses on and hitherto unsuspected explanations of the histories of the presently developed states are being generated. This technique has already been exemplified in a book praiseworthy for breaking ground in this direction, S. M. Lipset's *The First New Nation,* which casts a sophisticated eye on the United States in its own developmental period.[14] This exciting "new look" in a world-wide context of comparative social studies is just beginning, promising a breakthrough of great significance.

The Meaning of Political Modernization

The fact is that no society—regardless of how far it may have advanced toward self-sustaining rates of economic growth—can claim more than a partial and insecure resolution of such basic problems as the attainment of peace, plenty, freedom, full modernity. Whatever the form of economic or political organization, or level of industrial advance, substantial poverty and non-functional inequalities persist everywhere. Most men in all countries continue to accept and even embrace stifling discipline, taxing work, degrading status, and the short end of consumption, while yielding to others the right to make decisions, control resources, consume the major share of what is produced, and monopolize access to favored position. No sociological evidence points in the direction of a final withering away of stratification or other forms of social control, whatever the ideological guidelines or revolution-

14. New York, 1963.

ary capacity or intent of those leading change in any society.

The modern society now universally pursued will, under whatever guise it assumes, for a long time accommodate and sustain extreme inequalities, and the process of transition may create wider social gulfs than existed before the drive for modernism began. The study of development, then, cannot be approached as simply the examination of strategies and mechanisms of change through which ancient oppression and inequity will be made to disappear. The modern "developed" nation is a new arena in which the classic struggle between individual autonomy and social commitment, personal realization and social solidarity, freedom and participation will be played out. The question then becomes what kinds of freedom do development or modernization really provide? What new forms of discipline or submission do they impose? The option which the leaders of modernization have open to them is not one of total salvation by embracing one or another version of the "finished" society, but rather a choice between drift and the self-conscious effort to expand freedom and national capacity in determinate directions.[15]

Although the developed and the underdeveloped states face social problems so disparate as to be qualitatively distinct, they both share in the problem of the definition of goal, on deciding what a developed *person* is, and how change can be ordered to permit increasing development without constant institutional breakdown. One school of thought argues that a modern man is a relativist in the sense that he does not seek absolute truth in public affairs; thus he is willing to accept compromise solutions to social matters; in consequence of this relativism, he is also a secularist in his public beliefs, for otherwise he would seek to apply the necessary absolutes of theology to his political and

15. These two paragraphs are paraphrased from a section of the first chapter of a study of education and social development in Latin America which the author is preparing with Dr. Frank Bonilla, Associate Professor of Political Science at the Massachusetts Institute of Technology.

economic choices; social affairs remain limited in scope for him, then, and his acceptance of this limited system assumes that within it he will accept the rule of law as absolute. Students of this persuasion also argue that the developed society is characterized by a consensus system which supports the mechanisms required to incorporate fundamental institutional change without revolutionary breakdown or other fundamental dysfunction. Such a polity must, in its general outlines, encourage broad patterns of citizenship participation and depend heavily on acceptance of process and function instead of on deep faith in given, concretized situations.

The canny reader will immediately detect the Liberal bias in this construction; that is, a bias in defining modernization ethnocentrically in terms of the experience of Western Europe and its cultural offshoots. I have already argued that the drawing of such a baseline is imperative if we are not to have a kind of cultural relativism which will reduce the concept of modernization to "any change whatever," or to any auto-estimation of political leaders and ideologists. The argument is certainly not that the developing nations must attempt a carbon copy of American procedures, say, if they are to reach self-sustaining levels of industrial development. Rather, certain functions and relationships must be developed if nations are to develop the interplay of freedom and discipline and of individual fulfillment and national organization necessary to mitigate the costs of social relationships and harmonize individual and social interests.

The developed world would do well to be sufficiently introspective to learn what it is that truly characterizes a modern society. It is not machines, or easy beliefs in selfish motivation, or "blood." Rather, ethos and social organization have partially freed man to develop the power of his being. A determination for modernization is also a determination for the modernization of the individual. That is, this statement is so *if* the fundamental measure of contemporary society is thought to be the ability to sustain institutional change without breakdown into violence, misery, and more exquisitely worked irrationalities. The tools of modernization offer enormous opportunity for social evil. The people of modernity offer the only ultimate hope that the tools will be used to pursue the greater enrichment of man. This tension is as truly descriptive of the underdeveloped world as it is of the United States, the Soviet Union, or any other partially developed society.

III

National Change

7

AMERICA'S CITIES AND THE GREAT SOCIETY

FRANK SMALLWOOD

By focusing attention upon urban America as one of the most crucial challenges facing the Great Society, President Johnson has imbued the American city with a dramatic new sense of national urgency. Our cities, however, have long played a vital role in shaping the nation's destiny. Indeed, they have helped to mold our aspirations as a national, and even an international, power from the earliest days of the republic. In every decade since 1790, the country's urban population has grown at a rate clearly in excess of rural areas. The most dramatic urban shifts occurred prior to 1900, with the forty-year interval between 1880 and 1920 witnessing the most pronounced period of large-scale city building in the history of the United States.[1]

Despite such an impressive growth record, Americans have tended to underrate the significance of the city as a force in our national development. In large measure we have ignored the

1. Schnore and Petersen, "Urban and Metropolitan Development in the U.S. and Canada," *The Annals* (March 1958).

deeper national and international implications of our urban growth because of a predilection to view the city as a localized territorial and legal entity. In reality, the city has always been considerably more than this. From the very beginnings of human history, mankind's cities have been socio-economic in their fundamental orientation. Their primary purpose has been to bring together people and people, and people and goods, in order to facilitate the exchange of ideas, services, and commodities. In so doing, the city, despite its seemingly parochial leanings, has managed to exercise a vibrant magnetism over men and events far removed from the restrictive confines of its immediate territorial boundaries.

When the great classical cities of the past were able to translate their ideas and their economic strength directly into political power, this external dimension of urban life became fully obvious—witness the overarching influence that Athens and Rome were able to exert over their contemporary civilizations. Yet, even when the city has been subordinated to higher levels of governmental power (as has always been the case in the United States), it has still managed to shape, and to be shaped by, external events on a regional, national, and international level. This has been true of America's great cities of the past, and it is increasingly true today as these cities are subjected to the burgeoning forces of metropolitan growth that are transforming the face of modern America.

This external influence of the American city can be seen by viewing some of the primary roles our urban centers have been called upon to play since their original founding. Three such basic roles—the economic, the communicative, and the social—are particularly relevant in highlighting the interrelationships between our cities and our larger commitments in both national and international affairs.

The American City as an Economic Entity

America's first cities were founded as outposts of New World trade. As early as the mid-seventeenth century, the newly emerging Atlantic trade routes helped shape the character of urban development and the structure of society in the colonial settlements.[2] Some one hundred years later, by 1750, five coastal communities —Boston, New York, Newport, Philadelphia, and Charleston— had risen to positions of dominance in pre-Revolutionary America to a point where they provided the major links between the growing colonies and the outside world. Yet, as Carl Bridenbaugh has demonstrated in his brilliant analysis of *Cities in Revolt,* these same five communities were eventually destined to ignite the spark that led to the severance of our political links with this same outside world.[3]

One of the key catalysts leading to war with England came in the form of the coastal cities' growing economic grievances over the restrictive policies the English were adopting toward colonial trade. By the middle of the eighteenth century these coastal centers were totally dependent upon a free flow of trade for their economic survival.[4] The British, through a series of increasingly more severe economic restrictions, provoked a growing wave of resentment among their inhabitants. These new British revenue policies struck deeply at the roots of urban prosperity.[5]

2. Bernard Bailyn, "Communications and Trade: The Atlantic in the Seventeenth Century," *Journal of Economic History,* XIII (1953), 382.

3. Carl Bridenbaugh, *Cities in Revolt: Urban Life in America 1743-1776* (New York, 1955). See also *Cities in the Wilderness* by the same author for an account of American urban life from 1625 to 1742.

4. Richard C. Wade, "The City in History—Some American Perspectives," *Urban Life and Form,* ed. by Werner Z. Hirsch (New York, 1963), 62-63.

5. Arthur M. Schlesinger, "The City in American Civilization" in *Paths to the Present* (New York, 1949), 213.

Boston, which until the mid-eighteenth century had been the colonies' leading center, was especially hard hit. Following the Boston Tea Party, Parliament passed the Intolerable Acts which shut off the city from any external commerce. As this New England port began to lose its position of supremacy to Philadelphia and New York, the fires of revolt gathered strength. There is considerable evidence to indicate that the revolutionary spirit for which the Boston area is now so venerated was actually more a product of basic economic self-preservation than of lofty ideals or patriotic zeal. In no small measure, "Boston's primacy as the 'Cradle of Liberty' . . . sprung from her lagging progress in relation to other ports, inciting her at any cost to remove the obstacles that Parliament was thrusting in her way." [6]

Following the attainment of national independence, the seaport cities took on an even more important role in determining the future course of the nation's survival. As a consequence of the war, Americans found themselves excluded from the former trading privileges they had enjoyed as British colonies, shut off from trade with the British West Indies, and denied the opportunity to sell American built ships to British merchants. As a result, they were forced to establish new patterns of commerce and to find new markets for their products in order to pay for imports from abroad. The seaports were the key to this economic crisis. By 1800 American international commerce had survived thanks to aggressive trade policies pursued by seaport merchants who took advantage of the growing hostilities between England and France to restore a precarious balance-of-trade position with the outside world.[7]

Yet, while America's commercial position may have profited initially from the French-British struggle, in time this same conflict was destined to produce a new climate of international tension

6. Schlesinger quoted in Wade, *op. cit.,* 63.
7. C. M. Green, *American Cities* (London, 1957), 6-7.

which had a profound influence on the future economic development of the American city. The strains inherent in the deteriorating international situation eventually culminated in the War of 1812—a complex engagement that resulted from a variety of divergent forces. Not the least of the provocations that led to hostilities was the growing international conflict over neutral (i.e., American) commercial rights on the high seas. The British, determined to limit American trade with France, engaged in a series of actions which once again restricted the flow of American goods abroad and made international commerce an increasingly more hazardous undertaking for the new American nation.

The impact that such actions were destined to have on the future course of America's urban development can be seen most clearly in the shifting attitude toward the American city which characterized the position of Thomas Jefferson. In his *Notes on Virginia* (1784), Jefferson had produced one of history's most bitterly anti-urban tracts. Calling for the development of a simple agrarian democracy, Jefferson deplored the rise of the American city as a potential menace to be avoided at all costs, warning that "the mobs of great cities add just so much to the support of pure government, as sores do to the strength of the human body." It was Jefferson's original hope that the economic role of America could be limited to that of an agrarian supplier of raw materials to the manufacturing nations of Europe, which nations would then supply the finished products necessary to meet American domestic needs. In advocating this position, Jefferson stood in direct contrast to the Hamiltonian viewpoint which called for the development of an independent national manufacturing potential.

In light of deteriorating trade relations and the War of 1812, however, Jefferson was forced to subordinate his agrarian dream to the Hamiltonian concept, and in the process to re-evaluate the fundamental role of the city in the American economy. Writing in 1816, he moaned:

> But who in 1785 could foresee the rapid depravity which was to render the close of the century the disgrace of the history of man? . . . We have experienced what we did not then believe, that there exists both profligacy and power enough to exclude us from the field of interchange with other nations: that to be independent for the comforts of life we must fabricate them ourselves. . . . Experience has taught me that manufactures are now as necessary to our independence as to our comfort.

Although Jefferson retained his underlying distrust of the city's spirit, its manners, and its principles, "the international situation ultimately forced him to regard the city as an indispensable element of American life."[8] He came to conclude that only by developing an independent urban industrial base could we divorce ourselves from the violent political and economic upheavals that had come to dominate international commerce. In effect, the rise of the American industrial city would provide the growing nation with its own source of manufacturing strength, and thus hopefully free it from further entanglements with the embattled nations of Europe.

The development of this new manufacturing strength absorbed America's energies for the remainder of the nineteenth century. First came the New England mill cities—Lowell in the 1820's, Manchester in the 1830's, Holyoke in the 1840's. Then the railroads came to shape the nation's growing industrial cities; New York, Philadelphia, Baltimore, and Washington were the first to be linked. By 1850 some ten thousand miles of track had been pushed into the West to tie New York with Buffalo, Philadelphia with Harrisburg, Charleston with Atlanta, and Detroit with Chicago. The Civil War gave added impetus to this rapidly accelerating industrial growth, and after the war the railroads continued their restless march into the Far West. In 1870 the Western Pacific connected Kansas City with Denver; in 1873 the Northern Pacific

8. Morton and Lucia White, *The Intellectual Versus the City* (Cambridge, 1962), 18. The earlier Jefferson quotes appear on pages 14-18.

reached the tiny town of Tacoma, Washington; in 1876 the Southern Pacific pushed its way into Los Angeles.

By the turn of the century the total industrial output of these growing American cities already so outstripped that of any foreign country that the character of international trade was transformed.[9] And still the headlong rush toward urbanization continued. In 1900 some 40 per cent of all Americans lived in urban areas. By 1910 this figure had jumped to 46 per cent; by 1920 to 51 per cent; by 1930 to 56 per cent. Within the span of a century, America had been transformed from an agricultural to an urban nation.

The role the cities played in promoting this transformation was a crucial one. Not only did they house the massive new work force necessary for industrialization, but they provided the organizational scale necessary to accumulate the financial capital and to produce the mass urban consumer markets that have been an essential component of our modern corporate economy. Today, America's great metropolitan centers perform a vital service as the producers, dispensers, and consumers of our industrial wealth. As of 1960 these centers accounted for 78.6 per cent of all bank deposits in the United States and for 76.8 per cent of the value added by manufacture. They contained 67.2 per cent of the nation's manufacturing establishments, 73.8 per cent of the total number of industrial employees, and 78.5 per cent of all manufacturing payrolls.[10]

The international obligations that have grown out of America's

9. Blake McKelvey, *The Urbanization of America* (New Brunswick, 1963), 3, 17, 35-36.

10. Report of the Advisory Committee on Intergovernmental Relations, *Governmental Structure, Organization and Planning in Metropolitan Areas* (Washington, 1961), 8. It should be noted that these figures cover metropolitan areas rather than central cities alone. Some analysts are now arguing persuasively that the economic role of our central cities is changing away from manufacturing and back toward the commercial and managerial functions of the past. See, for example, Raymond Vernon, *The Changing Economic Function of the Central City* (CED, January 1959).

rush toward urban industrialization are highly paradoxical when viewed in light of Jefferson's original visions of national economic self-sufficiency. While our surging industrialization may well have limited our foreign political entanglements during the latter half of the nineteenth century, this new industrial growth was concurrently opening up a host of external commitments on a variety of other fronts. One way our surge toward industrialization led directly into increasingly closer contacts with other nations was through the tremendous influx of foreign immigration which flooded our cities in direct response to the need for a cheap industrial labor force. A second, and even more dramatic, external commitment growing out of this same industrialization was not destined to become fully apparent until the first half of the present century.

The very economic strength that America gained as a nation through the development of its urban industrial base has not only proven to be the decisive factor in the resolution of two world wars, but has also led to a series of more recent postwar foreign aid commitments that have kept us directly in the mainstream of world events for the past twenty years. When viewed in terms of both military and economic posture, the industrial strength provided by America's cities—the "arsenals of democracy"—has played a crucial role in the nation's rise as a great world power, and today this same strength stands behind the expenditure of billions of dollars in defense and foreign assistance in an effort to bolster a shaky non-communist world. In the long run, far from minimizing foreign entanglements, the rise of America's industrial cities has led to a new series of international commitments that are beyond the wildest dreams of Jefferson's world of 1784, or of 1812.

The basic international influence which America's cities have exercised in the economic sphere has been apparent throughout the nation's history. Originally these cities provided the commercial ties with other nations that were essential to the development of an emerging colonial society, and subsequently the stimulus that led to our independence as a nation. During more recent years they have provided the organizational base for a growing industrial economy that has permitted this nation to assume an increasingly more dominant role in all phases of world affairs. From the very beginning, the American city has played a vital role in shaping the nation's economic destiny.

The Communicative Role of the American City

In addition to its role as a producer, distributor, and consumer of goods, the city has always been preoccupied with the formulation and dissemination of ideas. Learning has always been one of the powerful lures of the city,[11] and through the dispersion of ideals and ideas the city has always possessed the ability to "both polarize a culture and raise its potential." [12] From its earliest formative years, the city has helped to shape, if not always to raise, America's social, economic, and cultural aspirations. Originally our cities concentrated almost exclusively on the importation of ideas from abroad, and in an attempt to imitate European—and more particularly British—cultural patterns, they tended to create the first significant cleavages in American society. Within a relatively short span of time, however, these same cities began to develop intellectual identities of their own, with crucially important consequences. By the time of the Revolutionary War, the cities served as the only significant points of communication that were able to transcend the growing geographical regionalism of an emerging colonial society.

The first period of intellectual importation and imitation of European ideas had become fully apparent as early as the latter

11. John Dyckman, "The Changing Uses of the City," *Daedalus,* Winter 1961, 123.

12. Sylvia L. Thrupp, "The Creativity of Cities," *Comparative Studies in Society and History,* IV, 1961-62, 53. Professor Thrupp is commenting on Lewis Mumford's views as expressed in *The City in History.*

half of the seventeenth century. The social and geographical cleavages that occurred at this time were to be seen in the marked differences that contrasted such growing urban centers as Boston with the more parochially oriented inland areas and minor ports. Fashion, styles of living, and intellectual attitudes followed the routes of trade, and throughout the colonial world they came to mark important social boundaries.[13]

During the next hundred years these embryonic social boundaries solidified along relatively clear-cut geographical lines. By the mid-1700's three distinct regions characterized America's colonial development: an urbanized section along the Atlantic seaboard; a settled but still rural section of agricultural countryside; and the sparsely populated districts of our back country.

Throughout the remainder of the colonial period, by means of their particular form of urban imperialism, the cities in effect came to dominate the other two sections. In retrospect it is now obvious that these cities represented the major grouping in pre-Revolutionary society that possessed the ability, in terms of both motivation and technique, to communicate coherently on an emerging national basis. Thus, within the span of a century, the cycle had come full circle. The same cities that had originally created the first "social boundaries" leading to the initial fragmentation of American colonial society subsequently provided the very base of communications that later led to the political consolidation of this society in the form of the new American nation:

> Constant communication, arising out of the needs of commerce, served to forge these communities into an integrated urban society—the only segment of colonial population so fused. In each of the cities certain common physical, economic, cultural and social characteristics accentuated the homogeneity whereas the other two sections exhibited vivid differences, north and south, in crops, architecture, people and customs. The achievement of the integration of urban elements was an essential prelude to independence. Otherwise the meeting of the First

13. Bailyn, *op. cit.,* 383-384.

Continental Congress appears as a cataclysmic event not subject to historical explanation.[14]

The cities did more than serve as mere vehicles of colonial contact, however, for they also supplied the intellectual content that gave this contact meaning. As already noted, a key catalyst leading to the Revolutionary War appeared in the form of urban economic grievances, but these pragmatic concerns were supplemented by a more general intellectual upheaval of significant proportions. The major influence at work here was decidedly European in its origins. Specifically, it was the emergence of a basic ideological unrest against monarchy, aristocracy, and other forms of political authoritarianism. Just as this ideological unrest had its origins in the principal cities of Europe, so its various manifestations first appeared in the five largest cities of the English colonies.

Thus the intellectual stimulus America's cities provided in inciting the Revolutionary War was every bit as crucial as their economic role. Nonetheless, during subsequent years three influences have prompted us to minimize the vital contributions the city has continued to make toward our intellectual development as a nation.

First, the growth of bitter inter-urban rivalries, especially in the economic sphere, has tended to characterize the city as a divisive, rather than an integrative, force in American society. While it is true that America's internal economic growth has led to a jockeying for position among different cities—for key transportation routes, industries, and the like—the transportation and communications networks that were forged to link the country's major urban centers have in fact performed a vital role in promoting a national sense of cohesiveness. Forces of localism and regionalism may have produced a somewhat irrational network of inter-urban contacts, but despite any aberrant elements this

14. Bridenbaugh, *op. cit.,* vii, 418.

network has played an essential role in providing a geographical sense of identity to America's emerging national society.

Second, a strong expression of anti-urbanism has characterized our intellectual attitudes toward the city, to a point where we have tended to underplay the key role that our urban institutions have actually performed as the creators and disseminators of ideas. As Morton and Lucia White point out in *The Intellectual Versus the City*, many of our most creative minds—Jefferson, Emerson, Thoreau, Melville, Adams, James, Dewey, and others—have harbored a basic bias against the city as a unit of human organization.[15]

This anti-urban intellectualism has tended to obscure the tremendous vitality and stimulus that the city has in fact provided to our national intellectual development. Just as in Medieval Europe the university was the creature of the city, so in Colonial America the city served as the home of our fledgling universities. Six of the nine pre-Revolutionary colleges—Brown, Harvard, King's College, Pennsylvania, William and Mary, and Yale—were urban in their early orientations. The cities, through their museums, galleries, and libraries, have always served as cultural storehouses, and through their theatres, as the developers of the dramatic arts. In the field of the printed word, the city has possessed the wealth necessary to publish the books, the journals, and the great daily newspapers that have shaped national thought. Under a flood of technological innovations during more recent years, most notably radio and television, the city has come to monopolize new media of mass communications that once again have had a profound influence in shaping our modern patterns of living. In spite of any anti-urban intellectual bias we may have harbored, we have looked to our cities both to create and to communicate the ideas which have dominated our cultural and social development since the founding of the nation.

The third influence that has tended to inhibit our appreciation

15. White, *op. cit.,* 1-2.

of the role which the city has played in integrating American society is to be found in our preoccupation with the West as the major determinant in American history. Following the formulation of Frederick Jackson Turner's classic "Frontier Thesis" in 1893, many Americans became intrigued with the idea that our Western expansion represented the keystone that could be utilized to interpret every phase of national development. In Turner's words, "The true point of view in the history of this nation is not the Atlantic coast, it is the Great West." [16] Through their fixation on the agrarian and rural influences of the frontier, Turner's disciples severely underestimated the significance of urban institutions in American life.

Actually, over the years Turner himself became considerably less adamant in defense of his thesis than many of his followers. By 1925 he had confessed the need for "an urban reinterpretation of our history," [17] but it is not until recent years that this reinterpretation has gained momentum. Today such contemporary historians as Richard Wade are providing new insights into the crucial role that the cities did, in fact, play in shaping the development of the Western frontier itself. As Wade has pointed out, "The towns were the spearheads of the frontier. Planted far in advance of the line of settlement, they held the West for the approaching population." [18] The later stages of our frontier development demonstrated these same characteristics of urban growth. By 1890 the Far West, "though the most sparsely settled area in the nation, was the most highly urbanized." Such urbanization was fed by the railroads that had come to criss-cross the continent.

. . . First the railroad, then the towns, then the farms . . .

16. Frederick J. Turner, "The Significance of the Frontier in American History" in *The Frontier in American History* (New York, 1920).

17. Schlesinger, *op. cit.,* 210.

18. Richard C. Wade, *The Urban Frontier: The Rise of the Cities in the West 1790-1830* (Cambridge, 1959), 1.

> The city stamps the country, instead of the country stamping the city. It is the cities and towns which . . . frame state constitutions, make laws, create public opinion, establish social usages, and fix standards of morals in the West.[19]

During the entire course of national development, the cities, in addition to formulating and disseminating their own ideas, continued to serve as the receptacles and communicators of ideas from abroad. Today, as in the past, the impact of foreign influences can be seen in every aspect of urban life, from the displays of the latest Parisian fashions to the cluster of foreign-language newspapers and cosmopolitan restaurants that have come to characterize the modern American metropolis. During more recent years this interaction between America's cities and the cities abroad has become increasingly more reciprocal. To cite but one significant illustration, nineteenth-century urban America was inundated by successive waves of Greek Revival, Mansard, and Victorian architecture. Today, however, for better or for worse, it is the American skyscraper which is influencing the profiles of cities throughout the world. Following the pioneering efforts of Louis Sullivan, the American city has become the exporter, as well as importer, of new forms of architectural expression.

This increasingly more reciprocal interaction between the American and the foreign city promises to open new vistas of international influence to our urban institutions in the future. Just as the development of radio and television have magnified the influence of the city at home, so the development of satellite communications and modern jet transportation promises to magnify the role of the city in promoting inter-cultural contacts abroad.

Lewis Mumford is among those who have prophesied that the great capital cities of the world, by bringing together the diversity and variety of different cultures, have unconsciously been "preparing mankind for the wider associations and unifica-

19. Josiah Strong, quoted in Wade, "The City in History—Some American Perspectives," 62.

tions which the modern conquest of time and space has made probable, if not inevitable."[20] Although Mumford's prophecy is perhaps somewhat premature, in the final analysis it would appear that the city does possess an extremely fruitful potential for promoting inter-societal contact. Karl Deutsch has characterized the metropolis as a "huge engine of communication,"[21] and as such it possesses a tremendous capability to bridge the social, ideological, and cultural diversities that have plagued mankind in the past. Under the stimulus of massive technological breakthroughs, the historic communicative role of the city has taken on both a new promise and a new urgency. Today man possesses the potential either to utilize his cities to improve his relations with his fellow men, or to obliterate these same cities, and himself, from the face of the earth.

The American City as a Vehicle of Assimilation

"Give me your tired, your poor, your huddled masses yearning to breathe free." These famous words on the pedestal of the Statue of Liberty represent the mythology, if not always the reality, of America's historic commitment toward foreign immigration. While our cities, and indeed our nation, were built upon immigration from the earliest colonial years, it was not until the mid-nineteenth century that the new waves of foreign-born descended on America's shores in flood-tide proportions.

The Irish and Germans were among the first of the pre-Civil War arrivals. The former, plagued by famine at home, poured into Boston, New York, and other eastern centers at a rate that added nearly two million to the nation's population between 1830 and 1860. The Germans, fleeing from bad crops and the avaricious remnants of a feudal landlord system that was breaking down

20. Lewis Mumford, *The City in History* (New York, 1961), 561.

21. Karl Deutsch, "On Social Communication and the Metropolis," *Daedalus, op. cit.,* 99.

under the new economics of European urbanization, added another one and a half million during these same three decades. The majority of these German arrivals settled in the Midwest to place their stamp on Cincinnati, Milwaukee, and other inland cities.

During the post-Civil War period the southern and eastern Europeans, led by the Italians, began to stream to America's cities. In the 1880's more than five million immigrants arrived, and although this number was temporarily checked by hard times in the 1890's, it surged to an all-time high of 8,202,388 between 1900 and 1910.

These tired and poor masses may well have come to America with a yearning to breathe free, but above all else they were attracted by the new economic opportunities that were an inherent outgrowth of America's urban industrialization. Robert Park, America's first great urban sociologist, has observed that cities have brought together people from the ends of the earth, "simply because they were useful to each other," [22] and the particular utility assigned to the foreign immigrant was that of providing a cheap source of human labor to power the country's growing industrial base. As such, his climb up the economic ladder was a long and difficult one, and the slum was as much a part of the New World city as was the promise to breathe free.

By 1910 the massive post-Civil War immigration had left a net total of 9,635,369 foreign-born in America's cities.[23] Differences in language, in habits, and in aspirations distinguished these new residents from earlier arrivals. Yet the old barriers were breaking down even while the last flood of immigrants was still pouring into the cities. Although by 1910 there were 9,600,000 foreign-born in our cities, there were also 12,346,900 first-genera-

22. Robert Park, "The City in Civilization," in *Human Communities* (Glencoe, 1952), 140.

23. McKelvey, *op. cit.*, 63. The earlier Irish and German estimates are taken from Arthur M. Schlesinger, "The Role of the Immigrant," in *Paths to the Present*, 59-60.

tion Americans of foreign or mixed parentage who were already beginning to integrate themselves into the larger economic patterns of American society.

The slowdown of foreign immigration during the First World War, and the restrictive immigration measures adopted by the federal government in the 1920's, halted the mass influx of the past and tended to simplify this process of assimilation. Although the road was by no means an easy one, by the time of World War II America's "huddled masses" were well on the way to becoming full-fledged citizens in every sense of this term. This process of assimilation has been accelerated even further by an era of postwar prosperity. During the past fifteen years there has been a radical transformation of the income structure of the large city which has enabled the great bulk of our earlier immigrants from abroad to aspire to propertied status.[24]

Before this process of economic accommodation was completed, however, these earlier immigrants had added a rich new cultural dimension to American life, not only through interaction with earlier arrivals but through interaction with each other. America's historic saga of urban immigration not only provided the new population necessary to man a burgeoning industrial base; it also added a new cosmopolitan flavor to our national life.

At the same time this process of foreign assimilation was taking place, our cities were experiencing the cumulative effects of a more recent surge of internal in-migration. Actually, by the end of the nineteenth century, the Negro was already beginning to move toward the city in relatively large numbers. In 1890 some 1,500,000 Negroes, or one-fifth of the 7,500,000 non-white population of the United States, were already living in urban areas. The migration of the Negro to Northern cities was heightened by the labor shortage resulting from the cut-off of foreign immigration during World War I. More than 400,000 Negroes left the South between 1914 and 1917, and this southern exodus

24. Oscar Handlin, "The Social System," *Daedalus, op. cit.*, 20.

continued during the depression until, by 1940, some 48 per cent of all the Negroes in our Northern and Western states were concentrated into only six cities.[25]

This more recent urban influx of Negro population has been supplemented by an immigration that began slowly in the 1920's. Unlike the Negroes, however, the Puerto Ricans have tended to cluster into one particular urban area. Following the pattern of the shipping lines that connect the island with the United States, the great bulk of these newer arrivals have located in the New York metropolitan region.

Both the Negro and the Puerto Rican movements were stimulated by the labor shortage of the Second World War, but it was not until the postwar period that these movements gained new momentum. During the past fifteen years the Puerto Ricans have continued to stream into New York to a point where they now form a sizable population group.[26] Their figures pale in comparison, however, to the growing Negro exodus to the urban North which has been spurred by an attempt to secure better economic opportunities and to break away from the formal patterns of racial segregation which have characterized Southern life. During the past decade 323,000 Negroes left the State of Mississippi alone, while substantial losses were also recorded in the Carolinas, Alabama, and Georgia. The impact of this Negro migration has become apparent in all major cities north of the Mason-Dixon Line. By 1960 over half of the twenty largest cities outside the Deep South could count non-white populations in excess of 200,000. The problems and challenges that have accompanied this great movement of non-white population to the North have been those of economic deprivation, and *de facto,* if not *de jure,* racial segregation.

25. Gunnar Myrdal, *An American Dilemma* (New York, 1944), 192. The six cities were New York, Chicago, Philadelphia, Cleveland, Detroit, and Pittsburgh.

26. Oscar Handlin, *The Newcomers* (Cambridge, 1959), Tables, 142.

CITIES OUTSIDE DEEP SOUTH
WITH OVER 200,000 NON-WHITE POPULATION[27]

	Non-White Population (1960)	Non-White % of Total (1960)	Non-White % Increase 1950-1960
New York	1,141,322	14.7	+47.2
Chicago	837,656	23.6	+64.4
Philadelphia	535,033	26.7	+41.2
Detroit	487,174	29.2	+60.4
Washington	418,693	54.8	+47.3
Los Angeles	417,207	16.8	+97.2
Baltimore	328,416	35.0	+45.3
Cleveland	253,108	28.9	+69.3
Houston	217,672	23.2	+73.2
St. Louis	216,022	28.8	+39.9

Economic deprivation is to be found in the fact that the estimated 20 per cent of the central cities that are blighted by slums and substandard housing contain 75 per cent of the urban Negro population. The United States Commission on Civil Rights estimated recently that if the population densities in some of Harlem's worst slum blocks prevailed throughout the rest of New York City, the entire population of the United States could be crammed into only three of New York's five boroughs! As a result of the social and economic squalor that characterizes these areas, their residents account for 60 per cent of tuberculosis cases, 55 per cent of juvenile delinquency, and 45 per cent of crime to be found within the cities. Although these substandard slum areas demand 45 per cent of total city costs, they yield only 6 per cent of real estate tax revenues.[28]

The effects of *de facto* racial segregation are hardly more encouraging. When the huge percentage increases that have characterized the non-white urban population growth during the past

27. Advisory Commission on Intergovernmental Relations, *op. cit.,* 7.
28. U.S. Commission on Civil Rights, "With Liberty and Justice for All," Abridged 1959 *Annual Report* (Washington, 1959), 148, 151.

decade are coupled with the tiny 1.5 per cent total population increase of the core cities during this same period, the pattern is clear. As the Negroes have moved into Northern cities in increasing numbers, the white population has moved out in increasing numbers. The result has been an ominous new pattern of residential settlement—the creation of the "white noose around the central city."

After years of apathetic resignation, if not complete acceptance, of these conditions, America's Negro citizens are now demonstrating a new air of militancy in their efforts to secure the promise that is inherent in the American ideal. The international repercussions that have followed in the wake of this development have been world-wide in their impact. Africans, Asians, and South Americans who have never heard of many of America's great Northern cities are already fully familiar with the racial strife that has ripped apart such communities as Little Rock and Birmingham. The challenge of the future, as non-white citizens continue to flood into the Northern cities, is that these cities will not, in fact, obtain the notoriety that has already come to their Southern counterparts.

The future challenges facing the American city as a vehicle of social assimilation are all too clear. Our great urban centers are only now beginning to come to grips with the massive task of integrating the non-white population into the economic and social mainstream of American life. The extent to which they are successful in meeting this challenge will have a profound impact on America's future leadership in a world that is more non-white than white. More than ever before in history, the eyes of this non-white world are being turned toward the American city in an effort to determine whether the mythology of our democratic heritage can be translated into reality.

Thus, once again, as was true in the fields of economics and intellectual life, the American city, through its assimilative role, has tended to take on a vital significance to our national and international development. It does so, however, from a position of political disability. For while the city has occupied a position of considerable influence, both internally and internationally, since the earliest days of our history, it has never achieved a formal position of political power that has been commensurate with its informal leadership.

The Political Position of the American City

America's cities from their earliest inception have always been the legal stepchild of some higher form of governmental authority. Even during the course of westward expansion, when the cities preceded the founding of the states and laid the groundwork for the states' incorporation into an expanding federal union, once the new states came into being they exercised a virtually complete political monopoly over the cities which had come before them.

This legal subordination of the city to higher levels of government is a direct result of the fact that only the national and state governments are recognized explicitly in the United States Constitution. In American law the city is regarded as a municipal corporation, created by virtue of soverign state authority and totally subordinate to this authority. This position has been upheld in state courts and, until very recently, in the Supreme Court as well.

The state court precedents of urban subordination to state authority hardened into a doctrine known as "Dillon's Rule," [29] which was subsequently confirmed in a series of higher court decisions that culminated in the case of *Trenton v. New Jersey* in 1923. Here, the Supreme Court declared that the city was "merely a department of the state, and the state may withhold, grant and withdraw powers as it sees fit." [30]

Thus, in terms of its legal status, the city has always occupied a position of marked inferiority to the states. What gave this situation a potent political significance was the fact that the

29. John G. Dillon, *Commentaries on the Law of Municipal Corporations,* 5th edition (Boston, 1911), I, Sec. 237.

30. *Trenton v. New Jersey,* 162 U.S. 182 (1923).

historical rural domination of the great majority of state legislatures continued to prevail in more recent years, despite the dramatic urban population shifts which had taken place during the past half-century. The reason was the so-called "silent gerrymander." Instead of compensating for the population exodus from farm to city and from city to suburbs, the states refused to reapportion their legislatures in any way that would have diluted rural control. By the mid-1950's rural overrepresentation had become predominant in practically every state legislature in the country, with the following representing the most severe cases of anti-urban bias: [31]

URBAN AREA UNDER-REPRESENTATION (MID-1950's)

State	Selected Urban Areas	Urban Area's % of Total State Population	Urban Area's % of Representation in State Legislature	
			House	Senate
Georgia	6 largest urban counties	32	9	7
Florida	9 most urban counties	60	23	24
Delaware	Wilmington area	59	23	24
Maryland	Baltimore and 3 largest urban counties	67	44	31
Connecticut	10 largest cities	46	7	46
Rhode Island	10 largest cities	77	67	34
New Jersey	8 largest urban counties	75	73	38
California	4 largest urban counties	59	59	10

31. Gordon E. Baker, *Rural Versus Urban Political Power* (New York, 1955), 16.

This anti-urban representative pattern was not confined to the states alone. The United States Congress also saw its share of rural overrepresentation. The Senate, with its constitutional emphasis on geographical, rather than popular, representation, has always displayed a significant disparity in this regard, but ironically it was the House of Representatives that displayed the greatest problem of rural imbalance at the congressional level. Since 1913, when they were first elected on a statewide basis, U.S. Senators have always had to pay attention to their urban as well as their rural constituents if they were to enjoy continued political success. This has been especially true of the smaller urban minority groups who could swing close state elections by means of their "bullet votes." As a result, during more recent years the Senate has displayed a considerably more liberal urban temperament than the House of Representatives. The members of the House, on the other hand, have long been elected from individual districts which are either totally rural or totally urban in character. Here again rural interests were able to take advantage of their strength in the state legislatures (which are also responsible for redistricting congressional seats) to exercise undue influence in the House of Representatives. During the 1950's, for example, the nation's thirteen largest urban congressional districts contained enough population actually to warrant twenty-two, rather than thirteen, Congressmen. Similar urban underrepresentation at the congressional level could be found in some medium-sized and smaller cities.

Rural influence in Congress has been further magnified by a seniority rule which allows representatives from "safe" districts to dominate key committee assignments and chairmanships. Since rural districts have demonstrated a much greater propensity to re-elect incumbents than their more competitive urban counterparts, spokesmen from these districts have long exercised a powerful influence over the congressional committee system. Hence, at both the state and the national levels, the political voice of the urban areas has been muted to a highly significant degree.

This situation was affected dramatically in 1962 when the Supreme Court rendered its historic *Baker v. Carr* decision. In effect, the Court ordered the lower courts to supervise a system of state legislative reapportionment which would reflect our more recent population shifts from rural to urban areas. In turn, *Baker v. Carr* was buttressed by a series of subsequent decisions, most notably *Wesberry v. Sanders* and *Reynolds v. Sims,* in which the Court emphasized the doctrine of "one man, one vote" in the reapportionment of congressional House districts, as well as in the upper houses of our state legislatures.

The Court-ordered reapportionments promise to have a major impact on the future course of American politics. Contrary to earlier expectations, however, it now appears that the nation's cities will not gain most of the new political power from electoral realignments. Rather, initial surveys indicate that the city's newer satellites, the exploding suburban communities, will be the big gainers in the reapportionment process. This development highlights the profound new pattern of urban settlement that has dominated America's postwar growth—a pattern of massive metropolitan sprawl that has sounded an ominous warning for America's urban future.

The City of the Future: Metropolis and Cosmopolis

The historic pattern of city building that marked the first three hundred years of the nation's growth was highly centripetal. Operating as huge vortexes, our historic cities sucked an ever expanding population into a series of increasingly more densely compacted urban clusters. Our more recent patterns of suburban growth represent a sharp contrast with this earlier model. Today's sprawling metropolis is the product of new breakthroughs in technology, most notably the technological destruction of distance via new modes of transportation and communications. Throughout most of human history, a natural tolerance level of physical inconvenience—especially the diminishing economic returns of distance of journey to work—tended to place marked restrictions on the city's natural size. The development of the automobile, the rapid transit system, and such modern means of communication as the telephone have broken these previous limitations on city scale so that the prevailing forces of suburban growth are now pushing out continually further from the core areas of the historic city centers.

Today, two-thirds of all Americans are clustered in some 216 "standard metropolitan areas" [32] that are scattered across the landscape from Boston to Los Angeles. The major growth patterns within these areas have been almost totally suburban in character. During the past decade, while these 216 metropolitan giants were accounting for some 84 per cent of the total national population growth, the central cities that constitute their core focus experienced a population increase of only slightly more than 1 per cent. In short, the United States was becoming an increasingly more suburbanized nation, and all indications are that this phenomenon is here to stay. By 1980 an estimated 190,000,000 people—three out of every four Americans—will be living within the giant metropolitan centers.

It was recognition of this fact that prompted President Johnson to focus upon the urban challenge as a number one priority facing his proposed Great Society. Despite the magnitude of the tasks they have performed in the past, America's cities today face a series of crises of truly staggering proportions. Giant strides will have to be made on at least four fronts before the cities can even begin to realize the type of Great Society the President has envisioned.

First, there is the growing financial crisis that has resulted

32. A "standard metropolitan area," as defined by the Bureau of the Census, is a county or a group of contiguous counties which contains at least one city of 50,000 inhabitants or more, or "twin cities" with a combined population of at least 50,000. The statistical data on SMA's is taken from "Governmental Structure, Organization and Planning in Metropolitan Areas," Report of the Advisory Commission on Intergovernmental Relations (Washington, July 1961).

from our headlong rush toward metropolitan living. The challenge here is twofold—an ever expanding demand for new urban services coupled with a rapidly deteriorating real property base in the historic central cities. Direct state and local government expenditures have soared by 187 per cent during the past decade (to a combined 1962 total of $70.1 billion), while local debt has increased by 216 per cent and state debt by a whopping 307 per cent (to a combined 1962 total of $81 billion).[33] At the same time the cities have been faced with these massive expenditures, they have been forced to wrestle with a growing deterioration of real property values resulting from urban blight and the exodus of wealthy population groupings to the more affluent suburban areas. Although the federal government has attempted to alleviate this financial squeeze by increasing its grant-in-aid payments to state and local governments from $1.3 billion in 1946 to $7.8 billion in 1962,[34] it is obvious that major new sources of state and local revenues must be found if local governments are to keep pace with spiraling expenditures.

A second major crisis area involves the physical deterioration that has grown out of the blight situations noted above. Stated quite bluntly, America's historic urban physical plant is now largely obsolete. Narrow and overcrowded streets, substandard housing, inadequate sewerage and mass transit systems plague virtually every major American city. It was a growing recognition of this physical deterioration that prompted the Congress to pass the 1949 Housing Act that has led to the great urban renewal effort of the past fifteen years. Since the inception of this program, the federal government has spent over a billion dollars on some 1,600 urban renewal projects in 777 U.S. cities. Yet the physical challenge that still remains is truly awesome. During the next

33. F. O. Woodward, "More Services Mean More Taxes," *Challenge,* February 1964; Frederick C. Mosher and Orville F. Poland, *The Costs of American Governments* (New York, 1964), 115, 172. See also Alan K. Campbell, "Most Dynamic Sector," *National Civic Review,* February 1964.

34. U.S. Bureau of the Census, *Statistical Abstract,* 1964, 422.

twenty-four hours New York City alone will dump some 500,000,-000 gallons of sewage into the Hudson and the East Rivers; during the next year the nation's army of bulldozers will push back another 500,000 acres of suburban land in their insatiable quest for new residential space; during the next decade the nation's suburban areas will grow by an estimated twenty-five to thirty-five million people. Small wonder that President Johnson has proposed that we will be forced to rebuild the entire urban United States during the next forty years.

As difficult as these financial and physical crises may be, they pale when viewed against the great social and human challenges that face urban America. Here again the problem is largely one of urban poverty that has resulted from the "second-class" stigma we have assigned to our Negro citizens. Today's median annual family income in central Harlem is 50 per cent lower (while substandard housing and unemployment are 35 and 10 per cent higher) than that of the rest of New York City.[35] We are compounding, rather than alleviating, the problems of the racial ghettos that we have permitted to fester in the hearts of our great cities through the suburban exodus of wealthier urban population. If 1950-60 residential growth patterns continue unabated in future years, by 1980 seven of the nation's ten largest cities (all except New York, Los Angeles, and Houston) will contain absolute non-white majorities.[36] The potential for racial violence that is inherent in these twin cyclones of Negro urban poverty and white suburban affluence is all too obvious. We must make major strides in inducing some of the wealthier suburban population back into the central cities, while opening up suburban communities to Negro citizens, if we are to avoid a racial explosion of truly disastrous proportions in future years. In order to achieve this end we will need to provide better schools, more effective building

35. *New York Times*, August 2, 1964.

36. Theodore H. White, "Rushing to a Showdown that No Law Can Chart," *Life*, November 22, 1963, 106.

and zoning controls, more creative utilization of architectural expertise, and more imaginative planning of parks, plazas, and open spaces so that we can revitalize the cities as attractive places in which to work and raise a family. At the same time, we must push our regional planning efforts in order to control the dismal sprawl and the monotonous and garish residential and commercial aspects of suburbia that Peter Blake classified under the apt description of "God's Own Junkyard."

In order to facilitate these tasks it will be necessary to come to grips with the newer governmental and political challenges that constitute urban America's fourth major crisis area. As a result of their historic growth patterns, the cities have adopted piecemeal systems of local government that no longer correspond to the economic, social, and political realities of the modern metropolis. Today some 1,467 local governmental bodies blanket the New York metropolitan area, while metropolitan Chicago is staggering under a similar burden of a thousand independent local governments. In all, it is estimated that over seventeen thousand local governmental authorities are attempting to wrestle with the needs of America's 216 standard metropolitan areas. The challenge here, quite simply, is that historic urban governmental systems were created in their essentials before the advent of the modern metropolis, and they are totally inadequate to meet the problems of today's urban leviathans. We have now begun to make a hesitant start toward new concepts of metropolitan government in such cities as Miami, Nashville, and Seattle, but we will need to show a markedly more inventive display of political creativity in future years before we can hope to resolve the great financial, physical, social, and economic crises that face modern urban society.

After viewing this massive backlog of problems, a number of observers have been prompted to speculate that the era of the historic city is now coming to an end, that we are about to enter into a new stage of post-urban civilization that will be quite unlike anything we have seen during the past five thousand years. It most certainly is true that new technological breakthroughs, such as the development of compact nuclear fuel sources, have now enabled us to devise totally new types of miniature portable "package" cities that could easily be shifted from one location to another as the need arose.[37] Indeed, one student of urban affairs foresees the complete obliteration of historic city life through a total dispersal of society into individually self-sufficient households. Noting that the day is not far off when only 1 per cent of the population will be able to produce our entire food supply, Professor Kenneth E. Boulding has speculated on "a society in which the population is spread very evenly over the world in almost self-sufficient households, each circulating and processing everlastingly its own water supply through its own algae, each deriving all the power it needs from its own solar batteries, each in communication with anybody it wants through its personalized television, each with immediate access to all the cultural resources of the world through channels of communications to libraries and other cultural repositories, and each basking in the security of an invisible and cybernetic world state in which each man shall live under his vine and his own fig tree and none shall make him afraid."[38]

Despite any such predictions regarding the disappearance of urban civilization, the city has displayed a remarkable resilience in meeting the challenges of past ages, and all indications today are that the city remains a highly vibrant institution, not only in the United States but throughout the rest of the world as well. In 1800 an estimated 15.6 million of the world's people were living in cities of 100,000 or more inhabitants. By 1950 this figure had jumped to 313.7 million—an increase of more than twentyfold. While much of this increase can be attributed to the general rise in world population during the past 150 years, the rate of world

37. J. Bronowski, "1984 Could Be a Good Year," *New York Times Magazine,* July 15, 1962, 41.

38. Kenneth E. Boulding, "The Death of the City: A Frightened Look at Postcivilization," *The Historian and the City,* ed. by Handlin and Burchard (Cambridge, 1963), 143-144.

urbanization has far outstripped general population growth. Whereas only one in every fifty persons was living in cities of twenty thousand or more in 1800, one in every five persons lives in such cities today. "Much of this increase has obviously come from rural-urban migration, clearly the most massive migration in modern times."[39]

Since rapid urbanization appears to be directly related to industrial growth, this migration pattern has tended to concentrate in the world's most highly developed economic nations. Great Britain has been in the vanguard of urban development since 1800, and today more than 80 per cent of its people live in urban areas—the highest concentration of urban population in the world. In Germany the urban population exceeds 70 per cent, while both the United States (69.9 per cent) and Canada (69.6 per cent) are at the very edge of this same 70-per-cent figure. The rapid industrialization of the Soviet Union is also leading to massive increases in urban population. The 1959 census classified some 99.8 million people, or 48 per cent of the USSR population, as living in urban areas—an increase of no less than 39.4 million over the last census in 1939—all the more impressive if one takes into account the heavy war losses the Russian cities suffered from 1940 to 1945.

As would be expected, the world's less industrialized nations are not this highly urbanized. Virtually all of the developing nations are now experiencing a tremendous urban boom, however, as they begin their long climb up the economic ladder. The urban population of India, for example, was estimated at only 17.3 per cent in the 1951 census, yet Calcutta and New Delhi each contained over two million inhabitants, and Bombay over four million. Likewise, Communist China listed an urban population of only 14.2 per cent in its 1956 census, yet this figure covered

39. Kingsley Davis, "The Origin and Growth of Urbanization in the World," *The American Journal of Sociology*, LX, No. 5 (March 1955), 433-434.

some ninety million urban residents, including such huge centers as Shanghai (seven million) and Peiping (four million). Thus, despite the fact that Asia has a smaller percentage of urban population than any continent except Africa, it already has more large cities and more people living in them than either Europe or North America.[40]

Asia has not been alone in experiencing the new forces of urbanization that have swept over the developing nations. In 1960 it was estimated that some 20 per cent of the world's population was living in cities of 100,000 or more inhabitants. By the end of this century it is estimated that this figure will jump to 42 per cent, a truly remarkable increase when one realizes that the current world population is expected to more than double during this same period. North America will be at the forefront of this urban explosion, but all of the other continents are also expected to experience sizable increases: [41]

ESTIMATED PERCENTAGE OF POPULATION LIVING IN CITIES OF 100,000 OR MORE INHABITANTS

Continent	1960	1975	2000
North America	60%	65%	77%
Latin America	25	39	50
Europe (inc. USSR)	30	36	48
Asia	12	22	39
Africa	8	16	25
Oceania	44	50	55

40. Figures on selected countries are taken from United Nations *Demographic Yearbook,* 1960, 373-390. It should be noted that there are wide variations in the way individual countries classify their "urban" populations. Many use the general criteria of "Cities and Towns," while others use population figures that vary from 1,000 in Canada to 20,000 in the Netherlands. The "urban" criterion for the United States is a community of "2,500 or more inhabitants," while the USSR uses "cities, towns, and urban-type localities," with no specified population requirements.

41. Homer Hoyt, *World Urbanization* (Urban Land Institute Technical Bulletin #43).

The above estimates have prompted such groups as the World Health Organization, a UN specialized agency, to declare that "after the question of keeping world peace, metropolitan planning is probably the most serious single problem faced by man in the second half of the twentieth century." Constantinos Doxiadis, the Greek city planner, is among those who have begun to recognize the full dimensions of this problem. Doxiadis forecasts that within the next hundred years the world's population may soar to twenty-five billion, and by then all of our major cities will have coalesced into one giant "cosmopolis," or world city. We must learn to direct these forces of cosmopolitan growth and establish meaningful new patterns of urban living. In order to promote this end, Doxiadis has founded a new science of "ekistics," governed by an organic theory of human settlement that provides for planning cities so that they will naturally adjust to technological change and population growth.[42]

Not all of these challenges, however, are grounded in the future. A great deal is to be found in the needs of today. Throughout history, man's approach toward the city has always involved an ambivalent lag between the ideal and the real—between his highest aspirations of urban beauty and the grim squalor of his existing urban world. More often than not, man's longing for the good life has found its clearest expression in urban symbolism:

> Visions of man's ultimate destiny on earth, and indeed often in heaven, have usually taken shape around the city. To build some kind of New Jerusalem or Celestial City has appeared to demand the most consummate artistry of which men are capable . . . Though these visions have been blurred by the mists and disillusionments of history, yet the dream continues to recur in ever new forms.[43]

42. For an interesting "Profile" on Doxiadis, see Christopher Rand, "The Ekistic World," *New Yorker,* May 11, 1963.

43. Humphrey Carver, *Cities in the Suburbs* (Toronto, 1962), 23.

The extent to which urban America is able to realize this dream within her own cities—and to provide the leadership that other nations of the world will require if they are to meet their own urban needs—may well determine whether we will be able to approach the ideals of the Great Society, not only at home but abroad.

8

TECHNOLOGY AND CHANGE: THE MEANING OF WORK

ROBERT H. GUEST

TECHNOLOGICAL innovation has been and will continue to be one of the most profound forces for change in Western society. Its effect is manifest today through the entire spectrum of human experience. Technology has revolutionized agriculture, industry, medicine, and education in a remarkably short space of time. The products of technology and their uses easily become matters of common knowledge. The secondary effects of technology on social institutions and on human interchange are also recognized, even if not fully understood until after they have become part of the total fabric of life.

Time and space have been shortened by the harnessing of the air waves and by the extraordinary developments in propulsion, but technology has also broadened social horizons and changed the core family and traditional kinship relations. Technology has measurably altered the size and function of urban living. Innovations in science and technology have not only enhanced the treatment of the sick but have substantially increased the span of life itself. And technology has now also made possible the total destruction of all life.

The crucial issue is not whether technology will continue to change at an accelerated pace; it will. Rather the fundamental question is whether society can create the social and political institutions needed to cope with technology's all-pervading effects.

This essay has a modest purpose. While viewing some of the large effects of technology somewhat impressionistically, it focuses on one aspect of the subject which has been neglected as an area of inquiry: man's direct relationship to the machine. How is modern technology changing the nature of work? What *meaning* does work have, other than the pay check, for the hundreds of thousands who spend such a large part of their adult lives in direct contact with machines? Why shouldn't the hours a man spends at work be considered as important to him and to society as the products and services which are consumed outside the work place?

Technology has given America its high standard of living, or more properly, its high level of consumption. But in a deeper sense the fulfillment of needs takes place not in leisure hours alone but at work as well. The notion that work is a means to other ends is deeply ingrained in the American ethos. There has also been a pervasive assumption that the benefits from the products of technology far outweigh the discontents that have been generated among those who produce the goods which they and the rest of society enjoy. But these assumptions conflict with another set of values related to man's "psychological health." We place a high premium on the notion of the "whole man." A psychologically healthy person is one who feels he has some control over his environment, and this control comes when he can utilize the full range of his capabilities.

The point has been made many times that the industrial revolution led to a fragmentation of work.[1] This fragmentation created a condition of alienation which was psychologically unhealthy for the worker. Alienation exists when a person feels powerless to control his immediate environment, when he can see little relationship between his immediate job and the purpose of the larger organization of which he is a part, when he feels isolated or remote from the larger society, and when work is only a means to some end outside of the work place—notably, his wages and what they provide him beyond the factory gates.

At least one observer has held that men were not alienated from work during the earlier *craft* period of technology. Alienation set in with increased mechanization of the work process. One of the central conclusions of this essay is that in today's most advanced sectors of technology there is the potential for a decrease in work alienation and an emancipation that may lead to a fuller life at the work place. But if modern technology is leading to greater utilization of man's capacities, it is at the moment more the result of accident than of design, and a deliberate effort will have to be made to exploit the potential advantages. Work continues to be based on certain rational and mechanical principles that pay scant attention to fundamental human needs. To understand this we need to begin with a brief historical overview of technical innovations, with special attention to the concept of work rationalization introduced at the turn of the twentieth century. We can then analyze the actual work environments created by modern technology and emphasize the opportunity and challenge we have to make work more meaningful.

1. Robert Blauner, *Alienation and Freedom: The Factory Worker and His Industry* (Chicago, 1964).

The Stages of Technology

A cursory knowledge of industrial history makes certain facts clear. The early days of industrialism saw many men, women, and children working under deplorable conditions. For those who worked in shops and factories there were few rewards: wages were low; hours of work were long; there was little security to employment. Many were driven to work out of sheer hunger and there were very few safeguards against hazardous conditions. Workers were regarded as so many "hands" whose only job was to keep machines running in return for modest wages.

The picture of the first hundred years of the Industrial Revolution is not all black, however. Many workers were still craftsmen in the true sense of the word: they had direct identification with the product. Craft skills were built up after years of apprenticeship, and control of both quantity and quality was vested wholly in the craftsman's hand. Production was not machine-paced.

The craftsmen were part of a stage of technological development that was soon overtaken, however. In American production, technology may be characterized by four stages of development.[2] The *craft* period falls in an early stage of low mechanization and hand tools. The introduction of steam power and mechanical devices for processing goods ushered in what might be described as the *machine* period. This phase dominated nineteenth-century technology and much of early twentieth-century industrial production. But the twentieth century also saw the introduction of *assembly-line* technology and, more recently, automatic continuous flow processes made possible by what is now known as *continuous-flow* technology, including the application of computers to the work process.

These four stages represent a kind of evolution through which

2. These technological stages are similar to Blauner's.

many industries have passed. Many industries originally started as a craft type, moved into a machine technology, expanded to the use of assembly lines, and later became automated. Shoe manufacturing and glass making began as simple craft trades and today have reached an advanced stage of mechanization. In some industries, such as printing, many of the work tasks continue to be carried out as craft functions. Other industries, such as automobile manufacturing, had very short periods of craft technology. They quickly moved into a more advanced stage. The stages may also overlap. Indeed, the elements of all four types of technology may be found in virtually all modern industrial enterprises.

These four stages or types of mechanization have distinguishing characteristics which help to explain the intrinsic nature of human work. They determine the degree of freedom and control men exercise over the immediate work environment. They call for different ranges of mental and physical skills required to perform tasks and hence different ranges of opportunity for achieving what was described earlier as psychological health. The type of technology determines the size, structure, and function of work groups, hence the social relationships. The division of labor required to carry out industrial tasks varies considerably with the type of technology. As will be seen later, the most extreme subdivision of labor is usually associated with the assembly-line type of technology. Also, as one views the four types of technology as they evolved historically, one can see that in the last half-century there has come about a systematic rationalization of work to the point where most work behavior is determined by carefully spelled-out rules and procedures, based on work measurement, which have tended to limit further the worker's controls over the immediate work environment. One of the questions this essay raises is whether the application of logic and scientific management to the design of work has fulfilled both the requirements for productive efficiency and the needs for self-fulfillment by the individual. And, as indicated, our special concern will be with the last two phases of technological progress, assembly-line technology and continuous-process technology, both of which are common to industrial work at the present time.

The period of craft technology extends back into medieval times. In America it was the primary type of technology at the time of the settlement of the colonies and lasting into the early 1800's. Most of the materials (iron, copper, and wood) were "worked" by hand and with simple tools. Power, whether for transportation or for tilling the soil, relied largely on the muscle power of animals. Water-wheel power was also employed for such tasks as wheat grinding and in the early days of textile manufacturing.

The shift from craft technology to machine technology came with the invention of the reciprocating steam engine which led to the mass production of spun yarn. It also created a new institution in the society, the *factory*. This came about primarily because central power required the concentration of manpower as well as machines in a central location. The former "putting-out" system was no longer feasible.

The rise of machine technology leading to the concentration of work in the larger factory organization was accelerated to some extent by an act of national policy in 1790, namely the Patent Act. Impressed by new developments in the grist mill industry, the significance of the steamboat, and other new inventions both at home and abroad, President Washington and members of Congress sought to encourage the development of new inventions through patent protection. Hamilton in his Report on Manufactures a year later recognized the economic benefits to the country by the increased production resulting from new inventions. The demand for greater production, Hamilton saw, would make for the employment of large numbers of workers.

Hamilton also recognized that the new technology would require new skills. Such skills were not readily available in the young America of the time. Both Hamilton and Jefferson, in one of their rare agreements, committed the nation to encouraging the immigration of skilled workers from abroad. America found it easier to "import" inventors and skilled craftsmen than it did the inventions themselves. In England, for example, Parliament had prohibited the exportation of inventions such as the power loom and the spinning jenny. But many inventors and craftsmen in England saw great opportunity for utilizing their skills in America. By the turn of the century, not only was American industry expanding by duplicating inventions from abroad but Americans, under the protection of the Patent Act, were also demonstrating a high level of creativity on their own part.

As the new inventions proliferated and factories were built, staffed by dozens and later hundreds of workers, the character of work itself underwent a basic change. Like the machine and the machine tool, workers became "instruments" of production. The home-spun era, although it predominated rural America, was phasing out during the first half of the nineteenth century. America was becoming a market economy. The factory organization was superseding the family as the basic work group even though the larger proportion of citizens was engaged in agriculture.

Adam Smith had been remarkably perceptive in seeing the implications of the centralization of production. He saw that the factory system would involve a division of labor determined by the imperatives of the machine. By the end of the first quarter of the nineteenth century, Andrew Ure defined the factory system quite simply by calling it "the combined operations of many work people, adult and young, attending with assiduous skill a system of productive machines continuously impelled by a central power." [3]

The degree of mechanization, which in turn determined the nature of the direct man-machine relationship, varied widely in the early period of industrial growth. In the textile industry there

3. Andrew Ure, *The Philosophy of Manufactures* (London, 1835). Quoted from John W. Oliver, *History of American Technology* (New York, 1956), 127.

had already evolved a high degree of job specialization. In other types of manufacturing, such as glass making, tanning, and iron production, the individual worker had to apply a variety of skills. He was more responsible for what may be described as the total product. It was the introduction of the basic machine tool, the machine lathe, that brought on changes having far-reaching effects on the organization of work at the factory level. The machine tool made it possible to turn out interchangeable parts. No longer were individual parts hand made. They could be standardized and turned out in large quantity. Eli Whitney, in his contract to produce muskets for the U.S. army, is given credit for having applied the concept of standardization to the mass production of firearms.

By the end of the first quarter of the nineteenth century, westward expansion was well under way and with it began a proliferation of small shops, many of which later burgeoned into large industries. Iron production on a modest scale sprang up in the Pittsburgh area and along the banks of the Ohio. Pottery plants were built in western Virginia. By 1811 Wheeling had four iron foundries and four woolen and cotton mills as well as a steam-engine plant. With the opening up of the canals and later the railroads, workers moved into Indiana, Illinois, Missouri, and other Midwestern states.

In the big cities other new industries were springing up, making possible such "modern" innovations as central heating, gas lighting, running water, and other consumer conveniences. Even before the mid-century London Exhibition, British observers were impressed by the many American technological innovations. Virgil Maxey was able to say in 1839, "The ingenious Americans with their new machines are rapidly gaining control over the power of the elements and are making fire, air, earth, and water their ministering servants." [4]

Although the new inventions in America were rapidly leading to a market economy with a broad industrial base, the era of large

4. Oliver, *op. cit.,* 112.

scale mass production (except in textiles) had not yet begun. America had yet to become an export nation. To the British and to the Europeans it seems to have been taken for granted that the Old World would continue to be the major exporter of both the ideas and the hardware of the new technology. This condition began to change in the 1840's and the late 1850's. Not only were Americans beginning to copy British locomotives, but these products could be produced in large quantity at low cost. By mid-century American locomotives were being sold in England itself. American engineers were hired by Czar Nicholas I to aid in the construction of the Moscow-St. Petersburg railroad. Friedrich List, the "father of the German railway system," developed his basic plans from his contacts with American experts. France, Austria-Hungary, and other nations were making greater use of American railroad technology.

American technology received its first dramatic exposure abroad with the London Exhibition of 1851. More than five major awards were given to American designs, the most outstanding being McCormick's reaper, labeled at first as the "ugly duckling." The successful tests of the reaper at the Exhibition won the unanimous praise of the judges. As Charles T. Rodgers put it in 1852, the McCormick reaper "mowed down British prejudice and opened the way for bringing our countrymen and their contributions before the public in a proper light." [5] The London Exhibition also revealed the remarkable technological developments in rubber technology, vehicles of many types, fire arms, machine tools, and various scientific measuring devices and compasses. To crown the American triumphs, the schooner *America* won the international yacht race at Cowes.

Continued westward expansion, a large population increase amplified by immigration from abroad, and foreign investment stimulated by technological progress—these forces brought America to

5. *Ibid.*, 255.

the verge of its great mass-production period. The Civil War gave it added impetus. As in later wars, the military requirements in the Civil War led to a "spin-off" of a number of inventions adapted for civilian use. Telegraphy and photography appeared for the first time on a large scale. The iron-clad ship was born. Basic industries that were formerly limited to isolated and small-scale operations grew in size and complexity. Steel making saw the introduction of large concentrations of manpower in the Bessemers, open hearths, rolling mills, and the fabricating component industries.

Subtle but important changes were also taking place in the man-machine relationship at the immediate job level. The need for craft skills continued on certain types of jobs, but the bulk of the work was performed with unskilled and semi-skilled labor. The technical processes were determining the character of the jobs, the pace at which men worked, and the degree of control workers could exercise. The blue-collar worker worked on a fraction of the product. Jobs were broken down into small segments. Industrial organizations were becoming complex bureaucracies. Administrative staffs were added. The maintenance of the total work processes required an increase in clerical staffs and auxiliary groups. The worker who formerly had a direct relationship to owner-managers lost what may be described as the social "connective tissue" to the larger organization.

The rise of vertically integrated mass production industries laid the groundwork for the assembly-line type of industrial operation. The classic example of such technology was the introduction of the assembly line by Henry Ford. The concept of progressive work flow along a moving sequence of operations was not new. The meat processing industry had adopted conveyor belt and continuous trolley mechanisms a quarter of a century earlier. Indeed, one can find examples of mass assembly as far back as the fourteenth century. The Venetians, for instance, were able to build, outfit, and provision vessels ready to sail at a rate of more than thirteen per day. But it was not until the twentieth century that assembly-line principles were adopted on a mass scale employing large numbers of the total working population.

For our purposes the most important development of assembly-line technology was not in machines and hardware alone but in the application of scientific measurement to human work itself, first introduced by the "father" of scientific management, Frederick W. Taylor. What Taylor did in applying systematic measurement to human work is, in many respects, as significant as Ford's introduction of the automobile assembly line. Taylor, and later Gantt and Gilbreth, came to realize that it was not enough to apply scientific reasoning in the design of the machine and factory layouts. There were gross inefficiencies in the human component of the man-machine system.

In essence Taylor's method for rationalizing work was through job analysis and time study. A job could be considered as the sum of many individual operations performed by both men and machines. Job analysis distinguishes what is essential to the completion of a task and what is waste motion. Once the individual operations are identified it becomes possible to time the components using a stop watch. The times can be added together, thus permitting a re-analysis and a re-combination of all elements in the most efficient manner.

The system permits a high degree of control. Standardized procedures can be instituted to minimize errors. Movements of machines and muscles can be synchronized according to predetermined metric units of time. The operator is relieved of the necessity to make individual judgments.

The rationale for the Taylor system of analysis and measurement was not new. It was a synthesis of ideas that had been applied formerly to machine processes themselves. It had its philosophical origins in eighteenth-century rationalism and nineteenth-century Benthamite utilitarianism. Yet as applied to human effort it was a cultural innovation of considerable importance in its own right. It created a system of human manipulation and control not only for workers but for vast numbers of people at all levels of our complex production organizations.

The Worker on the Assembly Line

The principal criticism of Taylor and of the work rationalization concept is that they ignored the workers' feelings and motivations. Taylor himself vigorously denied this. The basis for his denial was that men would respond favorably to the obvious logic of its benefits. The worker would certainly appreciate the elimination of wasteful and unproductive motions. He would be glad to have tasks simplified without having to make complicated decisions. He would welcome guidance as to the "best way" of performing the task. He would be given the right tools to do the job. Machines would be kept in proper adjustment. The worker would be paid fairly for his effort. Indeed, wage incentives could be established on a piece work basis so that extra compensation could be given for extra effort. He, like any normal human being, would respond to man's natural desire to benefit himself economically.

Frederick Taylor could never quite comprehend why the application of his theory of work measurement brought about such a strong reaction in those plants where the new scheme was tried out. The first major installation was made in 1908 at the U.S. army arsenal at Watertown, Massachusetts. It caused something more than just a strike. It brought on a congressional investigation resulting in legislation barring the use of work measurement systems in all government production facilities.[6] The law stayed on the books for thirty-five years. Unions became aware of a new

6. Hugh G. J. Aitken, *Taylorism at Watertown Arsenal: Scientific Management in Action, 1908-1915* (Cambridge, 1960).

threat. While continuing to fight for the usual economic and security benefits, a few unions took up the new challenge against the slide rule and stop watch. But most unions at the time were structured along craft lines; the large mass of industrial workers was not yet organized.

In the larger industries the Taylor movement gained strong support in management. An entirely new profession of time-study experts and industrial engineers came into being. Time and motion became the passwords of industrial efficiency.

By the mid-1930's the scientific management revolution was in full bloom. This was also the time of the rise of the industrial union as we know it today. The industrial union continued many of the basic traditional union functions: bargaining for wages, establishing grievance procedures, setting up agreements with respect to seniority, hours, and other general conditions of employment. From the beginning the industrial unions clashed head on with problems of work standards and wage incentives—problems whose origins could be traced in part to the Taylor movement of work rationalization.

Assembly-line technology continues to play an important part in the total production system even though automated, continuous-flow technology is gaining rapidly. It is also from the assembly line experience that one can find clues about the way to tap the potential benefits of the more advanced technology in terms of enriching the working hours. To do this, it is well to consider precisely how the worker views the world of the assembly line. A case that offers deep insights is that of the auto assembly worker on the "final line." "The extraordinary ingenuity that has gone into the construction of automobile assembly lines, their perfected synchronization, the 'all but human' or 'more than human' character of the machines, the miracle of a car rolling off the conveyor each minute under its own power—all this has caught and held the world's imagination for a quarter of a century. On the other hand, the extreme subdivision of labor (the man who puts a nut on a bolt is the symbol) conjoined with the 'endlessly moving belt' has made the [automobile] assembly line the classic symbol of the subjection of man to the machine in our industrial age." [7]

Utilizing the two basic principles of standardization and interchangeability, Henry Ford was able to work out and apply three additional "principles" of progressive manufacture in pioneering the automobile assembly line:

1. The orderly progression of the product through the shop in a series of planned operations so arranged that the right part always arrives at the right place at the right time.

2. The mechanical delivery of these parts to the operators, and the mechanical delivery of the product from the operators, as it is assembled.

3. A breakdown of operations into their simple constituent motions.

These principles are purely mechanical. Extended to the human component of the total work flow system, they mean the following for the worker:

(a) Mechanically controlled work pace
(b) Repetition of simple motions
(c) Minimum skill requirements
(d) Pre-determined operating procedures
(e) Small fraction of the total product worked on
(f) Superficial mental attention

How does the man on the line react? Here is one worker's response. It is typical of hundreds which this observer and others have heard in the course of their research.

The worker is J.D., a graduate of a public vocational training school, thirty-six years old, married, with two children. He makes

7. Charles R. Walker and Robert H. Guest, *The Man on the Assembly Line* (Cambridge, 1952).

good wages and is buying his own home. He is being interviewed at home.[8]

"Some years back I heard that they were hiring people for the assembly plant. Must have been thousands of fellows lined up for the job. The word got around that they were paying real good money. It was a big outfit, too. No fly-by-night affair.

"Figured I'd get any job and then, with a little electrician experience I had in vocational school, I could work my way up to a good job. And the idea of making automobiles sounded like something. Lucky for me I got a job and was made a spot welder on the front cowling. There wasn't much to the job itself. Picked it up in about a week. I tried to get into the Maintenance Department as an electrician, but there was no opening, so I went back to the line—we call it the iron horse. They made me a welder again, and that's what I have been doing ever since."

The worker then went on to describe his job:

"My job is to weld the cowl to the metal underbody. I take a jig off the bench, put it in place and weld the parts together. The jig is all made up and the welds are made in set places along the metal. Exactly twenty-five spots. The line runs according to schedule. Takes me one minute and fifty-two seconds for each job. I walk along the line as it moves. Then I snap the jig off, walk back down the line, throw it on the bench, grab another just in time to start on the next car. The cars differ, but it's practically the same thing. Finish one—then have another one staring me in the face.

"I don't like to work on the line—no man likes to work on a moving line. You can't beat the machine. Sure, maybe I can keep it up for an hour, but it's rugged doing it eight hours a day, every day in the week all year long.

"During each day I get a chance for a breather ten minutes in the morning, then a half-hour for lunch, then a few minutes in the

8. Parts of interview reprinted from *Personnel,* May 1955, with permission of American Management Association.

afternoon. When I'm working there is not much chance to get a breather. Sometimes the line breaks down. When it does we all yell 'Whoopee!' As long as the line keeps moving I've got to keep up with it. On a few jobs I know some fellows can work like hell up the line, then coast. Most jobs you can't do that. If I get ahead maybe ten seconds the next model has more welds to it, so it takes ten seconds extra. You hardly break even. You're always behind. When you get too far behind, you get in a hole—that's what we call it. All hell breaks loose. I get in the next guy's way. The foreman gets sore and they have to rush in a relief man to bail you out.

"It's easy for them time-study fellows to come down there with a stop watch and figure out just how much a man can do in a minute and fifty-two seconds. There are some things they can see and record with their stop watch. But they can't clock how a man feels from one day to the next. Those guys ought to work on the line for a few weeks and maybe they'll feel some things that they never pick up on the stop watch.

"I like a job where you feel like you're accomplishing something and doing it right. When everything's laid out for you and the parts are all alike, there's not much you feel you accomplish. The big thing is that steady push of the conveyor—a gigantic machine which I can't control.

"You know, it's hard to feel that you are doing a good quality job. There is that constant push at high speed. You may improve after you've done a thing over and over again, but you never reach a point where you can stand back and say, 'Boy, I done that one good. That's one car that got built right.' If I could do my best I'd get some satisfaction out of working, but I can't do as good work as I know I can do.

"My job is all engineered out. The jigs and fixtures are all designed and set out according to specifications. There are a lot of little things you could tell them but they never ask you. You go by the bible. They have a suggestion system, but the fellows don't use it too much because they're scared that a new way to do it may do one of your buddies out of a job.

"There's only three guys close by—me and my partner and a couple of fellows up the line a bit. I talk to my partner quite a lot. We gripe about the job 90 per cent of the time. You don't have time for any real conversation. The guys get along okay—you know the old saying, 'Misery loves company.'

"My foreman's an all right guy. I see him once in a while outside, and he's 100 per cent. But in the shop he can't be. If I was a foreman nobody would like me either. As a foreman he has to push you all the time to get production out so that somebody above won't push him. But the average guy on the line has no one to push—you can't fight the line. The line pushes you. We sometimes kid about it and say we don't need no foreman. That line is the foreman. Some joke."

The worker then discussed the general working conditions in the plant—the lighting, ventilation, safety conditions, cafeteria facilities, and the plant hospital. He thought these conditions were all good, but then added:

"But you know it's a funny thing. These things are all good, but they don't make the job good. It's what you spend most of the time doing that counts.

"My chances for promotion aren't so hot. You see, almost everybody makes the same rate. The jobs have been made so simple that there is not much room to move up from one skill to another. In other places where the jobs aren't broken down this way, the average fellow has something to look forward to. He can go from one step to another right up the ladder. Here it's possible to make foreman. But none of the guys on the line think there's much chance to go higher than that. To manage a complicated machine like that, you need a college degree. They bring in smart college boys and train them for the better jobs."

Interviewer: "What does your wife think about your job?"

At this point his wife spoke up: "I often wish he'd get another job. He comes home at night, plops down in a chair and just sits for about fifteen minutes. I don't know much about what he does at the plant, but it does something to him. Of course, I shouldn't complain. He gets good pay. We've been able to buy a refrigerator and a TV set—a lot of things we couldn't have had otherwise. But sometimes I wonder whether these are more important to us than having Joe get all nervous and tensed up. He snaps at the kids and snaps at me—but he doesn't mean it."

The worker was then asked if he had considered working elsewhere:

"I'll tell you honest. I'm scared to leave. I'm afraid to take the gamble on the outside. I'm not staying because I want to. You see, I'm getting good pay. We live according to the pay I get. It would be tough to change the way we live. With the cost of living what it is, it's too much of a gamble. Then there's another thing. I got good seniority. I take another job and I start from scratch. Comes a depression or something and I'm the first to get knocked off. Also they got a pension plan. I'm thirty-seven and I'd lose that. Course the joker in that pension plan is that most guys out there chasing the line probably won't live till they're sixty-five. Sorta trapped—you get what I mean?"

The subject of the worker's relationship to his union came up in the course of the interview:

"The union has helped somewhat. Before they organized, it was pretty brutal. The bosses played favorites—they kept jacking up the speed of the line every time after they had a breakdown. But the union can't do much about the schedule and the way a job is set up. Management is responsible for that.

"We'd had a walk-out last year. They called it an unauthorized strike. Somebody got bounced because he wouldn't keep up his job on the line. The union lost the case because it should have gone through the grievance procedure. The company was dead right to insist that the union file a grievance.

"But it was one of those things it's hard to explain. When word got around that the guy was bounced—we all sort of looked at each other, dropped our tools and walked. Somehow that guy was every one of us. The tension on the line had been building up for a long time. We had to blow our top—so we did. We were wrong —the union knew it and so did the company. We stayed out a few hours and back we came. We all felt better, like we got something off our chests.

"Some of these strikes you read about may be over wages. Or they may be unions trying to play politics. But I sometimes think that the thing that will drive a man to lose all that pay is deeper than wages. Maybe other guys feel like we did the day we walked out."

Toward the end of the interview, the worker spoke of the company he worked for:

"They are doing what they can—like the hospital, the safety, the pay, and all like that. And the people who run the plant I guess are pretty good guys themselves. But sometimes I think that the company doesn't think much of the individual. If they did they wouldn't have a production line like that one. You're just a number to them. They number the stock and they number you. There's a different feeling in this kind of a plant. It's like a kid who goes up to a grown man and starts talking to him. There doesn't seem to be a friendly feeling. Here a man is just so much horsepower. You're just a cog in the wheel."

Notice, first, that this worker's dissatisfaction was not due primarily to the things that are usually considered important to a job. This man's pay was good. His job was secure. He worked for a sound company. He had substantial seniority. He had a pension, hospitalization and disability benefits when he became sick, and a good boss; at least he did not hold the kind of job he had against his boss. Working conditions, heating, lighting, cafeteria facilities, and safety conditions were as good if not better than the average found in industrial plants. Yet J.D. despised his job.

The simple fact is that the impact of "sound" engineering principles, when translated into human experience, had a profound effect on his view of the meaning of work. In this interview we find most of the elements of *alienation* referred to earlier. Both the technical setup and the application of work rationalization principles made this man feel hardly more than an extension of the machine. The sense of anonymity implicit in much of what he said can be traced back to some of the basic characteristics of his immediate job.

The conveyor belt determined the *pace* at which he worked. He had no control over his work rhythm.

Because the task was broken down into simple motions, the job was highly *repetitive*.

Simple repetitive motions meant that there was little need to call upon a variety of *skills*.

The tools and the work procedures were pre-determined. And when techniques changed, it was the engineer—not the worker—who controlled the change.

He worked on a *fraction of the product,* which meant that he never felt a sense of the "whole."

Some attention was required—too much to allow him to daydream or carry on any sustained conversation with others, but not enough to allow him to become absorbed in the work itself.

The technical setup determined the character of his work relationships. This man identified himself with the partner who worked with him on the opposite side of the line, but beyond that he displayed almost no identification with a work group as such. Men on the line work as an aggregate of individuals, each man performing his operation more or less independently of the others. The lack of an intimate group awareness appeared to reinforce the same sense of anonymity fostered by the conveyor-paced, repetitive character of the job itself.

The worker's comments about promotion and job aspirations are also pertinent. He saw little hope for advancement because most of the production jobs paid about the same. By applying principles of work rationalization, the industrial engineer, in the best interests of efficiency, had simplified the tasks so that differences in skill from one job to the next were all but eliminated. It was difficult for the average worker to move vertically through a series of distinct steps in promotion.

This case is only one of over four hundred actual work careers that have been studied. Only a few had experienced any substantial change in job classification during a period of from twelve to fifteen years. Collectively, all the workers had improved their overall economic status; individually, few had experienced much change in their relative job status. The net effect of this condition was to increase the *de*-personalization of the job.

The case of an automobile assembly line worker is in many respects an extreme case in the application of the principles of work rationalization. There are many types and conditions of work in which the degree of dissatisfaction is not expressed as strongly as it was in this case. Nevertheless, there is little evidence that work in highly repetitive, conveyor-paced jobs is looked upon as a meaningful end in itself.

The Coming of Automation

Although the basic characteristics of assembly-line technology pervade many segments of industrial production, there are significant changes in technology which may lead to a new "emancipation" for the worker. Popularly known as automation, the new technology, like assembly-line technology, is based on the principle of continuous flow. What is new is that mechanical and electronic devices have been substituted for human organs of decision and effort.

Automatic continuous-flow technology came of age in the petroleum refining and industrial chemical industries. Later the same principles were applied in basic steel production and even to the machining and fabricating of metals. Materials are fed into and pass through a sequence of operations each of which is programed and controlled with a minimum of direct human intervention. In more advanced types of operations linked to computers, the equipment has "built-in" self-correcting devices which not only signal the need for mechanical adjustments but actually set in motion the mechanisms to make such adjustments. For many years the automatic continuous-flow principle was adaptable only to the large-scale production of identical or near-identical products. In small-lot production human skills were required to "re-set the job" for runs of different items. Today it is possible to program equipment automatically for short runs of products with different specifications for each run.

The immediate and pressing problem of the new technology is not usually seen in terms of its effects on the meaning of work. Rather it is related to the broad problem of displacement of men by machines. This is not only important as a matter of national employment policy; it also has an effect on those currently employed who see accelerated technical changes being made all around them. Uppermost in their minds is the question, "Am I the one to go next?" This question has a marked effect on how men look at work itself.

Technological displacement has been a fact of industrial life since the start of the Industrial Revolution. History is strewn with examples of attempts to arrest the installation of labor-saving devices. Riots by the Luddites to destroy new machinery in the early nineteenth century stemmed from the same fears of displacement reflected in the crippling strikes—or threat of strikes—in the 1960's in railroads, airlines, construction trades, the atomic production industry, and in disputes at missile launching sites.

Whole industries have experienced growth in productive capacity despite a sharply declining relative rate of employment. Automobile production increased 50 per cent from 1947 to 1960 while employment fell 2.9 per cent.[9] In five years prior to 1960, em-

9. Albert A. Blum, "America's Reactions to Technological Change and Automation: A Comparative View," *Management of Personnel Quarterly,* III, No. 3 (Fall 1964), 13.

ployment in the telephone industry dropped 5.5 per cent, or thirty-three thousand jobs, while business increased by 25 per cent. In a similar period employment among production and related workers in the electrical machine industry was down eighty thousand jobs—but productivity rose by 20 per cent. Similar trends can be seen in many industries, especially those rapidly adopting more advanced forms of mechanization. In spite of an overall increase in industrial employment from fifty-eight million in 1949 to sixty-eight million in 1963, the part of the work force without jobs increased to between 5 and 6 per cent in 1963. By the first quarter of 1965 the unemployment rate had declined to 5 per cent, but the absolute numbers of unemployed had increased.

Even the expansion of the service, communications, and transportation industries has not had a substantial effect on the unemployment picture. There is the additional problem of population growth with an estimated twenty-six million young men and women expected to enter the labor force during the 1960's.[10] In spite of efforts to expand markets, many consumer industries are approaching a saturation point. How many more television sets or automobiles can be sold? Even with the opening up of new markets for different products, the ratio of employees to units produced will continue to decline. Thus with little appreciable increase in total production there will continue to be a constant decrease in needed manpower.

It is also becoming quite clear which segments of the potential work force are hardest hit by the new automated technology. In 1963 the unemployment rate among teen-agers was 15 per cent.[11] The rate for Negro teen-agers has been twice that of whites. In depressed areas the general unemployment rate runs as high as 50 per cent.

Business, labor, and public authorities are now highly aware of

10. *Ibid.,* 15.

11. *The Triple Revolution,* A Report of the Ad Hoc Committee on the Triple Revolution (Santa Barbara, 1964), 8.

displacement problems associated with the new technology. There is growing realization that the economic and technological system does not have enough inherent "automatic" devices of adjustment and accommodation. Solutions will come only through deliberate and planned programs promoted by business, promoted through collective bargaining, or promoted at the highest levels of government as a matter of national policy.

Thomas J. Watson, Jr., president of IBM, a major manufacturer of automated equipment, has warned that adjustment to technological change cannot be left solely to the individual to work out his own problems.[12] He pleads for vast improvements in education and training, for relocation allowances, early retirement systems, a shorter work week, and fiscal reforms on a national scale. Unions have been especially outspoken in their demands to protect jobs or to negotiate agreements to cushion the effects of automation. They are asking for training programs to help displaced workers to be relocated. They are asking for the shorter work week, increased severance pay, guaranteed wages, longer vacations, and early retirement programs.

The President's Advisory Committee on Labor-Management Policy in 1962 put forward major policy recommendations. Legislation has since been adopted in the Accelerated Public Works Act, job retraining statutes, the anti-poverty bill, expanded social security, and many other programs. All are clearly directed at the central issue of machine displacement.

Many critics maintain that public and private programs now in effect or being considered merely scratch the surface of the problem. They call for a massive program of education, even suggesting the training of an additional 100,000 teachers a year over the present rate. They call for a public works program to create 200,000 jobs per year in the construction of dams, water and air pollution facilities, community recreation facilities, public buildings, and so forth. Public and private housing construction should

12. Blum, *op. cit.,* 15.

be increased, they say, to the rate of between 700,000 and 1,000,000 units per year. Urban renewal programs need to be stepped up, with basic support coming from federal funds. The list of suggestions is almost without limit.

Such proposals might go far in reducing the unemployment dislocations caused by technological change. But to adopt them on such a massive scale would require American society to accept an entirely new set of assumptions with respect to the role of government. It seems unlikely that, barring a major depression, Americans are willing to place such power in the hands of government at present, notwithstanding the powerful thrusts made under the Johnson administration.

There is also an international dimension to the problem. Failure to solve the problem of machine displacement, whether through public or private efforts, will have serious consequences beyond our borders. Nations eager to adopt American technology will be increasingly concerned with its social consequences. If America fails to come up with effective plans for coping with machine displacement, we have only added more fuel to the fires of today's frustrating anti-Americanism. It would be a sign that democracy is unable to meet the problems of modernization.

The big issue of displacement of men by machines is only one side of the dilemma, however. What about the question of automation in microcosm—the direct man-machine relationship among the large number of the working population who are not displaced? Is the new technology providing man with the opportunity for greater enrichment while at work, or is it leading into new eras of work alienation?

In a technical sense we have begun to acquire basic information about the characteristics of various types of automated technology. Unfortunately, data on the psychological and social effects is scarce and inconclusive. Most observers agree that the drudgery of the assembly-line technology is eliminated in the automated continuous-flow type of operation. Physical effort is no longer tied to machine pacing. General working conditions are considerably improved. At this point agreement ends. Some experts claim that work on automated jobs is merely a new extension of the work rationalization movement leading to a new kind of alienation. The argument here is that automated jobs for those directly linked to the production process do not call for a broadening of technical or intellectual skills. Limits of action are highly circumscribed by standard rules of procedure that allow for little deviation. Human control over the flow process is minimized because of "built-in" automatic feedback and self-correcting devices that eliminate the need for human judgment. Decision skills, it is said, can be programmed into computers which in turn are linked to the machinery. In short, the operator is reduced to the role of gauge-watcher and dial-setter.

On the basis of a limited number of interviews and observations in a dozen different types of highly automated operations, this writer would agree with some of the above speculations. In certain chemical operations, when experienced workers make the transition to almost fully automatic jobs, they complain that some of their former skills have been discarded. They imply resentment over the fact that engineers and specialists make the more important mechanical and electrical adjustments when serious problems arise. Interestingly enough, in a large pharmaceutical company it was discovered that many operators with no formal technical background could be trained to develop some highly sophisticated technical skills. The workers' reactions were enthusiastic.

In a newly automated seamless tube rolling mill in the steel industry, we found a similar pattern: resentment at the loss of some former skills, concern about reliance on engineers, and a certain degree of boredom at having to monitor gauges instead of the product itself. A similar pattern was observed among many workers at one of the most highly automated precision machining operations in the country.

On balance, however, most observations support the thesis that there is the potential, at least, for more work enrichment and less alienation from the job in many sectors of the new technology. Extrapolating from what is now known, some tentative predictions can be made. The worker will no longer be responsible for a small fractionated segment of the work process. He will be a "supervisor" of a more complex series of integrated operations. Unlike the man on the assembly line, he will have more freedom of movement. His pace of work will not be determined by the conveyor. Elimination of manual work in a prescribed job cycle will reduce the degree of repetitiveness. There may be relatively long periods of time with virtually nothing to do followed by periods of total involvement when the machinery runs into difficulties.

The worker will, moreover, have to be trained in a variety of maintenance and repair skills requiring technical judgments. The new technology may bring about a higher scientific orientation toward the total tasks. Improvements in the processes will mean periods of new training while employed. The integration of several presently separate operations will link the operator more closely with other operators, thus generating a sense of collective responsibility. In automated operations there is also a trend toward smaller plants, and these plants are being located outside the large urban concentrations. This could have favorable consequences leading to greater social identification with the work organization and the community.

Work measurement using standard motion and time techniques will be obsolete. This change could alter the entire concept of monetary payments for work performed. Piece work incentive plans, a persistent source of industrial unrest, will not be feasible in the automated continuous-flow type of operation. Even the age-old system of wage payment by the hour will become obsolete. Increased pressure by unions for a guaranteed annual wage is not simply a new bargaining device. It has a technological rationale. The new "equipment supervisor," as distinguished from the "factory hand," will not directly control given units of output. The metric hour for units produced will continue to be important for measuring machine output, but it is meaningless with respect to the "productivity" of the individual worker. In short, what an operator does to manage his part of a complex system will be hardly different from what managers and engineers are paid to do *by salary* in running their parts of the system.

Much of what has been said about the nature of work in the new technology is speculative. At best all one can do is to project possible consequences based on general trends. Just as government and private industry are collecting quantities of data on problems of unemployment because of technological displacement, so we need more detailed information about the nature of work itself on the new horizons of technology.

Collecting more information is not the only task. As stated earlier, what man does in his working life is just as important to him and to society as the goods and services he consumes in his leisure hours. This is a value accepted by the scientist, engineer, educator, manager, artist, politician, and many others who are not linked directly to the machine. Workers hold these same values, but too often technological constraints preclude their fulfillment. Does it have to be this way? This is the central question. Does technology have to be considered as a "given," meaning that humans as individuals, or as members of larger groups, must struggle to find *after-the-fact* ways to adapt? We think not. We believe that the same ingenuity and effort that has gone into the creation of our machines can be used to enrich the lives of those who operate them.

Applying the needed ingenuity is not an easy task. Old assumptions must be re-examined in light of new knowledge about human behavior. The function of work should be considered not solely in terms of immediate and measurable productive efficiency. The needs and potentials of humans *as humans* should be made a central consideration. The two are not necessarily antithetical.

There is encouraging evidence strongly suggesting how technical requirements can be met at the same time that a broad spectrum of human needs and aspirations are fulfilled.

Some years ago a department of a large American company began experimenting with a new idea which came to be known as *job enlargement.*[13] Dissatisfied with the application of scientific management principles in the design of tasks, the officials of the organization and a number of employees consulted on new ways of performing the required work. The workers convinced their superiors that instead of routinizing and fractionating work they would find it more challenging to work on a variety of tasks involving the production of a major component of the product. Management agreed—with reservations—and the experiment went forward. To management's astonishment not only was the rate of production maintained but the quality of work was vastly improved. Even more astonishing was the ingenuity of the workers in devising better ways of setting up the operations. They also made suggestions about the design of the product—suggestions which even design engineers had not thought of.

The experiment was observed by a group of social scientists who publicized it in an obscure academic publication.[14] In time a number of other experiments were conducted in other organizations. Although the proliferation of the job enlargement concept never took on the form of a great national "movement," it did shatter many assumptions held so strongly by the practitioners of scientific management. It gave encouragement to those who believed that human beings, even those with limited intelligence and education, were capable of being creative at work.

Job enlargement as a concept has been limited to fractionated tasks characterized by the assembly-line technology. It has not

13. See Robert H. Guest, "Better Utilization of Skills Through Job Design" in *Management of Personnel Quarterly,* III, No. 3 (Fall 1964), 3.

14. Charles R. Walker and Frederick L. W. Richardson, *Human Relations in an Expanding Company* (New Haven, 1947).

been deliberately considered in more automated operations, possibly because automated machine supervision, as noted above, does make use of an enlarged set of skills and capabilities. But again, this may be more the result of chance rather than of design. In most operations men are still viewed essentially as instruments performing work which the machine is not capable of doing itself.

The radical suggestion being made here is that we look first at the human needs and give men the fullest possible opportunity to express these needs in the work environment. This calls for something more than simply making jobs interesting. It involves a different relationship of workers to the whole system of organization. It calls for greater involvement in organizational as well as technical decisions by workers. It means a change in deeply held assumptions about competition between jobs at the work place. It calls for the elimination of many of the bureaucratic restraints and controls which those in positions of authority have felt are absolutely essential. It demands that the needs of higher level self-fulfillment must be met as well as the more basic security needs.

Finally, it should be recognized that as the level of education rises in our society there is a concomitant rise in expectations among the millions of youths seeking useful employment. On one hand the new technology demands this higher level of education and training for those who will become the scientists, engineers, and managers. But for the great majority more education could compound the frustrations of youth if, in their working lives, only limited use is made of their learning and of the full range of their human capacities. Surely, as the most technologically advanced society in the world, this is a challenge to which we can respond. It may mean a thoroughgoing shift in the motivations and bases of American industry. But it is obvious that these are already changing. Our task is to control change for the fuller life—at work and at leisure—that we can provide for all men.

9

THE STRUGGLE FOR CIVIL RIGHTS

VINCENT E. STARZINGER

THE concept of "civil" rights in America today is exceedingly broad and imprecise in contrast with what that concept has meant in other times. In early nineteenth-century Europe, for example, civil rights were defined usually as restraints against the possible abuses of a government in whose election the large majority of citizens had no voice. Even well into the century, the theory was that all individuals should have the right to free speech, worship, and jury trial, but that the right to vote could belong only to the upper classes who had demonstrated "political capacity" through the acquisition of property. In a sense, civil rights were a substitute for political rights.

In contrast, the attempt to guarantee every citizen an equal vote is at the heart of the civil rights cause in mid-twentieth-century America. That cause is directed against electoral discrimination based not only on race but on other factors such as rural or urban residence. That means, in turn, that the cause of civil rights is concerned with far more than mere checks on governmental power. It is also deeply concerned with the nature of the electoral system which defines a majority and which chooses those who wield power.[1]

Another expansion of the civil rights concept is the social and economic dimension which it has acquired in recent years. The target is no longer limited simply to abuses in the machinery of government and the electoral process. The goal now includes as well the elimination of a wide variety of racially discriminatory practices by individuals and groups within the private sector of society. Witness, for example, the present fight to guarantee Negroes equal access to housing, employment, transportation, restaurants, theaters, and hotels. Although some of these facilities can fairly be described as "public" in nature, the fact that they may be neither state owned nor operated has not deterred the advocates of broader civil rights.

Even within the conventional view of civil rights as restraints on purely governmental power, the complexity of American society and the role which our nation now plays in the world at large have created a range of problems which those who framed the Bill of Rights could hardly have foreseen. As the late Mr. Justice Jackson observed on one occasion, it has really become impossible at mid-twentieth century to define the limits of free speech in America without at the same time trying to calculate national security requirements which "baffle the best informed foreign offices." Or, to take quite another issue, the Supreme Court's historic declaration a decade ago that segregation in public schools was unconstitutional was based on the careful assessment by the Court of a large body of extremely complex, subtle, and sometimes contradictory sociological evidence concerning the impact of segregated education on the intellectual development of Negro pupils. Finally, even the seemingly simple question of what amounts to a constitutionally fair arrest and trial for a defendant in a criminal

1. Or, to return to Roger Brown's theme of republicanism, the cause involves a search for the very electoral criteria which define what a republic is in the first place.

prosecution can involve an exceedingly difficult balancing of the claims of the individual against the need for adequate law enforcement in a society menaced by organized crime syndicates, virulent juvenile delinquency, and other forms of violence.

Thus the cause of civil rights today is by no means simple in nature or narrow in scope. That cause touches practically every phase of contemporary American life and poses profound challenges for practically every American citizen. In fact, this situation seems to suggest that no detailed list of specific rights can yield a meaningful definition or understanding of civil rights in general. But an alternative remains. That, quite simply, is to define the cause of civil rights as an attempt to rearticulate and fulfill the American dream of individual freedom and equality.

If that definition seems overly general, it nonetheless cuts to the heart of the civil rights struggle. For it is obvious that those fighting today for broader freedom and equality feel that the full meaning of those two ideals is not embodied in America's past or present institutions. In turn, the crucial question to ask is what the terms "freedom" and "equality" mean in a conceptual or analytical sense. If we can answer that general question at the outset, we will hopefully then have some working tools with which to examine what exactly is involved in the attainment of freedom and equality within specific areas of the contemporary civil rights movement.

The Concepts of Freedom and Equality

Usually people think of freedom and equality in negative terms —the first as the *absence* of coercion or tyranny or oppression, the second as the *absence* of discrimination among individuals. At the same time practically anyone would recognize instances in which the coercion of individuals and the unequal treatment of individuals can be justified. Few would argue, for example, that a minor should have the same legal and political rights as an adult or that a citizen should be free to refuse to pay his taxes whenever he disagrees with the policy of his government. More fundamentally, it is a fact of life that, regardless of justification, a good deal of coercion and inequality in human society can never be eliminated. The day will never come when the individual can choose whether to be born or who his parents are to be. Even the free choice by an individual of the country in which he lives is exceedingly rare, for the societal and political pressures against expatriation are formidable indeed.

As for equality, even if one adheres to the normative proposition that all men ought to be treated equally, the fact remains that if we factor out all the different talents and attributes from any group of individuals, there is very little left to justify any claim that men are equal. We may be left with the notion of the sanctity of man's soul, but belief in that is itself a value judgment or act of faith. Despite these qualifications, however, most people seem to stand by the negative definition of freedom and equality and insist that the task before us is simply to reduce to an absolute minimum whatever coercion and unequal treatment exist in society.

My approach is rather different. My thesis is not merely that the *exceptions* to the general rules—"men ought to be free from coercion" and "men ought to be treated equally"—turn out to be more important than those imperatives themselves. I will also argue that institutionalized coercion is really the only technique by which any meaningful experience of freedom can be achieved, and that institutionalized discrimination among individuals is often the only technique by which any meaningful experience of equality can be achieved. In what might seem a paradox: freedom through coercion; equality through discrimination.

To consider freedom first, there is a direct relationship between the realization of freedom in a society and the conformity which that society imposes upon the individual. Americans, for example, are terribly proud of their freedom from governmental prescription of each and every detail of daily existence. Yet in a profound sense the state can and has abdicated from that task precisely because societal and other coercions have already done the job instead. We can be trusted with freedom because so few of us are likely to turn out to be communists, fascists, anarchists, or arsonists—because the overwhelming majority is fairly certain to exercise freedom in conformity to accepted standards of morality and reason. And indeed most regimes extend a generous measure of freedom to groups and individuals only when they are fairly certain in advance what those groups and individuals will do with freedom. The point is that, whether he realizes it or not, the very individual who boasts of freedom from the state is often already *un*free in the sense that he is caught in the grip of social custom and conformity.

To leave the relation of freedom and coercion with that statement, however, is hardly enough. Surely the problem of individual freedom involves more than the recognition of the community's need for some measure of conformity. Surely freedom means that an individual ought indeed to have some range of choice about what he does with his life. Yet even here coercion remains an indispensable and positive instrument of freedom. It is inadequate to say simply that freedom means the minimizing of coercion wherever it exists and the maximizing of every individual's range of choice.

True freedom must presuppose the individual's ability to calculate and understand the implications, the meaning, and the consequences of the various choices available to him. And there is, in any given situation, some limit to the number of choices for which an individual can make such calculations. To make that statement is not to scorn man's reason, but rather to recognize that despite impressive human achievements which can be attributed to reason, that faculty has also often proved tragically fallible. Man simply seems not to be a "lightning calculator" even of his own self-interest. Nor is there any magically precise range beyond which one's grasp of alternatives always fails. Nonetheless, as the range widens, the job of calculation becomes increasingly difficult and must eventually reach a point at which one's choice cannot be based on reason. And that, in turn, can place a person in intolerable agony. Indeed, Durkheim, the French sociologist, regarded suicide as a response to a range of choice beyond a person's power of rational deliberation. That solution and the alternative of basing choice on sheer guesswork are hardly acts of meaningful freedom.[2]

If, then, individual freedom means neither the opportunity to do only *one* thing with one's life nor the choice to do *anything,* any society committed to freedom must provide the individual with a limited or middling range of choices whose implications he can understand. And that is the point at which, in the most significant sense, the individual begins to realize freedom through institutionalized coercion. For the very job of structuring and limiting the range of choices assumes the need for some form of social order, and that involves coercion. Consider, for example, the contribution which a system of political parties makes to the democratic electoral process. Parties usually make a free franchise more meaningful than it would otherwise be by structuring the electoral alternatives and establishing some framework within which elected officials can be held responsible. Nevertheless, any party system is also "coercive" in the sense that the particular alternatives which it offers at a given election can never please everyone.

That fact of political life illustrates the more general problem: any finite range of choices presupposes certain value judgments. If men are not free to do anything and everything, the kinds of choices open to them will invariably reflect a value-laden decision

2. For an interesting discussion of this general point, see Lon L. Fuller, "Freedom—A Suggested Analysis," 68 *Harvard Law Review* 1305 (1955); also, S. I. Benn and R. S. Peters, *Social Principles and the Democratic State* (London, 1959), 196 ff.

which has been made somewhere, somehow, about how men ought to live. Even when all the members of a given society participate in that decision, it will still involve a large measure of coercion. For at one given moment not all individuals will be satisfied, and many of those who are satisfied will become disenchanted as time goes on, only to find that the earlier scheme of things cannot be quickly or easily undone. Any society stands in fairly heavy bondage to the value judgments of the past. To suggest some illustrations, a society with a Puritan ethos will obviously take a rather different view than a hedonistic society toward the individual's free access to alcohol, gambling, and similar diversions. A society which places the value of monogamous marriage above the complete freedom of religion will banish polygamy. A society which glorifies the competitive acquisition of wealth and the proposition that every individual ought to provide his own security for personal crises will likely prefer a laissez faire economy which gives freedom from statism, rather than a welfare state which gives some freedom from the harsh breakdowns of an unregulated economy. The point, in brief, is that any given society at any given time will usually prize certain human attributes, interests, and forms of self-fulfillment more highly than others. Thus the real question is not freedom or coercion. It is instead the attributes, interests, and values in terms of which coercion is to be structured.

That question is also the clue to an understanding of the concept of equality. Not only do the exceptions to the rule that all men ought to be treated equally seem to be more important than the rule itself; it also seems that institutionalized discrimination often gives us a meaningful experience of equality, so long as the discrimination is rationally justifiable in terms of a value or attribute which we esteem. We feel more equal because we are being treated unequally. Look, for example, at the very earthy business of prize fighting. If all men were treated equally in prize fighting, no weight classifications would exist. The size and weight of a man would simply be ignored. What would be the result? Everyone in the game would feel and be inferior to whatever giant had the greatest sheer brute strength. But we do have weight classifications in boxing, and even some other minimal rules of conduct both in and out of the ring. These weight classifications and rules treat individuals differently. But do they give men a feeling of inequality? Quite the contrary. They treat people differently in order to afford opportunity to a talent which we prize: pound-per-pound boxing skill. And because weight classifications have that rationally justifiable purpose, they hardly make boxers feel unequal. Instead they give the good lightweight or middleweight—the Sugar Ray Robinson—the feeling that he too has a place in the sun along with a Joe Louis or Cassius Clay.

Turn from boxing to the American dream of "equal opportunity," and the same pattern emerges. What that magic phrase means is that every individual should have the opportunity to develop certain human attributes which, as a society, we approve of, provided that he possesses those attributes and is indeed able to develop them. As Herbert Hoover once put it, each of us should have the chance to win "that position in the community to which his intelligence, character, ability and ambition entitle him." [3] If those are noble words, the hard fact is that they encourage discrimination. Surely one must be concerned with education. Surely the poor must receive a chance for first-class schooling along with the rich. That means scholarships for the poor, but not for the rich. And that is discrimination. But not scholarships for all the poor at every level of education. Only those who turn out to possess such attributes as Hoover glorified will be so favored. And that is more discrimination.

If all this seems remote from the cause of civil rights, the purpose of these innocent illustrations is to remind us in indisputable terms of what we seem so easily to forget in the struggle over civil

3. Quoted by Arthur E. Sutherland, *The Law and One Man Among Many* (Madison, 1956), 23.

rights. That is the egregious unreality of pretending that equality is in any sense an absolute. It is important, for example, to recognize what the person who presses for "equality of opportunity" today is really demanding. He is, of course, urging that such factors as birth, wealth, and race, which have in the past determined much of an individual's opportunity in life, be neutralized. But he is also assuming that those factors should be replaced by discrimination according to some other standard, such as intellect. He is criticizing existing or past criteria of inequality in favor of others which he considers more rational.

There is nothing wrong in that gambit per se. But his statement of his case in terms of "equality," when he really wants to substitute one set of discriminatory standards for another, is misleading not only to others but usually to himself as well. That is true even if his new criteria are a more rational, more authentic fulfillment of the American ideal of equality than those he is attacking. For to imply, as is so often done, that equality means the absence of differentiation among individuals is like defining freedom as the absence of coercion. For one thing, both definitions promise more than we can ever have. No absolute tide of freedom and equality is coming in. Indeed, the ever increasing complexity of modern society will probably bring more, not less, control over our lives by society, and more, not less, differentiation among its members. For another thing, if that is the prospect, it is all the more important that the problem of freedom and equality be seen not in the simplistic terms of banishing coercion and discrimination from the earth, but rather in terms of a never-ending attempt to structure coercion and discrimination so that they serve and do not thwart the human values and attributes which we cherish.

Racial Discrimination

One value judgment dominates the present struggle in America for broader rights and opportunities for the Negro: the rejection of race as a relevant or rational basis for the discriminatory treatment of individuals. That means that the fact of Negro racial origin is no justification for limiting an individual's freedom of self-fulfillment to second-class citizenship and a life of social and economic degradation. Conversely, the fact of Caucasian racial origin is no justification for permitting other individuals the freedom to maintain political, economic, and social privilege.

Why has the problem of race become so acute in America in the years since World War II? There are many related reasons. Surely one is the very background of World War II, in which America called for—and received—common sacrifice from its citizens of all races in order to defeat a Nazi regime which explicitly preached and practiced racism. Surely the background of the present Cold War is also important. For America has been badly embarrassed by communist success in advertising to the world the discrepancy between our ideal of equality and our practice of racial discrimination. The embarrassment has become all the sharper since the emergence of the newly independent nations of the non-Western world.

But it would be false—and cheap—to explain our sensitivity to the problem of race only as a matter of foreign policy. Within America itself there has always been a deep strain of Negro bitterness and white self-reproach that the noble words of the Declaration of Independence and the Constitution have somehow turned out to be "for whites only." The development of American society over the last quarter-century has deepened both the bitterness and the self-reproach. The tremendous expansion of American industrialism, for example, has had at least a fourfold impact. First, the industrialization of the South has badly shaken the traditional, parochial nature of society there and given the Southern Negro new mobility and new perspective. Second, industrialism has produced formidable concentrations of Negroes in urban areas, concentrations which have aggravated racial tensions and given the Negro far greater political power than he ever had before.

Third, the affluence with which booming industrialism has blessed American society in general has dramatized the squalid existence of those who lack decent educational and economic opportunities. Finally, many who formerly insisted on the racial "inferiority" of the Negro have had to face the fact that, where racial barriers have indeed been lowered, an ever increasing number of Negroes have made outstanding contributions to American life.

Yet, having said all this, one must also face the fact that large sectors of American society are not yet ready to reject race as a basis for the discriminatory treatment of individuals. Many still cling to explicit or tacit theories of racial inequality; many others who pay lip service to racial equality refuse to implement it in practice. That is why the cause of Negro rights has been in crisis these last years, and it suggests again the relation between coercion and freedom. Each side in the present struggle is forever accusing the other of the use of coercion—especially governmental coercion. The accusation is accurate. The federal government has resorted to a wide array of measures, ranging from judicial process to armed force, in order to achieve integration, and the South continues to rely on the power of state governments to resist integration.

What is patently false, however, is the implication that the resort to coercion is per se a betrayal of freedom. Were American society in happy agreement on the means and ends which should resolve the racial crisis, then government at all levels could conform to the classic negative definition of freedom: simply leave private individuals free from all such coercion. But the lack of agreement—indeed, the threat of virtual civil war in society itself—has meant that government has not been able to leave society to its own devices. No society can claim that privilege, nor can any government tolerate that privilege, unless its citizens have first accepted the self-discipline of at least a common point of moral reference. To cast the cause of Negro rights in the simplistic terms of freedom versus coercion is thus unreal. For if coercion is inescapable, the real question is how American society and government can resolve the conflict of values which lies behind its use.

Where we are today may well help answer that question. However slowly desegregation may be proceeding and however unresolved the problem of purely private discrimination may be, one doctrine seems irrevocably established today. Discrimination on the basis of race by state or federal government violates those provisions of the Constitution which guarantee to every individual "due process of law" and "the equal protection of the laws." I do not mean that all citizens yet accept that interpretation of the Fifth and Fourteenth Amendments. But it seems clear today that a vast majority do, and that resistance to that interpretation can now be no more than a futile delaying action. How that victory was won suggests some important guidelines for those who seek to broaden Negro rights beyond the explicitly public domain.

It may seem overly legalistic to begin by saying that the landmark decision in the Negro victory over public discrimination is, and probably will always be, the Supreme Court's 1954 declaration, in *Brown vs. The Board of Education,*[4] that segregated public education violates the Constitution. But America is in general a highly legalistic nation. As de Tocqueville remarked in an often quoted line, "Hardly any question arises in the United States that is not resolved sooner or later into a judicial question." The civil rights cause has been no exception, for despite the sporadic violence of the last years, it has been fought largely through the judicial or legal process. And however profoundly the two sides have disagreed in their interpretations of the Constitution, that document has dominated both judicial and congressional attempts to resolve the problem of race.

Because of this background of legalism, one cannot really understand the Court's 1954 decision without also understanding its genesis. The purpose of the NAACP, which spearheaded the Negro drive in education, was to establish the normative proposi-

4. 347 U.S. 483.

tion that the Constitution required integrated schools. Now it is a matter of logic that a norm or value judgment can never be derived from empirical fact, but only from another norm or value judgment. That means that one could document *ad infinitum* the fact that segregated schools did not provide equal education, and yet, in logic, fail to establish the proposition that they ought to be integrated. What the NAACP needed was the prior normative imperative that public schools *ought* to be equal. And ironically the doctrine which the South itself professed before 1954 provided that premise. For however much the mind and heart of the South may have believed in the inferiority of the Negro and in the justice of white mastery, the South had long ago come to accept, as a matter of necessity, what was called the "separate but equal" rule. Formulated by the Supreme Court in 1896, that rule declared that the equal protection clause of the Constitution could be satisfied by segregated public facilities, provided those facilities were also fully equal in nature.[5]

With that premise (even though the South's adherence to it may often have been insincere) the issue was rather more pragmatic: could segregated educational facilities *ever* be fully equal? Since judges necessarily know and understand legal education, it is not surprising that the first Negro push and breakthrough came in that field. In the late 1930's Missouri denied a Negro admission to its only state law school but offered to pay his full tuition at the non-segregated law school of a neighboring state in order to satisfy the "separate but equal" formula. Neither the Negro nor the Supreme Court was satisfied. The Court held that Missouri's failure to provide legal education for Negroes within its own boundaries, and the alternative of attending the school of another jurisdiction, violated the equal protection clause. Although the decision was limited in the sense of not emphasizing the disadvantage to a prospective Missouri lawyer of being trained

5. *Plessy v. Ferguson,* 163 U.S. 537.

in the law of another state, it did imply the Court's willingness to recognize non-bricks-and-mortar factors in education.[6]

In 1950 that willingness became explicit in the case of a student who had been admitted to Texas' all-Negro law school, but claimed that the school was markedly inferior to the state's all-white law school. The Supreme Court did more than agree that the two schools were unequal in size of faculty, library, and curricula. More important, Chief Justice Vinson stressed that the white school offered to a far larger degree "those qualities which are incapable of objective measurement but which make for greatness in a law school"—for example, the reputation, as well as size, of the faculty, the position and influence of the alumni, and the opportunity to develop one's legal skill not in isolation but in association with the racial group which constituted 85 per cent of the state's population and which would provide the vast majority of judges, lawyers, witnesses, and jurors with whom the student would later deal as a lawyer.[7] With that, the Supreme Court virtually announced that separate legal education could never meet the requirements of equality. In another case the same year, the Court again stressed the importance of intangible factors in barring the intramural segregation of a Negro who had been admitted to the graduate school of the University of Oklahoma but was then deliberately isolated by the school from any social or scholastic association with white students.[8]

From these decisions it was a far shorter and more plausible step than many Americans perhaps have realized to the conclusion that all state-imposed segregation in education involves inequality. For when the NAACP moved from higher to lower education, its strategy was already cut out for it. The job was to marshal extensive evidence that even at the grade school level

6. *Missouri ex rel. Gaines v. Canada,* 305 U.S. 337 (1938).
7. *Sweatt v. Painter,* 339 U.S. 629.
8. *McLaurin v. Oklahoma State Regents,* 339 U.S. 637.

segregation stamped the Negro child with a lasting sense of inferiority detrimental to the child's motivation to learn and to his future intellectual development. And that was precisely what the NAACP managed to do to the satisfaction of a unanimous Supreme Court.

Although many have tried to denigrate that evidence by calling it "sociological," the truth is that all law relies heavily on such evidence. The purpose of law, after all, is to structure and order society. And to deny those who interpret law the right to examine the nature of society itself would be ridiculous. If that were the rule, the Supreme Court would not be permitted to know any economic facts about a given industry when it decided whether the industry was part of interstate commerce within the meaning of the Constitution. Nor would the Court be permitted to know anything about the organization and tactics of the Communist party in deciding whether certain restrictions on the party should be upheld.

The only fair objections to the evidence in the *Brown* case are rather more marginal. First, some of it had not been subjected to adequate cross-examination—i.e., counter-argument—in the trial courts before the *Brown* case finally reached the Supreme Court for review. Second, the Supreme Court itself was perhaps not sufficiently explicit in emphasizing the broader context of the evidence. For example, one can conceive of a society in which the Negro, enjoying educational, political, and economic opportunities fully equal to whites, might voluntarily adopt separatism without either race considering it a stigma. It is therefore difficult to argue in an abstract, absolutist sense that racial separatism is per se—always and everywhere—invidious.[9] In terms of the back-

9. Nor is it quite true, as is often said, that the law should necessarily be "color blind." For classifications based on race can sometimes be "benign." For example, under "busing" plans designed to overcome *de facto* school segregation, a pupil's race is one factor which determines whether and whither he is bussed.

ground of the *Brown* decision, however, the crucial fact of American history was that one race had for centuries kept the other in a position of educational, political, and economic subservience, and that state-imposed segregation was both a symbol and an instrument of that status. It was within that context that segregated schools stunted a Negro child's development and were therefore "inherently unequal."

That context is also the explanation for the later extension of the *Brown* decision to bar discrimination in other public facilities, including playgrounds, swimming pools, parks, golf courses, and municipal auditoriums.[10] The experience of constructive leisure complements and conditions the experience of formal education. After all, a Negro pupil can hardly forget in some magic fashion during his six or so hours a day in school what the rest of his daily existence offers him. And it would be a mockery to deny the state the right to discriminate in public education, yet permit it to reimpose that stigma relentlessly at every turn as soon as the Negro stepped from the classroom.

To sketch this evolution of constitutional doctrine is of course hardly to imply that the Supreme Court's imperatives have yet been fully realized in American society. They have not. Ten years after the *Brown* ruling, only 10 per cent of the Negro pupils in the entire South (not just the ex-Confederacy) were in integrated schools. In both the North and South those who resist school integration seem not yet to have run out of evasive tactics, and even those who genuinely favor integration have yet to find a really satisfactory solution to the problem of *de facto* school segregation which reflects not the deliberate action of public authority but simply the existence of separate Negro and white residential areas in most large cities.

But the constitutional ruling against state-imposed discrimina-

10. For example, see *New Orleans City Park Improvement Association v. Detiege,* 358 U.S. 54 (1959); *Holmes v. Atlanta,* 350 U.S. 879 (1955); *Dawson v. Baltimore,* 350 U.S. 877 (1955).

tion is so well established that integration can only go forward, not backward.[11] It is accepted by the vast majority of Americans, and even those who resist must know that the game is lost. That is no mean victory. And it is a victory which reflects the strategy that won it. The Negro leaders were extremely shrewd, first, in selecting their field of battle, for there are few subjects to which the American conscience is more sensitive than the importance of education. Second, they were shrewd in starting from the "separate but equal" premise and then documenting exhaustively the self-contradiction of that formula. It was a strategy of patience, reason, and pragmatism on which one can look back today almost with nostalgia.

The Negro today also seems to be winning what can only be an inevitable victory in his struggle for equality in the political franchise. Again, this struggle must be kept in perspective. If many Southern states continue to discourage Negro voting through a variety of devious strategies, the registration of Negro voters in the Old South has nevertheless increased by over 40 per cent in the last five years. When one looks back even further, progress is all the more impressive. Although it may seem almost incredible today, the Supreme Court until 1944 permitted the exclusion of Negro voters from primary elections and party conventions in the South on the ground that these were purely "private affairs." [12] In the days of strict one-party rule in the South, when the Democratic candidate invariably won the November election, that meant that the Negro's right to vote was virtually meaningless. Today the integral relation between the nomination of candidates and the electoral process is firmly established doctrine, and both the Court and other federal agencies, like the U.S. Civil Rights Com-

11. An indication of this trend is the Court's present apparent willingness to move against state laws barring interracial marriage and cohabitation—an emotion-laden subject which the Court took pains to side-step a decade ago.

12. *Smith v. Allwright,* 321 U.S. 649, was the decision which overruled this doctrine.

mission, have been vigilant in attacking attempts to maintain or reintroduce discrimination in voting. A recent example is the Court's invalidation of Louisiana's requirement that the electoral ballot specify the race of candidates for public office.[13]

If the Negro's ultimate victory over state-imposed segregation seems fairly well assured, that can hardly be said of his struggle against *privately* imposed discrimination. Certainly he will win broader rights in the social and economic realm, but what will the final terms and conditions of those rights be? There are a number of reasons for this uncertainty. To be legalistic again, the 1964 Civil Rights Law does seem to overcome a major barrier which protected private discrimination so long as the Fourteenth Amendment was the only constitutional weapon which could be used against that target. The problem was that the Fourteenth Amendment is explicit only in barring *state* action which deprives a person of equal protection, and it takes a good deal of stretching to apply that language to the discrimination of a private employer, real estate dealer, or hotel proprietor. But even if Congress and the Court now seem to have solved that problem legally by resting the Civil Rights Law on the plenary power of Congress over interstate commerce, it is still too early to be certain how broad a range of private discrimination will be struck down by actual enforcement of the law. That same uncertainty exists in the case of much recently passed state legislation against private discrimination.

The deeper problem is that it is one thing to bar government itself from imposing discrimination on society, and quite a more formidable task to transform government into a positive instrument with which to fight discrimination throughout society. Many people who are quite ready to deny the state the right to discriminate, deeply resent losing that right themselves. It is not simply

13. *Anderson v. Martin,* 375 U.S. 399 (1964). President Johnson's voting rights bill, still pending in Congress at this writing, seems assured of passage in some form which will go well beyond earlier measures to guarantee the franchise.

that emotion and prejudice become all the more explosive as the cause of civil rights moves from the public to the private sector. The problem is that in the private sector the Negro's demand for equal treatment confronts a rational counter-argument that cannot be dismissed out of hand. That is the argument that every individual has a certain right to choose freely those with whom he associates, a right to privacy, and a right to free use of his own property—and that imposed integration in the private sector of society threatens these rights. Even if one admits that these alleged rights cannot be absolutes and that appeal to them is often nothing more than a cover for sheer bigotry, they do have a history in the American creed of individualism which far antedates the present racial crisis. The latest phase of the civil rights cause thus involves a more acute confrontation between conflicting values and rights than did the earlier phase.

The way to resolve that confrontation is not to pretend that it does not exist and to reach for some automatic, mechanical solution. Yet it is probably fair to say that this was what the Supreme Court seemed to do in the first important step that it took after World War II in the field of private discrimination. One of the early civil rights thrusts on this front was against the so-called "restrictive covenant," in which a number of private homeowners agree among themselves not to sell to non-Caucasians. Often the covenant "runs with the land" and is therefore binding on future buyers. The constitutional question was how this kind of discrimination could be brought within the scope of the Fourteenth Amendment ban against state action which deprives a citizen of equal protection. The Court's answer in 1948, in *Shelley v. Kraemer,* was that the *enforcement* by a state court of such a covenant against a home owner who welched and sold to a Negro constituted state action in violation of the Fourteenth Amendment, even though the covenant itself was valid before its enforcement.[14] This ruling, which seized on enforcement per se

14. 334 U.S. 1.

rather than the nature of the discrimination itself, carried the implication that *any* exercise of an individual's right to free association, privacy, or property becomes state action as soon as he calls upon the law to vindicate the right.

As such, the *Shelley* rule proved a Pandora's Box of unhappy lessons which are still relevant today in terms of how *not* to deal with the problem of private discrimination. For one thing, most Americans—on both sides of the civil rights issue—probably still believe that the individual is prior to the state in a philosophic sense. To put it differently, they believe that individual rights are derived from the sanctity of the individual himself, not from the state, and that the state exists only for the fullest possible implementation of those rights. To say, however, that the state's vindication of an individual right through legal procedure transforms the exercise of the right into state action is seemingly a betrayal of that premise. The next step would be to announce that, even when enforcement by the state is absent, the mere toleration by the state of certain forms of individual conduct transforms that conduct into state action. With that, all action would become state action, and the line between government and society would become meaningless.

A second, more practical objection to the *Shelley* rule is that it left no basis for distinguishing between radically different situations or assessing the validity of an individual's claim to free association, privacy, and property in those situations. Again, we meet the supreme importance of context and degree in attempting to realize the concept of equality. For example, however much one detests racial bigotry, it is difficult to deny an individual home-owner the right to select those who are guests or servants in his home. It is also difficult to deny a private social club the free choice of its members.

However, the claim to free association, privacy, and use of property is hardly convincing in the case of a large number of home-owners, many of whom may never know or speak to one another, who enact what really amounts to a private zoning ordinance by restricting all future property sales in a residential area. Nor are these claims of individual right at all impressive in the case of a Howard Johnson-type restaurant, most hotels, and most department stores. For usually such businesses will serve any and all members of the general public, except Negroes; usually their customers are transient and have no social intercourse among themselves; and often such businesses are owned by neither their employees nor managers, but by distant stockholders who may number in the thousands and be scattered across the nation. On the other hand, the neighborhood barber shop or rooming house or coffee spot can involve such highly personalized relations among customers and proprietors that the claim of free association and privacy may well have some validity.

The *Shelley* rule, however, seemed to draw no distinction between almost totally impersonal economic situations and exceedingly intimate face-to-face relationships. The implication was that in *any* of these situations private discrimination became unconstitutional as soon as a policeman or court acted against a trespasser whom an owner—even a club or home-owner—wished to bar because of race. And that absolutist implication was surely an important reason why the Court never resolved the basic problem of the many "sit-in" cases which came to it under the Fourteenth Amendment before the passage of the 1964 Civil Rights Law. Boxed with an unrealistic rule, the Justices went through incredible contortions to dispose of these cases on technical, legalistic grounds—claiming, for example, that the evidence in the record was inadequate to support a conviction, straining the construction of local ordinances to find some shred of "state action" behind private discrimination, or dismissing the case for lack of jurisdiction.[15] All this was to leave unsolved the essential

15. For example, *Garner v. Louisiana,* 368 U.S. 157 (1961); *Lombard v. Louisiana,* 373 U.S. 267 (1963); *Bell v. Maryland,* 378 U.S. 226 (1964); *Griffin v. Maryland,* 378 U.S. 130 (1964).

question of discrimination by businesses which may be privately owned, yet are open to all the general public except Negroes.

Yet all along there has been a common sense alternative to the mechanical *Shelley* formula—an alternative which could have solved the question under the Fourteenth Amendment and which, in a sense, Congress adopted in the Civil Rights Law. That is to shift the focus from the *Shelley* factor of court enforcement of private discrimination to the nature of the discrimination itself. Or, to put it differently, the alternative is to recognize pragmatically that private discrimination does occur in radically different contexts. In some contexts the claim to equal treatment regardless of race clearly seems to deserve more protection than the claim of privacy or property or free association, but in other contexts the latter claim may well deserve to prevail, even if it must be enforced by the state.

Although the Justices themselves could have adopted that selective approach, it is probably fortunate that the future of Negro rights need not now rest upon a purely judicial reinterpretation of the Fourteenth Amendment. For the declaration that many privately owned businesses are so public in the nature of their operation that their discrimination amounts to "state action" would have been controversial indeed. The reliance of the Civil Rights Law on the interstate commerce power of Congress in order to strike at such private discrimination is a far happier solution. For one thing, the crucial mandate behind that law is not simply its passage through Congress by overwhelming majorities. It is rather that the Supreme Court, in upholding the law's public accommodations section, could base the exceedingly broad commerce power of Congress on venerable constitutional precedents which date from the era of John Marshall.[16] For another thing, the Civil Rights Law itself conforms rather well to the situation-oriented approach which I have suggested. Usually

16. *Heart of Atlanta Motel v. U.S.,* 379 U.S. 241 (1964); *Katzenbach v. McClung,* 379 U.S. 294 (1964).

businesses which are part of or affect interstate commerce *do* have an impersonal, public character. More than that, the law explicitly excepts from its scope certain intimate, face-to-face situations—for example, the private club and small owner-operated rooming house. Finally, the law—as interpreted by the Justices—"abates" or strikes from court dockets the large number of "sit-in" cases which have never reached final adjudication. Although arguable in a legalistic sense,[17] that gloss is probably a shrewd, happy settlement of those cases. For it virtually makes an anachronism out of the mechanistic trap of the *Shelley* rule and the Fourteenth Amendment "state action" issue.

At the same time, having finally escaped that particular trap, we must be careful not to fall into another. We must not assume that the problem of private discrimination will be automatically solved simply by the existence of either the 1964 Civil Rights Law or new state and local ordinances.[18] The pattern of voluntary compliance with and public enforcement of that legislation has yet to emerge. And that pattern can prove successful only if we all sustain an attitude of realism and flexibility. That means keeping always in mind at least three facts of life which have too often been obscured. First, the present crisis will not be resolved unless the Negro is extended far more equal opportunity in employment, union membership, housing, and public accommodations than he now possesses. The right to the franchise and education are precious, but after all no citizen spends his entire life in the voting booth or in school. What responsible Negro leaders today demand is no utopia of complete social and economic equality in which all differentiation among individuals would end. What they demand is rather that the differing opportunities and rewards

17. See the dissenting opinions in *Hamm v. Rock Hill* and *Lupper v. Arkansas,* 379 U.S. 306 (1964).

18. Already every Northern industrial state has an enforceable fair employment law, and in the single year of 1963 twenty-five states strengthened their anti-discrimination statutes.

which society affords an individual should depend on his ability and industry, not his color.

Second, no viable solution can be reached without continued action by government at all levels. To say that is not to betray the meaning of freedom and equality. As we have seen, those ideals are realized not through the absence of coercion, but through the rational use of coercion. Lastly, we must remember at the same time the limits of both public and private coercion. Neither can change easily or quickly the deeply held prejudices which men carry in their minds and hearts. And even if they could, the belief in individual self-determination includes values other than the Negro's demand that racial prejudice be banished from society. That belief also includes the notion that every individual should be left at least some small authentic realm of daily personal experience in which neither the state nor any other group can dictate his most private likes and dislikes.

It may have been tempting on occasion during these last years to wish that somehow America had been born and had lived always in bland innocence of the race problem. But that kind of escapist thought is at odds with the belief that America's greatness has always reflected the diversity of her ethnic groups, and with the truth that greatness in any society usually comes out of the crucible of high challenge. It would be fatuous to suggest that Americans ought to be thankful for the crisis in which they now find themselves. But it is also fatuous for Americans not to realize that the resolution of that crisis will make them a far richer society—richer in the fullest possible development of the talents of all individuals and richer for having successfully come through a searing trial of conscience which forced them to rethink their commitment to freedom and equality.

Legislative Apportionment

Another unfinished civil rights cause is the attempt to end the inequality in voting which results not from racial discrimination but from malapportioned legislative electoral districts. Usually malapportionment reflects the failure of state legislatures over the years to redraw the boundaries of districts in response to population shifts. Since the last decades have brought an immense movement of population from rural to urban areas, the urban voter has been the chief victim. In California, for example, electoral districts are so unequal that some fifteen thousand people in a rural county command the same representation in the state senate as the county of Los Angeles, which has a population of six million. In Florida, at least until quite recently, districting was so heavily weighted in favor of rural areas that a mere 15 per cent of the state's voters could elect a majority of the lower house of the legislature. In many states the same inequality exists among districts for election to the lower house of Congress. In 1960 Michigan's 16th Congressional District had a population of over 800,000, while its 12th District had about 175,000.

For the voter in the larger urban district, the penalty in each case is clear. His vote counts only a fraction—and often an egregiously small fraction—of the ballot cast by a rural voter. And for the burgeoning metropolitan areas of the nation, which struggle with ever increasing problems of housing, education, traffic, racial tension, and crime, the penalty is also clear. Heavily underrepresented in state legislatures and in Congress, the cities simply have not received the financial and other outside help necessary to solve these problems.

It is not difficult to understand how this state of affairs developed. Even though most state constitutions require some form of reapportionment every ten years, state legislators who had become entrenched in power under cover of unequal districting were hardly eager to reapportion themselves out of power. Usually they refused to act at all or made only negligible changes in the old electoral map. As for Congress, it has no clear constitutional power over state legislative districting, and it has never enforced the power which it does have over the size of a state's congressional districts. For years the Supreme Court also refused to plunge into this "political thicket," doubting both its own constitutional mandate and also its ability to devise or enforce standards of equitable apportionment.[19] It was not until 1962, in *Baker v. Carr,* that the Court reversed its position, declared that malapportioned districts could indeed violate the equal protection clause of the Fourteenth Amendment, and assumed on behalf of the federal courts jurisdiction to pass on the constitutionality of state electoral systems.[20]

The *Baker* decision, which left uncertain exactly what kind of an apportionment would satisfy the Court, soon prompted lawsuits attacking the districting systems in over three-quarters of the states. When the Court began to pass on these cases, the full implications of *Baker* became clear. In *Wesberry v. Sanders* in early 1964, the Court held that the congressional districts within a state must be based upon the equality of population principle.[21] Then later in the year, in *Reynolds v. Sims,* the Court extended that requirement to *both* houses of every state legislature.[22] Although the Alabama electoral disparities in *Reynolds* were so remarkably bad as to be beyond any reasonable justification, the Court at the same time, in a companion case, struck down a Colorado apportionment with far less serious disparities which had been approved in a popular referendum by a two-to-one

19. See especially *Colegrove v. Green,* 328 U.S. 549 (1946).
20. 369 U.S. 186.
21. 376 U.S. 1.
22. 377 U.S. 533.

majority of Colorado voters, including a majority in every county in the state.[23] The "one man, one vote" tenor of these decisions is perhaps best caught in Chief Justice Warren's declaration: "Legislators represent people, not trees or acres. Legislators are elected by voters, not farms or cities or economic interests." [24]

Although the Court's stringent standard of electoral equality caused surprise and shock in both political and scholarly circles, one fact should be recognized at the outset. The apportionment issue does not involve the same measure of deeply felt emotion, prejudice, and conflict of values which is evident in the struggle against racial segregation. There is nothing in American experience to match, for example, the persistent defense of a highly restricted franchise which one finds in European development. As we noted at the outset, the right to participate at all, much less equally, in the process of election was not considered a civil right in France and England until well into the nineteenth century. At the very time the framers of the American Constitution were providing that representation in the lower house of Congress should be apportioned among the states according to population, both Whigs and Tories in England still defended a crazy-quilt electoral system in which a relatively few members of the aristocracy, controlling so-called "rotten boroughs," could determine who filled a very substantial number of seats in the House of Commons. Even in the more open constituencies, there was an incredible variety of property and other requirements for the franchise. And when the vote was finally extended to the bulk of the middle class in England and France in the early 1830's, it was only after deep political crisis and only on the assumption (at least of the ruling classes) that the property-based, middle class franchise would be a "final solution."

In America the notion that all men might have certain civil rights, such as free speech or worship, but that only the few

23. *Lucas v. Forty-fourth General Assembly,* 377 U.S. 713 (1964).
24. *Reynolds v. Sims,* 377 U.S. 533, 562, 580 (1964).

geography. Although Chief Justice Warren has found that factor "unconvincing" because of modern transportation and communication, one can argue effectively that vast, sparsely populated rural or mountainous areas, islands, and remote peninsulas deserve special consideration precisely because the job of campaigning, getting voters to the polls, and representing those areas is rather more difficult than in compact urban districts. Interestingly enough, Great Britain made a commitment some twenty years ago to a mathematical concept of equality quite analogous to the Court's present view. Yet Britain has all along conceded special overrepresentation in the House of Commons to the islands and agricultural counties in the far north of Scotland.

Still another factor is the value of maintaining a coincidence between the boundary lines of legislative districts and those of local units of government, rather than permitting the former to criss-cross the latter in cavalier fashion. It is generally true that the organizational responsibility of parties is fragmented when district lines do violence to those of local government. Also, a coincidence of boundaries facilitates the common practice by which state legislatures charge local units of government with responsibilities for the operations of state government. Although the Court's majority does seem impressed by this factor, it is not yet clear what measure of electoral disparities would be tolerated for the sake of preserving the integrity of local boundaries. Again, it may be worth noting that this consideration was the basic reason that Great Britain found unworkable and abandoned a requirement that, aside from special geographic cases, constituencies should not deviate in either direction by more than 25 per cent from the ideal of absolute equality. Today, with no percentage formula specified by statute, the factors of geography and local boundaries have created a range of deviation of roughly 50 per cent in each direction. Although that range is fairly close to the electoral disparities which the Court rejected in the Colorado case, practically all students of British apportionment seem content with it.[27] Even if one were to balk at that degree of inequality in America, the British experience would seem to call into question the realism of any narrow mathematical formula—including, for example, the proposal now before Congress to establish for each state's congressional districts a limit of 15 per cent on variations from absolute equality.

Finally, sheer movement of population over the years in such a highly mobile society as Britain or America means that we must live with a certain measure of inequality in the periods between general reapportionments. If there are good reasons against too *in*frequent change in the electoral map, there are also good reasons against too frequent change. Even relatively slight changes can involve partisan squabbles which distract legislators from substantive law making and can unsettle the stability of local party organization. Although Chief Justice Warren expressed suspicion in *Reynolds* of a longer than ten-year period between apportionments, the British have replaced a "not less often than seven years or more often than three years" formula with a ten- to fifteen-year period between general reviews.

These comments are not meant to suggest that the Court will or should retreat from the general standard of electoral equality. One can only be thankful that the irrational disparities which have long existed in many states are now soon to end. But one can suggest that in future cases the Court might be more flexible and pragmatic than it has been thus far. This means a greater tolerance than it has indicated it would be willing to give to deviations from equality which can be explained in terms of relevant, legitimate purpose, or in terms of the reasoned balancing of conflicting values. Just as the mechanical rule of the *Shelley* case proved no answer to the subtleties of private discrimination, no similar formula makes sense in the apportionment problem. Yet, in turning to what Justice Stewart, in dissent, has called

27. For an analysis of English experience, see David Butler, "The Redistribution of Seats," *Public Administration,* XXXIII (1955), 125.

"the simplistic and heavy handed application of sixth grade arithmetic," the Court almost appears to be repeating its mistake in *Shelley*. One can only hope that the Justices will somehow develop more sensitivity to the very real complexity of the process of representative government.

If one hopes for that, one must also wonder what impact the final resolution of the apportionment issue will have on American political life. It takes little imagination to guess that urban areas will be advantaged in terms of political power, and rural areas disadvantaged. But with more and more of the nation becoming urban and with the large scale, quasi-industrial farm replacing the old small family farm, one wonders how much difference that result of reapportionment will really make. Also, one can doubt that any shifts in strength between the major political parties will be terribly significant. Indeed, my guess is that the impact of the present controversy will be far more subtle. In an era in which executive and administrative power is gaining at the expense of legislative power, the insistence on more equal, rational standards of representation suggests the continuing dedication of American society to the concept of republican government. More than that, it demonstrates America's readiness to rethink in searching terms what that concept means. And that in turn may be a hopeful sign for the continued survival and vitality of representative institutions.

Free Speech

The right to free speech in America is a curious phenomenon. Compared with the millions of citizens who are directly affected by the cause of Negro rights and the cause of equal voting, very few Americans ever feel they are suffering any direct or unjust infringement of their right to free expression. In a sense this is a tribute to American government at all levels. But in another sense it simply raises once again the relation between freedom and conformity. One crucial reason that government has shown such seeming tolerance of free speech in America has surely been that in general Americans have exercised that freedom within a commonly accepted framework of ideas about what constitutes a good society. They have been permitted to speak freely because what they said or would say was so predictably non-subversive of the existing order.

Although the problem of race has been an exception, America has seldom experienced either the range or sharpness of political, social, and ideological antagonisms which marked the development of most European nations in the nineteenth and twentieth centuries. That fact has resulted in a strange ambivalence in our attitude toward free speech. For if conformity in America is one explanation for our usually large measure of freedom, that same conformity has also meant that as a people Americans are apt to be peculiarly *in*tolerant when they confront someone who dissents from consensual values. There is so much agreement on those values that dissent or eccentricity is all too easily equated with sin. And as the witch-hunting eras after both world wars suggest, that proclivity is especially strong when the nation is under challenge from abroad.[28]

Today we have been under such challenge for so long that it is somewhat difficult to know how dearly or precisely in what sense America prizes free speech. Surely it is more difficult than a generation ago. Even in the era of World War I, those sensitive to the problem of free speech seemed more certain of themselves than we do today. Take, for example, the celebrated and stringent rule that Oliver Wendell Holmes and Louis Brandeis propounded —to limit the infringement of free expression only to those situations where the words uttered constituted "a clear and present danger . . . of substantive evils." That rule implied two fundamental beliefs: first, the idea that free expression was indispensable

28. For an interesting treatment of this point, see Louis Hartz, *The Liberal Tradition in America* (New York, 1955), especially Chap. 1 and 11.

and precious in individual self-fulfillment; second, the belief that the best test of the truth of an idea was its ability to win acceptance in free competition with other ideas. To elaborate the second point, the faith of Holmes and Brandeis was that if the danger feared were sufficiently distant to leave time for further free discussion, true ideas would triumph over false ideas and avert the danger.

Yet a generation later the Supreme Court upheld the Smith Act's restrictions on certain forms of free expression and association by stripping the Holmes-Brandeis test of the requirement that the danger must be "imminent" as well as "clear." Now the danger need only be "clear and probable" In contrast to earlier decisions there now appears more than a hint of uncertainty that truth will indeed triumph over falsity, even if time remains for further discussion. That uncertainty is, moreover, strengthened by recent arguments that there can be no logical proof that free discussion *does* lead to truth rather than falsity.[29] If one concedes that point, about the only logical defense of free speech is to claim that the silencing of discussion necessarily implies an infallibility on the part of the silencer, which is at odds with what we know about human nature. Since, however, one can imagine situations in which the need for action or decision of some kind could be so compelling that one might demand an end to discussion without any pretense of infallibility, it is easy to be disconcerted by a defense of free speech which really lacks faith in its efficacy. Finally, it is even easier to be disconcerted by Walter Lippmann's words immediately after the assassination of President Kennedy: "In the light of this monstrous crime, we can see that in a free country, which we are and intend to be, unrestrained speech and thought are inherently subversive." [30]

29. For an articulation of this argument, see The Editors, "The Constitutional Right to Anonymity: Free Speech, Disclosure and the Devil," 70 *Yale Law Journal* 1084 (1961).

30. "Murder Most Foul," *New York Herald Tribune* (European edition), November 27, 1963, 4.

If Lippmann's words were written in shock, there still seems to be a general mood of skepticism about free speech which deserves more than passing comment. Surely the Cold War is part of the explanation. When any society becomes increasingly preoccupied with its own survival, it is likely to take more and more for granted the truth of its own ideology and to prize the bonds of community over and above the sanctity of the individual. But the Cold War is only part of the background. The discoveries of modern psychology and sociology, as well as the uses to which we have seen mass communications and propaganda put in these last decades, have also laid bare rather frightening depths of human irrationality. Of course one can always defend the efficacy of free discussion by distinguishing between "rational" and "irrational" discussion, but that is a difficult line to draw and itself reflects disillusion with our past faith.

The decline, the fall, and the aftermath of the "clear and present danger" rule are an apt illustration not only of how Americans have been cut loose from the certainty of the past, but also of how we have failed to devise any new, viable concept of free speech. The problem is not that we have suddenly become "anti-libertarians," but rather that the problem of free speech over the last generation has proved too complex for any formula as simplistic as the "CPD" (clear and present danger) test. Once again, it is probably fair to suggest an analogy with the inadequacy of the mechanical state-action formula of the *Shelley* case in the area of private racial discrimination. Although the CPD test by no means gave free speech the absolutist protection for which some liberals—notably Justices Black and Douglas—still plead, it did place free speech in a "preferred position." It did that by implying an a priori presumption of unconstitutionality against governmental restriction of speech and by seeming to require an extremely strong showing of danger before that presumption could be overcome.

If that seems eminently plausible at first glance, one must

remember the particular situation for which Holmes and Brandeis first propounded the CPD rule in the era of World War I. That was a series of cases in which the free speech claims of a relatively few isolated individuals, who were criticizing the draft, urging strikes in munitions plants, or advocating anarchism, confronted the state's interest in restricting such speech in order to preserve its own security during crisis.[31] Although the average citizen may have little sympathy for the person who speaks out against his nation's war effort or its form of government, the fact remains that the lone individual who chooses to oppose the organized state on those terms faces a terribly formidable antagonist. In that radically unequal confrontation, there may be special reason to shield the individual's liberty in heavy armor by requiring that his words must indeed constitute a clear and present danger before he can be punished for them.

But as Walter Berns has argued in a brilliant analysis of the CPD test,[32] the problem of free speech does not always involve the pitting of an individual claim against the state's interest in its own security during an emergency. Far more often the confrontation is simply between one individual claim of liberty and *another* individual claim, with the state acting only as a balancer or umpire. And the fate of the CPD test in later years was its use by the Court in precisely such situations—situations, indeed, for which the test had probably not been originally intended. One example was the confrontation between a union's claim to be free to advertise its side of a strike by picketing an employer with placards, and the employer's claim to be free from the economic coercion which picketing constitutes.[33] Another case involved the freedom of the Jehovah's Witnesses to disseminate their ideas

31. For example, *Schenck v. U.S.*, 249 U.S. 47 (1919); *Abrams v. U.S.*, 250 U.S. 616 (1919).

32. *Freedom, Virtue and the First Amendment* (Baton Rouge, 1957), *passim.* I am deeply indebted in my own analysis to the major themes of this volume.

33. *Thornhill v. Alabama,* 310 U.S. 88 (1940).

through daytime house-to-house doorbell ringing in a factory town where many workers were on a night shift and had an obvious interest in uninterrupted rest and privacy during the day.[34] A somewhat analogous case pitted the freedom to broadcast by soundtruck against the right of citizens to enjoy noise-free tranquility.[35] Finally, in a rather different situation, the freedom of the press to advise a judge how he ought to decide a pending trial confronted the claim of a defendant to enjoy a trial free from such external influence.[36]

What was the result when the Supreme Court applied the CPD test to cases like these? Clothed in the protective coat given it to face the state in crisis, the claim of free speech almost always triumphed over those opposing claims which were far less formidable than the state's right to self-preservation. The question is not whether the Court's decisions were right in all cases. Rather, the question is whether the use of the CPD test at all in these cases made sense. As time went on, more and more doubt began to be voiced. As Mr. Justice Jackson complained in one of his dissents, the Court's majority seemed to have "a conception of free speech so rigid as to tolerate no concession to society's needs for public order." [37] What he meant was that in a real society the problem of free speech is far too intricate for any mechanical rule which always gives one claim of freedom an a priori presumption over and against all other legitimate claims. The CPD test may have been plausible for the original situation for which it was devised. But once one moves from that to other situations, it becomes clear that the job of government, acting not in its own self-defense but as an umpire of individual interests, is constantly to balance and rebalance a variety of values, including property, privacy, tranquility, fair trial, and so on.

34. *Martin v. Struthers,* 319 U.S. 141 (1943).
35. *Saia v. N.Y.,* 334 U.S. 558 (1948).
36. *Bridges v. California,* 314 U.S. 252 (1941).
37. *Terminiello v. Chicago,* 337 U.S. 1, 14 (1949).

Once again, meaningful freedom does not mean simply the absence of coercion. For the claim to unrestricted speech comes no closer to exhausting the full, complex meaning of individual self-determination than does the demand for equal treatment regardless of race. Ultimately the Supreme Court itself, after a decade of CPD test supremacy, came to accept these propositions. Starting with a reversal in the late 1940's of one of its earlier soundtruck decisions, the Court began to abandon the test in cases which involved essentially a confrontation between two individual claims of freedom.[38] From that date on, the Court has turned more and more in these cases to the "*ad hoc* balancing" approach—that is, the pragmatic, case-by-case assessment of competing claims of freedom, without a pre-determined presumption in favor of or against any one kind of freedom.

There are certainly difficulties in the *ad hoc* approach, but first a final chapter in the saga of the CPD test remains to be told. That is its virtual abandonment in 1951, in *Dennis v. U.S.*,[39] in a situation which at first glance may seem analogous to the early World War I cases in which Holmes and Brandeis devised the test. For when the Court upheld in the *Dennis* case the Smith Act's bar against the advocacy of ideas directed at the violent overthrow of government, the interest of the state in its own self-preservation was obviously once again involved. But there the resemblance ends. For who were the other claimants in the *Dennis* case? They were not the lone, isolated, harmless, crackpot individuals of the earlier cases. Instead, the other claimants were the top American leaders of the Communist party—a highly disciplined organization whose advocacy of subversion is explicit and whose efforts toward subversion are backed by an international movement and a nation with whom we are at cold war.

The real question, then, in the *Dennis* case was whether the

38. *Kovacs v. Cooper,* 336 U.S. 77 (1949); also *Breard v. Alexandria,* 341 U.S. 624 (1951).

39. 341 U.S. 494.

armor with which the CPD test protects the claim of free speech could be realistic when the state faced that kind of challenge. The problem was not simply that this was an unprecedented situation which the generation of Holmes and Brandeis had never foreseen. The problem was also that the CPD test had bowled over so many antagonists in confrontations with private claims of freedom that one could doubt as of 1951 that it was any longer possible to use the test *negatively*. As Walter Berns has written, "It was not [Chief Justice] Vinson's fault—in the *Dennis* case—that the test was not the chaste, unsullied debutante of 1919; it had after all spent over thirty years in the streets." [40]

What was Vinson's solution? After recounting the federal trial court's assessment of the menace of Soviet Russia and the Communist party, he accepted a modified test of constitutionality which Judge Hand had propounded in reviewing the *Dennis* case at the federal circuit court level. That test turned essentially on one question: "whether the gravity of the 'evil,' discounted by its improbability, justifies such invasion of free speech as is necessary to avoid the evil." And Vinson's answer in *Dennis* was *yes*. That question and answer stripped the CPD test of its most objective, stringent component: the requirement that the evil feared be "present" or "imminent." While the evil still had to be clear and serious, the new test required it to be only a probability in the indefinite future, not an imminent threat. True, both the *Dennis* and later Smith Act cases have been explicit in insisting that a defendant's advocacy of subversive ideas could not be punished unless he actually intended to accomplish the violent overthrow of government. Purely abstract advocacy, without that intent, is still protected by the First Amendment's free speech guarantee.[41] Nevertheless, the substitution of "probable" for "imminent" gave the Supreme Court such increased flexibility in Cold War cases

40. *Op. cit.*, p. 57.
41. For example, *Yates v. U.S.*, 354 U.S. 298 (1957).

that the "clear and probable danger" test has really amounted, in practice, to the same thing as the *ad hoc* balancing test to which the Court has resorted in other free speech cases.[42]

The implications of the *Dennis* decision, however, are more profound than the Court's abandonment of the CPD test in the soundtruck and doorbell-ringing cases. For in the latter cases one can defend certain restrictions on the right of free expression without questioning the intrinsic importance of the right itself. The objection in those cases is merely to a particular *form* which free speech takes, and leaves open innumerable other media of expression. The objection does not really question the classic liberal belief that free speech is precious to individual self-fulfillment, that it is indispensable to the democratic political process, and that it is the best route to truth. In the *Dennis* case, however, one can find more than a little skepticism about these propositions.

First, a clear conclusion of the decision is that to extend unrestricted free speech to a movement like the Communist party is to betray, rather than fulfill, individualism and democracy. Second, as suggested earlier, the new "clear and probable danger" rule suggests some very real uncertainty that truth will indeed win out over falsity if only there is time for free discussion. Surely the sheer military power behind international communism was part of the background of Vinson's opinion. But one also suspects that he was not oblivious to what the last decades have taught us about the depths of human irrationality and the fanatic hold which political ideology can acquire over men's minds.

Third, despite the distinction between advocacy which is purely abstract and that which is actually directed toward unlawful results, the restrictions now placed on the Communist party have implications for free thought throughout American society. For human thought, abstract expression, the intent to act on ideas,

42. For example, *Barenblatt v. U.S.,* 360 U.S. 109 (1959).

and overt action all lie along a spectrum in which it is exceedingly difficult to draw sharp lines of distinction. Whether free discussion takes us closer to truth or not, it is a right which both encourages men to think and helps them elaborate the ideas which they do think. But usually men want more than the opportunity to voice ideas in a purely abstract fashion. Usually they also have some hope or dream of acting upon their ideas, or of seeing others translate them into reality. It is thus fatuous to pretend that there is always a clean line between thought that is purely abstract and thought which is action-oriented.

Just as the state discourages free thought when it denies free expression, so it also discourages free thought and expression when it punishes those who attempt to implement their ideas through certain forms of political organization—whether the punishment be a jail sentence under the Smith Act, the loss of union office under the Taft-Hartley Act, or the public ostracism which a man may suffer from a congressional investigation of his past or present beliefs and affiliations. The effect, inevitably, is to encourage safe intellectual conformity and reinforce the American proclivity to equate dissent of any kind with sin. These, then, seem to be the deeper, more subtle corollaries of the *Dennis* rationale.

Whether one feels this rationale is or is not justified by the Cold War, there are some narrower comments which one can confidently make in appraisal of the *ad hoc* balancing approach which the Supreme Court now takes to the problem of free speech. On the one hand, that approach gives the Court the option to consider realistically a wider range of relevant factors in any given case than more rigid tests allow. On the other hand, experience with the test thus far suggests that the Court has not always exercised that option realistically or consistently, and that the *ad hoc* approach can itself involve some real dangers because of its very flexibility.

One such danger is the Court's inconsistency in dealing with statutes which are so loosely worded as to provide no clear standard of guilt and encourage indiscriminate dragnet operations by government. For example, the Court recently read greater specificity into the Smith Act's proscription against *ordinary* membership in certain organizations (a different clause than the top leaders of the Communist party were tried under in *Dennis*) by requiring proof of activism and subversive intent on the part of a defendant.[43] At the same time, though it could surely do so, the Court has thus far refused to find constitutional fault with the exceedingly vague charters with which Congress often authorizes investigations by its own committees.[44]

Secondly, the *ad hoc* approach would also seem to give the Court the right to look behind the alleged purpose of infringements of free speech or association. But again the Court has not been consistent. In the case of congressional investigations there has been no satisfactory attempt to draw a line between those which have legitimate legislative purpose and those which are engaged in exposure purely for the sake of exposure.[45] On the other hand, the Court refused a demand by the state of Alabama that NAACP membership lists be made public record, by arguing that Alabama's true interest was not in its own security against subversion but rather in making life intolerable for members of the NAACP.[46]

A third difficulty of flexibility is illustrated by obscenity decisions in which the Court has come to rely on the "audience-medium" and "community standards" tests. When a novel is clearly directed at an average adult audience, for example, the fact that it might arouse lascivious or lustful thoughts in the minds

43. *Scales v. U.S.*, 367 U.S. 203 (1961); *Noto v. U.S.*, 367 U.S. 290 (1961).

44. For example, *Barenblatt v. U.S.*, 360 U.S. 109 (1959).

45. *Ibid.*

46. *NAACP v. Alabama ex rel. Patterson,* 357 U.S. 449 (1958).

of juveniles or perverts is no longer sufficient proof that it is obscene.[47] But matters are not always so simple. For example, do motion pictures, because they communicate to mass audiences through direct visual portrayal, belong in a special category which justifies some form of prior censorship? Finally, the Court's competency in balancing relevant factors varies widely from situation to situation. The Justices may be peculiarly skilled in judging the impact which unrestricted press comment can have on the fairness of a pending trial. But are they as competent to judge whether a book or movie violates the prevailing standards of a given community by appealing to "prurient interests"? The question of competency becomes even more acute in cases involving national security. Thus the balancing approach would seem to imply a larger measure of deference to legislative and executive judgment in some areas. Nevertheless, that deference can easily become a contagious attitude which spreads from cases in which it is justified to others in which it is not.

Thus, although the *ad hoc* approach has its virtues, it also has its weaknesses. The basic problem is not that the Court has not in actual practice always considered all the factors relevant to given cases. In a deeper sense, the problem is that the *ad hoc* test is really *too* flexible. It casts issues in such broad and unstructured terms that one can really wonder whether it is a "test" at all. As a practical matter, it permits the Court to decide almost any case either way. And that has helped foster the popular notion that caprice, not reason and doctrine, rules the Court—an impression which is unfortunately reinforced when decisions turn on five-to-four majorities or on changes in the Court's personnel. Although that impression is far from fair, it is probably the very flexibility of the *ad hoc* approach which explains why neither liberals, conservatives, nor moderates are quite satisfied with the Court's performance in the free speech field.

47. *Roth v. U.S.,* 354 U.S. 476 (1957).

The solution is *not* a return to the rigid doctrines of the 1940's, however. One can hope of course that whenever the situation for which the CPD test was originally devised rearises, the Court will treat it differently from the Communist party. One can also hope that if and when the climate of the Cold War alters significantly, both Congress and the Court will be sensitive to the change. But above all, one must insist that while working within the *ad hoc* approach, the Court shall indeed balance *all* the relevant factors in given cases, be explicit in explaining its decisions, strive for consistency and predictability within particular areas of free speech, and not use the balancing test as a screen for caprice or sleight of hand. After all, it was the complexity of the free speech problem which led the Court to the *ad hoc* approach in the first place, and it would be inexcusable for the Court now to pretend that that complexity does not still exist.

But it is hardly enough to place these injunctions on the Court alone. For the Justices cannot for long preserve *any* civil right unless society at large shares their concern. Amid all the controversy over Negro rights and reapportionment, it is terribly important for all Americans to remember that the problem of free expression not only still remains, but in certain senses is *more* complex than those other causes.

Ironically, the words of the Constitution are misleading on that score, for the First Amendment protection of free speech seems far more explicit than the Fourteenth Amendment language on which those other civil rights turn. Yet in the real world it is a good deal easier to define the meaning of racial or electoral equality than it is to define the extremely subtle concept of free speech. There is not only the difficult relation between thought, expression, and action but also the fact that some forms of human expression, such as obscenity, have never been considered part of free speech in America. At the same time, there is as yet no clean, viable definition of obscenity; and until we have that and a number of other definitions of what is *not* free expression, we still lack a definition of what *is*.[48] Another complication is that although the imperatives of racial and electoral equality often confront other legitimate values, they do not have to face—at least today—the supremely formidable antagonist with which free speech must often struggle: the state preoccupied with its own security.

Within these complexities, Americans must forever resist complacency over the fact that the vast majority of us go through life without ever experiencing any direct abridgement of free expression. It is too glib to say simply that we live under a state which tolerantly permits us to voice whatever eccentric ideas we have in our heads. We should also recognize that very few of us indeed ever have any eccentric ideas to voice in the first place. And however happy or unhappy one may be about that, it is obviously no justification for callously disregarding the fate of the few who do dissent. We must remember not only that indifference to the occasional violation of a right can easily be the first step toward wholesale violation, but also that the preciousness of a right can never be measured by the number of people who claim its violation.

Conclusion

Free speech, legislative reapportionment, and equal treatment regardless of race obviously do not constitute the full range of civil rights in America today. As I suggested at the outset of this essay, one could detail such rights almost *ad infinitum,* and surely a complete catalogue would include, for example, freedom of

48. For an interesting recent free speech case, see *New York Times v. Sullivan,* 376 U.S. 254 (1964), in which the Court reversed an Alabama judgment against the paper for carrying a paid advertisement which libeled public officials in the state. The Court held that such a judgment could be constitutional under the First and Fourteenth Amendments only if "actual malice" on the part of the paper were proved.

worship and assembly, freedom from unreasonable search and seizure, the right to counsel and jury trial in criminal cases, and the privilege against self-incrimination.

But the purpose of this essay has not been to catalogue all those rights which can be called "civil." Instead, I have attempted to deal analytically with the concepts of freedom and equality, and then consider in depth the problems and dynamics which their attainment in several particular areas involves. For this purpose I think that the three civil rights which we have considered are by far the most important and that an analysis of these three yields the same essential insights which one would gain from going on to further problem areas.

My thesis throughout has been the non-absolutist nature of freedom and equality. By that I do not mean that coercion and differentiation can never be totally banished in any real society. That is of course true, but it is not enough to dwell only on the practical impossibility of maintaining absolute equality among electoral districts, of guaranteeing that no individual will ever suffer discrimination of any kind because of race, or of tolerating complete freedom of expression. My more basic proposition has instead been that it is wrong to define freedom and equality negatively as the absence of coercion and differentiation. For often it is their very presence which gives us a meaningful experience of freedom and equality—provided of course that the coercion and differentiation are rationally structured to serve some human purpose or value which we prize.

To look back briefly, although a malapportioned district system surely frustrates electoral equality, even a well-apportioned district system is a departure from the simplistic equality of an election at large. Yet the district system can be justified on the ground that it undoubtedly gives most citizens a far more meaningful sense of equal participation in the process of representative government than they would otherwise have. Again, the demand for equal treatment regardless of race is not a demand that differentiation among individuals be banished from society, but rather that it be based on individual talent and achievement instead of race.

If indeed the experience of equality is inseparably linked to differentiation—and thus to discrimination—it is also inseparably linked to the problem of freedom. Grant that it would be intolerable for any society to single out one particular talent or skill and then favor it to the exclusion of all others, there is also some limit to the range of opportunities for self-development which can exist in a given society at a given time. If my general discussion of freedom left any doubts on this score, surely the particular problem of free speech suggests that the right of self-expression cannot be an absolute, and that the job of assuring that it does not infringe other legitimate rights invariably involves coercion.

The result of this analysis, hopefully, has been to place the civil rights controversy in a somewhat clearer focus than that in which it is often seen. The controversy is not a simple one between those who are "for" and those who are "against" freedom and equality. For these have turned out to be highly instrumental concepts whose meaning depends on the substantive content which we pour into them. The real issue is to decide what human purposes and attributes should be afforded the opportunity for self-fulfillment, and how the elements of coercion and differentiation in our society can best be structured to that end.

Cast in these terms, the civil rights controversy lends itself to a rather more pragmatic dialogue than we have often heard in recent years. For one thing, both sides stand on some common ground in most of the questions with which they struggle. For another thing, most of these questions involve evidence which is susceptible, in some degree, to dispassionate analysis. In the case of public school segregation, both sides accepted—at least in theory—the proposition that the Constitution did not permit the white race to impose on the Negro race inferior educational opportunity. That forced the issue to turn on evidence concerning the tangible and intangible quality of segregated education. In the case of Negro demands for equal access to "public accommodations," both sides must also surely agree that every individual possesses some legitimate claim of privacy, property right, and free association. The pragmatic question is the point at which that claim becomes more convincing than the claim to equal treatment regardless of race. Again, in the case of legislative apportionment, precious few really espouse the absolute equality of at-large electoral systems, or on the other hand reject the essential premise of self-government. In each case the common ground makes the issue essentially one of practical engineering over which men can reason in common-sense fashion.

If one looks to other civil rights areas which we have not discussed in depth, much the same approach seems feasible. Take the problem of whether evidence obtained through an unreasonable search and seizure, in violation of the Fourth Amendment, should nevertheless be admissible in court against a defendant. No one wants to encourage violations of the Fourth Amendment; also, few concur in seeing a guilty man go free because the constable has blundered. Grant that, and the relevant questions to ask are quite practical: Does the use of such evidence actually seem to encourage—and its exclusion from court *dis*courage—police irregularity? And are there measures other than the exclusion of such evidence which can effectively deter police violations of the Fourth Amendment? Again, even in the sporadically explosive problem of prayer and released-time religious instruction in public schools, the real issue does not lie between those few who may want to establish a "state religion" and those few who may wish to convert us all to "atheism." The real issue is the impact—intellectual or psychological or other—which school sponsorship of such an exercise can have on the non-believing pupil, even when he is permitted not to participate, and, to turn matters around, whether the school's withdrawal from such sponsorship in any way infringes the believing individual's right to religious self-fulfillment outside the school.

If my argument has seemed to amount to an espousal of pragmatism, two closing admonitions must follow. First, the very nature of pragmatism is to shun definitive or absolutist solutions. Its technique is to take one step at a time on the basis of the best evidence available, to see issues in terms of what is practical and possible, to move forward through the adjustment and balancing of competing claims, and always to recognize that the future is certain to bring new problems as difficult as those which we face today. All this means that however superior the pragmatic approach may be to emotionalism, we should not expect from it more than it can give us. It can hopefully contain the civil rights controversy within the orderly process of law and reason, but it can never banish all human frustration and tension. It can never promise a world without problems.

Second, for all its hardheadedness, pragmatism almost paradoxically requires a certain commitment of faith. If indeed both sides of the civil rights controversy do today share at least some common ground, that, I would submit, reflects what has been and still remains a pervasive consensus in American society on at least three basic tenets: belief in the intrinsic dignity of the individual *qua* individual; belief in the efficacy, if not the infallibility, of human reason; and belief in the moral imperative of self-government. True, we may often quarrel about the particular interpretation or application of these norms, but it is our prior agreement on them which makes our quarrels amenable to pragmatism. For only when men agree in some measure on such fundamental values can they deal with issues in terms of technique, of what will "work," of what will take them one step forward. Without that consensus, every issue becomes a confrontation between philosophically irreconcilable antagonists and pragmatism proves futile.

Thus the civil rights controversy is, in the most profound sense, a challenge to both the common sense and the faith of America. If our fundamental faith in human dignity, reason, and self-government remains firm, there is every reason to believe that common sense can and will prevail in today's crisis. If not, the prospect may well become one of permanent crisis.

Index

A Note on the Contributors

Rowland Berthoff was born in Toledo, Ohio, and studied at Harvard University. He is the author of *British Immigrants in Industrial America, 1790-1950.* He is at present Associate Professor of History at Washington University, St. Louis.

Roger H. Brown was born in Cleveland and studied at Harvard University. He is the author of *The Struggle for the Indian Stream Territory* and *The Republic in Peril: 1812.* He is at present Associate Professor of History at the American University, Washington, D.C.

Meredith O. Clement was born in Colusa, California, and studied at the University of California, Berkeley. He is the author of *An Economic Evaluation of the Federal Grant-in-Aid Programs in New England.* He is at present Associate Professor of Economics at Dartmouth College.

Robert H. Guest was born in East Orange, New Jersey, and studied at Amherst College and Columbia University. He is the author of *Organizational Change: The Effect of Successful Leadership* and co-author of *The Man on the Assembly Line* and *The Foreman on the Assembly Line.* He has served as adviser to the President's Committee for Better Utilization of Manpower Resources in Government, and is at present Professor of Organization and Administration at Dartmouth College.

Gene M. Lyons was born in Revere, Massachusetts, and studied at Tufts University, the University of Geneva (Switzerland), and Columbia University. He is the author of *Military Policy and Economic Aid* and co-author of *Education and Military Leadership* and *Schools for Strategy.* He has served as a member of the secretariat of the

International Refugee Organization, and is at present Orvil E. Dryfoos Professor of Public Affairs at Dartmouth College.

HARRY N. SCHEIBER was born in New York City and studied at Columbia University and Cornell University. He is the author of *The Wilson Administration and Civil Liberties* and editor of *United States Economic History: Selected Readings*. He is at present Associate Professor of History at Dartmouth College.

KALMAN H. SILVERT was born in Bryn Mawr, Pennsylvania, and studied at the University of Pennsylvania. He is the author of *The Conflict Society; Chile: Yesterday and Today;* and *Guatemala: A Study in Government,* and editor of *Expectant Peoples: Nationalism and Development* and *Discussion at Bellagio: The Alternatives of Political Development*. He is at present Professor of Government at Dartmouth College.

FRANK SMALLWOOD was born in Ridgewood, New Jersey, and studied at Dartmouth College and Harvard University. He is the author of *Greater London: The Politics of Metropolitan Reform* and *Metro Toronto: A Decade Later*. He is at present Associate Professor of Government at Dartmouth College.

VINCENT E. STARZINGER was born in Des Moines, Iowa, and studied at Harvard University. He is the author of *Middlingness: Juste Milieu Political Theory in England and France, 1814-48*. He is at present Associate Professor of Government at Dartmouth College.